LACQUER OF THE WEST

LACQUER OF THE WEST

THE HISTORY OF A CRAFT AND AN INDUSTRY · 1550–1950

HANS HUTH

THE UNIVERSITY OF CHICAGO PRESS

CHICAGO AND LONDON

Library of Congress Catalog Card Number: 73-130185
The University of Chicago Press, Chicago 60637
The University of Chicago Press, Ltd., London W. C. 1

Published 1971
Printed in Germany
ISBN: 0-226-36315-5

TO MY WIFE MARTA HUTH

CONTENTS

ACKNOWLEDGMENTS

Publication of this book was made possible by a grant provided by The Joseph and Helen Regenstein Foundation of Chicago. For this I am most grateful. To Mrs. Joseph Regenstein, Sr., I offer my sincere thanks for her concern and interest.

I am grateful to all those who allowed me to see the lacquer objects they own as well as to the many who provided me with information in matters of lacquer. To the following I owe particular thanks:

Mr. Winslow Ames, The Honorable Gavin Astor, Prof. Dr. Hans Aurenhammer, Mr. Alexander Ball, Mr. Richard Ball (†), S. A. Urbano Principe Barberini, Mr. G. Barzan, Messrs. Batsford, Dr. Eckart Berkenhagen, Dr. Alfred Berner, Dr. B. Bilzer, Mr. Gudmund Boesen, Comte J. de Borchgrave d'Altena, Mr. Robert D. Buck, Mrs. Shirley Bury

Mr. R. L. Charles, Messrs. Christie, Mr. Andrew S. Chiechanowiecki, Dr. Tove Clemmensen, Dr. Armin Conradt (†), Dipl. Ing. Trude Cornelius, Mr. Charles Cunningham, Mr. Carl C. Dautermann, Mrs. Hélène Demoriane, Mr. Ivan Dethier, Dr. Florens Deuchler, Mrs. Shirley de Voe, Dr. Ludwig Baron Döry, S. D. Alexander Fürst zu Dohna, S. A. Orietta Principessa Doria-Pamphilij, Dr. Hans Martin Freiherr von Erffa, Prof. Dr. Richard Ettinghausen, Prof. Dr. Italo Faldi, Mr. Ralph Fastnedge, Mr. Alan Fern, Prof. Dr. Herman Fillitz, Mr. Karl Fischer-Böhler, Dr. W. Fleischhauer

Mr. Joseph Graham, Prof. Dr. Ernst Grube, Dr. Helmuth Hager, Dr. Luisa Hager, Dr. Rolf Hanstein (†), Dr. Julie Harksen, Mr. John Hayward, Dr. Georg Himmelheber, Monsignore Hermann Hoberg, S. D. Constantin Prinz zu Hohenlohe-Langenburg, Mr. G. Isachenko, Mr. Martin Kemp, Dr. Bernhard Kerber, Dr. Erich Köllmann, Prof. Dr. Jiri Kotalik, Dipl. Phil. Arno Krause, Prof. Dr. Heinrich Kreisel, Dr. Margarete Kühn

Prof. Dr. Heinz Ladendorf, Messrs. Lempertz, Mr. Karl Leuthenmayer, Dr. Norbert Lieb, Mr. Adolph Loewi, The Lord Chamberlain's Office, Prof. Dr. Wolfgang Lotz, Dr. Frits Lugt, Dr. Th. Lunsingh Scheuerleer, Mr. John MacGregor, Messrs. Mallett, Dr. Giovanni Mariacher, Prof. Dr. Edward A. Maser, Dr. P. W. Meister, Dipl. Ing. Gisela Messner, Mrs. Alexandra Michailova, Mr. Robert de Micheaux, Prof. Dr. Ulrich Middeldorf, Dr. Lieselotte Möller, S. A. Le Duc de Mouchy, S. A. Dre. La Duchesse de Mouchy, Mr. Abel de Moura, Prof. Dr. Wilhelm Mřazek, Prof. Dr. Theodor Müller, Mr. Charles Nagel, Le Vicomte de Noailles, Prof. Dr. Carl Nordenfalk, Mr. Gregor Norman-Wilcox

Mrs. Irina Ouchanova, S. A. Elena Principessa Pallavicini, Mr. James Parker, Miss Helena Mendes Pinto, Dr. Pavel Preiss, Mr. James I. Rambo, Mr. and Mrs. William J. Robertson, Dr. Marvin Ross, Dr. Rainer Rückert, Madame Georges A. Salman, Dr. Günther Schade, Mr. Paul Schaffer, Mr. Hans Schedelmann, Miss Vivian Scheidemantel, Dr. Eberhard Freiherr Schenk von Schweinsberg, Dr. Günther Schiedlausky, Prof. Dr. Arno

Schönberger, S. E. Dr. Karl Graf von Schönborn-Wiesentheid, Mr. Donald A. Shelley, Mr. Laurence Sickman, Mrs. Tullio Silva, Messrs. Sotheby, The Right Hon. Lord St. Oswald, Mr. Francis Spar, Miss Edith M. H. Strässer, Mr. Max Terrier, Prof. Dr. Bruno Thomas, Dr. Christiane Thomas, Mr. P. K. Thornton

Mr. Pierre Verlet, Prof. Dr. Vittorio Viale, Mr. Francis J. B. Watson, Mr. E. G. Williams, Prof. Dr. W. Willvonseder, Miss Alice Winchester, Dr. Franz Windisch-Graetz, Mr. Marcel Wolfers, Mr. and Mrs. Charles Wrightsman, Dr. Federico Zeri, Dr. Friedrich Zschocke, and Dr. Valentin Count Zubow (†).

My most sincere thanks go to Miss Helen Perce who prepared the manuscript with the greatest of care.

I wish to thank my wife who contributed a number of photographs and cooperated in many ways.

H. H.

CHAPTER I LACQUER IN THE SEVENTEENTH CENTURY

> Tout serait à étudier dans Venise . . .
> qui s'en va pierre par pierre
> EMILE MOLINIER, 1889

As presented here, the history of European and North American lacquer deals with decorated objects made of wood, papier-mâché, tin, leather, and earthenware. Lacquer of course is a medium in which a resin has been made soluble by the addition of suitable ingredients before application in several coatings to objects decorated in color. The period with which I am concerned extends from about 1550 to the present day. Since it is not always possible to determine whether the surface of an object has been suitably prepared before lacquer is applied or whether it has simply been painted with oil colors and then heavily varnished, I propose to treat as lacquer those pieces that to all intents and purposes have been decorated to produce the highly polished effect of lacquer; objects lacquered solely for protection will not be taken into account.

During the development of this technique in Europe in the late seventeenth and early eighteenth century, artisans sought to give their work an exotic appearance by combining color, decoration, and luster in the style of the Orient. In the late eighteenth century, lacquered objects lost much of their foreign character and more closely followed the general trend of European fashion. The popularity of lacquer in the Western world reached its peak around the middle of the nineteenth century; today, with few exceptions, its production is alive only in Russia.

The fashion for lacquer spread over Europe in two waves that differed considerably one from the other, the second coinciding at times with the popularity of *chinoiserie*. The first wave came without much fanfare during the second half of the sixteenth century and lasted less than three generations, to about 1630. The new process, reaching Europe from the Near East and spreading throughout Italy, was mastered by Venetian craftsmen, who used it together with motifs from the same region to decorate caskets and other traditional objects they had been producing for centuries. As lacquered works became greatly prized elsewhere in Europe, the technique was soon adopted by craftsmen abroad. During the second quarter of the seventeenth century the trend lost its momentum, but within the span of another generation, around 1660, there was a revival of interest. This time lacquerwork came in Far Eastern guise, in appearance more spectacular, and its popularity proved to be lasting.

Lacquered objects from the Far East had been shipped to Europe as early as the end of the sixteenth century, at first spasmodically and then in constantly increasing quantities as they were the more highly appreciated. The supply of Chinese and Japanese lacquer was never equal to the demand, and thus arose the inevitable question: could Oriental lacquer techniques be copied by Europeans? It was obvious that several problems had to be solved: first, how could the hard and lustrous lacquer, rather different from the sort used earlier, be produced with materials available in Europe? Second, how well could Oriental patterns be copied? European artisans would be forced to compete with their Oriental prototypes, and this presented a number of complications. Many craftsmen, artisans, alchemists, and scholars sought to solve the difficult problems of technique, and at length they succeeded: by 1680 European-produced lacquer rivaled that imported from the Far East. Although European craftsmen professed to believe that their patterns were shaped completely "in the foreign manner," nonetheless they could not escape entirely the influence of the styles of their own period. Nineteenth-century critics, who were to note these discrepancies, coined the term *chinoiserie* when referring to work done "in the manner of" or "in allusion to" the Far East. By the end of the eighteenth century European lacquer was no longer dependent upon Far Eastern designs, and what was once a craft developed gradually into a large and flourishing industry.

Ever since the thirteenth century, when the indefatigable Marco Polo first journeyed to China, the city of Venice had been the European point of departure for and the port of entry from the Orient. It was by way of Venice that goods from the Levant – earthenware, metalwork, textiles, and such precious items as jewelry and lacquerware – were introduced into Europe. Venice was also the one place in Europe where, over the centuries, the greatest body of knowledge concerning varnish and lacquer had accumulated.[1] We have the date 1283 for the oldest known Venetian document having to do with the varnishing of caskets, tables, and woodwork: it consists of rules for the *depentores*, a guild composed of painters, miniaturists, gilders – in fact, anyone who could wield a brush. The guild remained intact until the year 1691, when the painters of pictures withdrew, ostensibly because they believed the other members of the guild to be "of a lower standing" and by this means sought to end the association.

Unfortunately, there is no known document to tell us when the varnishers among the *depentores* began to decorate their wares instead of simply applying a protective coating of varnish. From existing evidence we assume that it must have been during the middle of the sixteenth century and that the artistic stimulus came from the Near East.

As a token of their common interests, Orient and Occident were joined at an annual fair in Venice held on the day of the Ascension of the Holy Virgin. The Piazza San Marco was crowded with displays of merchandise – metalware, textiles, lacquer, pearls and jewelry, ceramics, spices, and a wealth of other items from both East and West. The vendors were solely Venetians. All foreign merchandise entering Venetian territory had to be sold to resident merchants and at no other places than the inns (called *fondachi*) at which merchants from far lands were required to stay under threat of heavy punishment should they seek to evade this mandate. In they swarmed, Arabs, Armenians, Turks, and Persians, to the *fondachi* allocated to foreigners, under strict government surveillance, each inn teeming with customs officers, brokers, and guards. One such inn, later known as Palazzo Correr, a museum of natural history, can be dated from 1621; it was set aside for Turks and Persians, although they were kept apart.[2]

A Syrian craft which may well have inspired Venetian artisans working in lacquer was the practice of damascening, with its emphasis upon vivid patterns and contrasting color effects, glittering metal inlays and dark backgrounds. This technique was known in Venice and in other cities such as Milan as early as 1300, with the first importation of damascened vessels from such places as Herat in easternmost Iran. Best known today among the makers of such wares was Mahmud al Kurdi (pl. 4) who flourished during the first half of the sixteenth century and who signed some of his pieces. Both damascene patterns and techniques were adopted by Venetians. The craftsmen who practiced this art were called *azziministi*. These were all Venetians or Italians, since no oriental craftsman resided in Venice.[3] The only signed piece known today is a casket that once belonged to the Trivulzio collection in Milan, but has disappeared since (pl. 10). It is signed *Paulus Ageminius*, probably standing for Paolo Rizzo who in 1570 had his workshop "at the sign of the dove" in the *Ruga dei orefici* at the Rialto.

Another Oriental craft introduced and of influence in Venice from the end of the fifteenth century was the practice of fashioning elaborate bindings for books.[4] Venetian copies or adaptations of lacquered bindings "in the Persion style" date from the middle of the sixteenth century. One such binding (pl. 1) contains an official document from the period of Doge Aloysius Mocenigo (1570–77) and shows the arms of Venice amid sunken panels with raised designs lacquered in blue and red and decorated in gold. As will appear, lacquerworkers often used tooled and lacquered leather for the decoration of wooden cabinets. Such work shows the close relation between the Near East and Venice and the strong influence of the Near East on Venetian crafts (pls. 1, 2). The influence was not entirely one-sided: there was a considerable trade in jewels and finely executed weapons exported from Venice to Turkey, especially during the reign of Sultan Solyman the Magnificent (1520–1566). Like Venetian jewelers and arms makers, the glassworkers of Murano, forbidden to go abroad by strict ordinances, or to sell the secrets of their craft, exported their wares to the Near East.

All of these contacts between Orient and Occident leave no doubt that the craftsmen of Venice were ready to learn artistic techniques brought from afar, to which they would add their own creative skills, just as we know that the crafts of Venice spread into Syria and other Near Eastern countries. A contemporary Venetian chronicle quoted by Lavoix characterized the mingling of peoples and cultures in the following manner: "One sees our estates and gardens in Rumania, Greece, Trebizond, Syria, Armenia, and Egypt; there we gain profits as well as pleasure of life, there we live for many years, our children as well as our nephews."

Trade routes to the Near East had been established as early as the thirteenth century, or earlier. The bone carvings of the Embriacchi family, for example, were typical of the early craftwork of Venice known throughout the Mediterranean. The carvings were produced on order for individual customers, but a fair supply reached the open market in the seaport of Venice. Given these circumstances it seems advisable to examine lacquered objects that survive and are decorated in the fashion of the Near East and consider their possible relationship to the products of the artisans of Venice in the sixteenth and seventeenth centuries, although many are scattered in various collections and bear a variety of labels.

After all, Near Eastern motifs were introduced into Europe at many times and places. European engravings based on Moresque designs, such as those by "the Master F," were circulating in Italian workshops as early as 1520. Prints of this kind were emulated by Jacques Androuet I. Ducerceau around 1540 (figs. 3, 4). In turn, Ducerceau prints were copied by the French master, Thomas Geminus, who lived in London in the period 1524–63 and published a collection of "Morysse and Damashin" designs.[5] In Germany, Peter Flötner (d. 1546) and Virgil Solis (1514–1562) adapted Moresque patterns (fig. 1).

Definitely established as being Venetian work are a number of shields (pl. 3) ordered in Venice in the last quarter of the sixteenth century for the horsemen of the bishop of Salzburg, Wolf Dietrich von Raitenau (1587–1611). These shields, now displayed in a number of museums, are made of wood covered with parchment since turned brown; the design is of interlacing Moresque scrollwork. The general pattern as well as the details – knotwork and scrolls – are closely related to shapes seen on Mosul vessels such as the one in the Victoria and Albert Museum (pl. 4). Tiny areas between the scrolls, colored in white, red, and green, shine through the varnish and produce the effect of lacquer. This translucency must have been most striking before the parchment darkened. Another shield utilizing the same technique was apparently made for the state of Venice. Both shield and matching quiver show the symbolic lion of San Marco on a ground of brilliant red and green lacquer as well as ornamentation, typically Islamic in character, often found on bookbindings (pls. II, 6). A number of these shields are still to be seen in the *armeria* of the Doge's Palace.

Ornamental effects akin to those of the Salzburg shields are to be found in the decoration of a toilette box, still equipped with all its accessories, which once belonged to Archduke Ferdinand II of Tyrol (1529–1596). It came from his *Kunstkammer* in Ambras and is now displayed in Vienna (pl. 7). The tradition that it was made in Venice is most convincing. Its body, fashioned of wood completely covered with bone, is decorated with intertwining spirals and tiny translucent color areas of lacquer similar to the ornaments of the shields, though here they stand out the more brightly against a light background. The box may be of an earlier date, perhaps around the middle of the sixteenth century, since some of the ornamental elements which reflect Renaissance style appear on the box but not on the shields. The somewhat oriental character of the design takes on significance when we realize that its presumed original owner, Ferdinand II, was involved in the wars of Transylvania between Turkey and the Roman Empire and that he was the first prince to capture a considerable amount of Turkish booty (in 1556 and again in 1566). A lacquered quiver case, acquired in 1566, is covered with exquisitely executed ornamentation in the Turkish style (pl. 5). The border design is related to that of a number of Venetian caskets, to be discussed presently.

Here it might be well to mention a lacquered folding table once at Ambras and now in Vienna (pl. 29). Julius von Schlosser was the first to call attention to it in 1908 as an example of early European *chinoiserie*, but later it was generally considered to be a Chinese product.[6] The piece is mentioned in an inventory of Ambras made in 1596 as having been given to Ferdinand by his son, Cardinal Andreas of Burgau (b. 1558). In 1591 Ferdinand's son was Bishop of Brixen, and in this city not far from Venice he built an elaborate palace, although his duties frequently compelled him to live elsewhere. It may well be that the table was acquired in Venice, where lacquer was produced at this time. In any case, the roughly prepared undercoating of this piece speaks against possible Far Eastern origin, and a chemical examination has shown that the lacquer was not made with the resin of the *rhus vernicifera* tree. As far as the "Chinese" motifs are concerned, they may have traveled to the Near East and there been used on Persian ceramics, Turkish bindings, and other objects of the kind, only thence adapted by Venetians. The classic border on the table (even though it is rather limping) would never be found on a Far Eastern piece dating from the sixteenth century. Since the table cannot be shown to be closely related to other lacquer assumed to be of Near Eastern or Venetian origin, the idea that it is also Venetian can be no more than a suggestion; we simply do not know enough about pieces of this period. Another tabletop, possibly Italian and contemporary to the table from Ambras, was exhibited in 1936 in London (pl. 30). It incorporates Near Eastern motifs such as plants and animals, has a border of Renaissance character, and has no Chinese elements in its decoration. One may ask if Turkish objects were available for copying at that time, and the answer must be in the affirmative. By 1562 recipes for the kind of lacquer used in the Near East had been made known by the scholar Leonardo Fioravanti whose book *Secreti* was published in that year.[7] Fioravanti informs his readers that the Turks lacquer their bows and arrow with a solution of three parts *pece greca* (a fir resin later called colophonium) dissolved in one part linseed oil in which color had to be mixed.

Closely allied with the toilette box mentioned above is a small upright case (pl. 8). Again there are the same ornamented lines and little areas of color appearing like gems against a background of white bone. Both boxes are set with similar brass lion heads which serve to anchor the cord with which the cases were to be carried. In his classic essay on the use of mirrors and toilette boxes in Renaissance Venice based on analysis of inventories and last wills, Gustav Ludwig distinguishes several types of boxes.[8] The smallest were the *casse da petteni* used for combs, brushes, and other small objects – like the boxes mentioned above. Another casket of much larger dimension has similar decoration as well as the same attempt to create the effect of lacquer, though the casket itself is of a different shape and equipped with handles (pl. 9). It is probably representative of the type Ludwig calls the *cassa da conzar il cao* (abbr. *conza da cao*), in other words a box containing utensils to dress the hair, *cao* being the Venetian form of *capo*. Among other items a lady might keep in this box would be hair dye and bleach. How this was used is illustrated in a Venetian woodcut of 1522 in which "a girl doing her make-up" (*la fanciulla a farsi bella*) sits in the sun bleaching her hair spread out on a hoop.[9] By her side is a *conza da cao*, though in simplified form (fig. 2). All the objects mentioned thus far provide strong evidence of Near Eastern influence in design and, since the middle of the sixteenth century, evidence of attempts to master the lacquer technique.

Next should be mentioned a somewhat different and probably slightly later group of objects of various types and various quality and workmanship, from the simpler to the most elaborate, all of which illustrate an increasing use of lacquer. There can be hardly any doubt that these too owe their existence to Venice, the commercial as well as the cultural focus of the Mediterranean world; this is most evident when, after examining them singly, they are compared, even though there is no document to prove that any of these pieces were created in Venice. The claim for Venice as point of origin rests upon an analysis of their style and some few bits of circumstantial evidence.

A box, *cassa da petteni* (pl. 12), intended to be carried by cords, appears to be the same type as the two square boxes decorated with bone (pls. 7, 8), discussed earlier. Although Moresque motifs appear in the decoration, the figure set in the center square is in the Renaissance style that made its appearance in Venice after the middle of the sixteenth century. The attempt to create a lacquer effect is carried out with success. In a portrait of a lady at her toilette table, possibly painted by Bernardino Licinio before 1550, we note a little toilette box with combs and other utensils closely related in its decoration to the box just mentioned (pl. 11). A similar box is described in an entry in Lorenzo Lotto's account book of 1538 in which payment is listed for a *cassa da petteni* decorated on the sides "with a grotesque design done in oil colors at a great loss of time" (*frissi grottesche*).[10] It is quite possible that the phrase *frissi grottesche* is the equivalent of "in the Persian manner" (*alla zemina*), used of a comb box listed in an inventory of 1547, or that of another object mentioned in the 1579 inventory, "in the Turkish manner" (*petteniera turchesca*).

Closely related to this group are certain frames, once holding mirrors and now used for pictures; framed mirrors of the period have become exceedingly rare. Some like the so-called Venetian *restello*, mirrors framed with paintings by well-known artists, are virtually non-existent, although the Victoria and Albert Museum owns a small mirror on a stand which in its decoration is closely related to the frames to be discussed (pl. 13). Of frames found not infrequently, one should mention those most often associated with portraits of the school of Corneille de Lyon (pl. 14). These paintings date from around 1580 and thus offer an approximate date for the frames. The design is purely architectural, in the Italian Renaissance style, lacquered in black and decorated with ornaments in gold, enhanced with colorful marble slabs cut into roundels and squares and arranged very much like those seen on the façades of Venetian palaces of the early sixteenth century. Such frames are found in the collections of the Louvre, the Art Institute of Chicago, the Museum of Fine Arts in Boston, and elsewhere. Frames utilizing the same architectural decoration, though without the marble inlay, were used for embossed wax portraits executed in Venice by Francesco da Segala toward the end of the sixteenth century, now to be seen in the Kunsthistorisches Museum in Vienna (pl. 15). The frames were also used for *églomisé* paintings popular in Venice throughout the sixteenth century. Examples are on display at the Art Institute of Chicago (pl. 16).

What is important about most of these frames in a discussion on lacquer is not their architectural structure, though this does help to place them, but rather the way their cornices and moldings are decorated. All are lacquered in black and decorated in gold with ornaments classical in character as well as with Moresque patterns. It is more than likely that this decorative scheme, lending shine and sparkle to the wood, was intended to produce an effect akin to the kind of lacquer known in Venice from Turkish bookbindings, weapons, boxes, and other trinkets which make use of the repeated patterns usual in Islamic art. Presently we will see other objects of undoubted Venetian origin which make it most convincing that frames of this kind originated in Venice. That the frames are most often used in conjunction with paintings originating in France does not prove France to be the source of the frames themselves, although this has been claimed on occasion. A similar frame used before 1538 by Albrecht Altdorfer for a colored woodcut of the *Schöne Madonna* of Regensburg was undoubtedly Venetian in inspiration. An arrangement in which several frames are united in one façade decorates a cabinet in the Museum für Angewandte Kunst in Vienna (pls. 17, 18), a smaller cabinet at the Palazzo Doria-Pamphilij in Rome (pl. 19), and another in a collection in Los Angeles (pl. III). This employment of a marble inlay is reminiscent of a similar use of marble in fifteenth-century church façades attributed to Pietro Lombardi. The Doria cabinet is covered with embossed and impressed leather and fits into a box, the doors of which are lost. The designs on the top of the Doria cabinet as well as on the doors of the Vienna cabinet (pl. 17) follow the traditional design of oriental bindings, using a central ogival medallion and corresponding ornaments at the corners but unconventionally adding a number of pendants to the central motif. The Vienna cabinet has a domed top covered with leather and tooled with Moresque patterns. In all three pieces the desire to give the effect of lacquer is obvious. Some ornaments, notably the rosettes at the base of the portal and those in the corners of the entabulature, are related to the ornaments on the two boxes mentioned earlier. It should be noted that all three cabinets are similar in style but vary in quality and value. This too must be considered as evidence that such products were made in Venice for a market with a variety of demands.

In Venice there could have been nothing more suitable for sale both to the illustrious and the more humble than these magnificent cabinets. There is good reason to believe that cabinets of this kind were produced shortly after the middle of the sixteenth century.[11] One such cabinet of similar style is on display in the Hearst Collection at San Simeon, although it is decorated with enameled plaques from Limoges, some using subjects from classic antiquity, others simply ornamental (pl. 20 a). They are signed and dated (I. C. 1562) by Jean Le Court, the well-known painter of Limoges. We can infer that both Venetian frames and Venetian cabinets were copied in France. Judging from this cabinet, the lacquer decor was much coarser than similar products made in Venice.

The fact that colorful stone and wood were combined to decorate boxes in Venetian tradition is confirmed by an inventory of 1554 in which a *conza da cao* is described as being made of walnut with insets of porphyry and serpentine.[12] A rich casket now displayed in Vienna at the Geistliche Schatzkammer combines stone and wood in following an architectural scheme not unlike that of the two cabinets (pl. 22). The sides are made of sardonyx and lapis lazuli slabs, held in place by black lacquered woodwork covered with a gilded decoration of Moresque ornament.

Related in style to the objects just discussed and yet rather different in character is a group of eight lacquered caskets dating from about 1600.[13] They have yet to be studied and compared in spite of their considerable artistic value and probable historic significance (pls. I, 23–26). They vary in size, and in length range from 28 cm to 96 cm. The larger of these sumptuous caskets, designed in Renaissance style, are truly impressive. The body is placed on short gilt-bronze supports, the lid is hinged and domed. The casket has a wooden framework lacquered in black and decorated with gilt ornaments occasionally enhanced by accents of red luster, much of which shows the influence of the Near East. Encased by this framework are rock crystal slabs of square and oval shape and rosettes cut in diamond fashion. Turned rock crystal columns, generally paired, are set in front of the façades in architectural order. The entabulature, capitals, bases, and moldings are made of richly ornamented gilt-bronze. The inner framework is similarly lacquered. The bottom is covered with silver or gilt-bronze slabs ornamented with engravings or utilizing elements of north European origin. For example, the bottom of the Astor casket is inlaid with stonework in a geometric design.

Two pieces of evidence furnish hints to the dates and provenance of this group of caskets. One is given by the historian Francesco Sansovino who prepared a history of Venice published in 1581.[14] Among the jewelers of the Ruga dei Orefici, he visited the shop of Antonio Maria Fontana and was impressed by a large casket of rock crystal made in such a manner that the contents could be seen through the crystal windows as if sculptured within (*una cassa di cristallo molto grande fatta di modo che le cose che si ripongono dentro appariscano tutti scolpiti di fuori*), a description which provides a telling picture of the unusual character of the casket—indeed also of the others here under scrutiny.

The second piece of evidence is provided by a painting, late sixteenth century, showing a version of Titian's portrait of his daughter Lavinia, originally painted around 1550.[15] In the later picture, a casket has been exchanged for the platter of fruit in the original (pl. 21), and in many ways the casket resembles those we are discussing. Following these indications it seems possible to claim that caskets of this kind were in vogue in Venice toward the end of the sixteenth century; indeed, they must have enjoyed a certain reputation to have been deemed worthy of mention by Sansovino as well as incorporation in the copy of Titian's portrait.

The question arises: what purpose did these caskets serve? Might they have been reliquaries? It would seem unlikely, since for primary relics such as bones or skulls their uniform shape and unusually large size would have been unsuitable, and for secondary relics such as pieces of wood and other artifacts they would have been too large. The fact is that these caskets, though open all around, would not have allowed a proper view of an object of veneration. Furthermore, none of the caskets is decorated with religious symbols, inscriptions, or any other indication that they were to serve as reliquaries. Nor was suitable space allowed to apply a notice of the contents, as would seem indispensable.[16] It also appears unlikely that these caskets were used as jewel cases. Their large size, lack of handles and inside partitions as well as their transparency would not have recommended them for this purpose. The function of the casket must have been a very special one, not easy to isolate. In order to solve the problem one must piece together the purported facts of their history, fragmentary though they are. Let us start with the traditional story associated with a casket belonging to the Duc de Mouchy. This piece has been in the possession of the Ducs de Mouchy, members of the illustrious Noailles family, since the period of Louis XVI, when it was acquired by marriage from one Prince de Beauvau-Craon, the last in his branch of another great family of France. A reproduction of the casket was published in 1873 with a caption saying that it had once contained the baby linen of King Henri IV of France. For explanation we must turn to a long-forgotten custom of the popes. In the period 1601–1880, it was the custom of the Vatican to present clothing (called *fascie* in

Italian, *langes* in French, *mantilla* in Spanish) to the first-born heirs to certain thrones of Catholic princes.[17] The clothing received the blessing of the pope in a very elaborate ceremony and thereafter was known as *fascie benedette*. This gesture followed the papal custom of blessing swords, ducal hats, golden roses, and other objects the popes were wont to present to distinguished personalities. By this act the *fascie* lost their homely character and became symbolic of a spiritual gift to the newly born, embraced by the Holy Church. In view of the splendid ceremonies accompanying the presentation of the gift by a *Nunzio extraordinario*, the symbol obviously required a repository worthy of its contents. So far we have come across no descriptions of the containers used for very early presents, but at least we do have knowledge about the elaborate cases in which later caskets containing the *fascie* were bedded.

The first to suggest this kind of gift was Queen Margaret of Spain, the spouse of King Philip III, who was expecting a child in September 1601. This wish was transmitted to Pope Clement VIII (Aldobrandini) by the papal Nunzio Ginnasio in a letter from Madrid. The pope agreed at once and wrote in the margin, "We will do it, order it" (*Lo faremo ordinatelo*). As it happened, Queen Marie de Medici, the spouse of King Henry IV of France, also was expecting a baby in September of that year. It would never have done to honor one queen and not the other, and accordingly a second set of *fascie* was ordered and presented to the royal couple at the Louvre on 16 December by the papal delegate Maffeo Barberini, who later became Pope Urban VIII.[18] To get an idea of what this set of linen consisted one may consult a record of the nine items presented to the Queen of Spain on 30 September. They included *un manto di tela d'argento* (a coat of silver cloth) and *una fascia di lama d'argento ricamato con l'imagine del S^{mo} Presepio del Signore in mezzo* (a *fascia* of silver cloth embroidered with a picture of the Holy Manger of the Lord). Such a rich array demanded a receptacle of equal splendor. This being so, there should be no question that the Mouchy casket with its tradition of having been the container of a king's baby linen can hardly be other than that which was sent by the pope. In order to accept this interpretation we need not be given pause by the family tradition that mistakes Henry IV for Louis XIII, since we know the gift was made to Henry IV. Sansovino's description of the casket he examined now has particular significance: what more appropriate container could there have been in order to let the glittering array be seen and at the same time protect it from profanation in a casket of rock crystal? The fact that more than a century later the casket ceased to be a part of the royal treasury can be paralleled by another instance in which a crystal casket from the Royal Treasury was presented in 1702 to the King of Siam – possibly the one presented by the pope to Louis XIII in honor of his son the Dauphin.[19]

We know that this kind of crystal casket was not devised solely for the papal gift (Sansovino's description must be dated prior to 1581, some twenty years before the first gift was made). We also know that there was not sufficient time to design two caskets and have them made for these royal occasions. It seems most likely that the caskets were ordered in Venice from already existing designs. If we trust this conclusion, we may claim that the Mouchy casket was made in Venice in or before 1601. It became the prototype for other caskets which may have served the same purpose even at considerably later dates. We know that the protocol of the first presentations remained the same for at least a century, and it seems likely that the design of the casket also remained unchanged. Therefore some of the other caskets in this group of eight may also have been papal gifts, and in fact two of them (n. 13 c, h) carry traditions touching on the theme of nativity gifts.

A smaller and much less pretentious casket, though similar, should be mentioned. Displayed in the museum at Salford, Lancashire, is a casket both transparent and lacquered (pl. 20 b). In spite of its unassuming character, it does full justice to the creative spirit of Venice. It represents one of the very early European pieces to rely entirely on lacquer for its artistic expression.[20]

There is another group of Venetian caskets of lesser splendor though of greater elegance which shows exquisite workmanship. Generally they are called jewel boxes, although this may be a mistake; a Venetian lady would be more likely to consign her treasures to a strong box (*scrigno*). All the same, the boxes may have been used for lesser finery or possibly for certain toilette articles. The boxes differ in shape and in the manner in which a variety of techniques, among them lacquer, is used. An especially rich piece owned by the Metropolitan Museum has the general appearance of a Renaissance chest with pilasters dividing the sides into panels (pls. 2, 27). Each panel is covered with a pattern of Near Eastern design, once more showing striking similarity to the designs utilized in Turkish bookbinding as well as some relationship to the Vienna cabinet (pl. 17). The casket is made of wood painted black and covered with Moresque ornaments in gold and silver with the usual intermingled accents of red, the whole treatment producing the effect of lacquer. The finely wrought handles and hinges of gilt-silver are of Renaissance design. Another casket, now in West Berlin (pl. 28), is also designed in the Renaissance style with some figural motifs, yet it also incorporates some Near Eastern features; once again, blue and red color elements give the impression of lacquer. Very likely this piece should be dated before the middle of the sixteenth century. Finally, an Italian cabinet on a stand, now in East Berlin and dating from before 1600, is related to Venice in the style of its ornaments, though in general it appears to be of North Italian origin, if we take account of its rather rigid Renaissance appearance (pl. 37).

Near Eastern motifs once accepted and adapted in Venice doubtless radiated to other centers in Italy. We find these ornamental trends in the decoration of such musical instruments as the virginal, one of which was owned by Queen Elizabeth and is now in the Victoria and Albert Museum (pl. 31). This instrument was made in 1570 (the outer case is of later origin). Three others, by Benedetto Floriani, Venice 1571 (University Museum at Leipzig); Giovanni Antonio Baffo, Venice, 1574 (Victoria and Albert Museum); and Giovanni Celestini, Venice, 1593 (Royal College of Music, London), utilize Near Eastern motifs in their decoration (pls. 32–34). At the same time, the instrument made by Baffo has a polychrome design on a bone ground in the fashion of the toilette boxes mentioned earlier (pls. 7, 8). In this connection note should be taken of a harp (pls. 35, 36) made for Duke Alfonso II of Mantua in 1587 and possibly decorated by Giulio Marescotti, if we may thus interpret an entry mentioned in an account.[21] In any case, the decoration is executed with great subtlety and the design of some areas seems close to Moresque engravings by Virgil Solis (fig. 1). Both Oriental motifs and Renaissance ideas inspired the artist; the desire must have been to produce something like lacquerwork. Undoubtedly these musical instruments, most frequently exported, helped to spread the Venetian style and technique to foreign countries. Whether the lacquer trend continued in Italy after the first quarter of the seventeenth century and whether it lingered on in Venice up to the middle of the century, as well it may, so far remain uncertain. The fact is that at present we do not know of any lacquer objects that may have been produced in Venice in the time between the first quarter of the century until the 1660s when the second wave of orientalism, this coming from the Far East, began to be evident.

A much quoted date, formerly accepted though in error, was the year 1615 for the *chinoiserie* decoration of the lacquer paneling in the bedroom at Rosenborg Castle in Copenhagen (pls. 262, 263). Some documents, previously misinterpreted, prove that the decoration was executed later.[22] The Dutch scholar Theodor Lunsingh Scheurleer also discovered that some of the designs were copied from John Nieuhoff's book on China, published in 1665. With the date 1615 no longer valid to prove the existence of lacquer *chinoiserie* early in the seventeenth century, there still remains the date 1619, the year in which the ballot box of the London Saddlers' Guild was made according to the date on the box (pl. 38). This date is often quoted to prove the existence of early lacquer decorated with *chinoiserie*. Considered to be closely related to the ballot box in style as well as in technique are two cabinets and a round box inclosing a set of trenchers inscribed with verses taken from a book printed in 1611 (pls. 39–44). The door of one of the cabinets is decorated with vases of flowers in conventional Flemish style (pl. 41). The inside of the door of the other cabinet is decorated with houses, a windmill, a beacon, and a gibbet placed on undulating horizontal lines to represent a landscape (pl. 40). In addition, we note on both the doors and the trenchers solitary plant forms with feathery leaves and circles representing cumulus clouds. A *guilloche* pattern forms the borders of the trenchers and of the drawers of the cabinets. Some of the human figures are dressed in Renaissance style and others in somewhat exotic raiment though by no means in the Chinese manner. It is significant that the scheme of decoration on the lid of the ballot box shows a pointed oval motif of Islamic origin with the usual triangular ornaments filling the corners of the area dominated by the central motif. True, this oval motif is also to be found on Chinese products of the sixteenth century, but it is most unlikely that during this period such products were imported in any considerable quantity. Chinese products began to reach Europe somewhat regularly only around 1600 and then in very limited quantities. It is quite possible that one or another piece was copied or matched for some specific reason, but at this time there was certainly no public demand for Far Eastern products or copies thereof. The average lacquer workshop would have had no patterns available.

All of these objects – ballot box, cabinets, and trencher box – are decorated in silver and gold on a black lacquer ground with an occasional touch of red. Both the Near Eastern motifs and the rest of the decoration, as well as the absence of Far Eastern motifs, place this group with those objects of Venetian origin examined earlier. Nor do their shapes make concession to foreign influence. At one time these objects possessed more brilliance and luster than they have today; particularly when set against dark oak furniture and wainscoting, they must have produced the desired exotic effect of lacquer.

To a certain extent, the relationship of this group to the Far East has been questioned, and indeed it was claimed that these pieces showed "no specifically Eastern feature." Nevertheless, the pieces forming this group were always considered incunabula of *chinoiserie*, although Ralph Edwards did note "a certain Italian influence."[23] This observation can be fully justified by what has been stated about the Venetian lacquer style and the way it spread throughout Europe. Once it is agreed that this English group offers no evidence of Far Eastern influence early in the seventeenth century, such a theory loses its last support. Nor do documents, inventories, and last wills provide evidence of influence, although there is, for example, an often quoted inventory made up for Henry Howard, Earl of Northampton, in 1614. Here we find listed a "China gilt Cabinette upon a frame" as well as a large, square "China worke table and frame of black varnish and gold and another small table of Chinaworke in golde and colors with flies and wormes."[24] Finally, there is a field bedspread of "China worke, black and silver branches with silver with the arms of the Earl of Northampton on the head piece." The cabinet may have been an imported piece, with the others made in England to match it. From the meager description it is to be doubted whether the domestic products offered a very "Chinese effect."

From France a similar case is reported by Louis Battifol. It concerns Marie de Medici, the recipient of the pope's *fascie benedette* in 1601, who employed one Etienne Sager, skilled in the imitation of Chinese lacquerwork.[25] Sager was paid to make "with lacquer gum and gold" decorations in the Chinese manner for "cabinets, chests, boxes, paneling, ornaments for churches, chaplets, and other small articles and Chinese goods..." It is not readily clear why he should have decorated ornaments for churches and chapels in the Chinese manner if plain lacquerwork is not meant. One also learns from Battifol that a chest decorated by Sager in the Chinese style was set in the bedroom of the queen at the Louvre, while in the queen's private chamber there was a genuine Chinese desk presented to her by the general of the Jesuits. How faithfully this information was transcribed from contemporary sources is hard to tell, but at least it leaves the impression that in this instance there was both a genuine Chinese desk and a chest made in France in a related style.

Both Marie de Medici and the Earl of Northampton were the owners of precious Far Eastern pieces. This might explain their desire to provide these curios with a suitable background. Until we have proof to the contrary, the meager data we have do not allow us to assume that there was much copying of Far Eastern lacquer in the first decades of the seventeenth century. Certainly those few items of the period we happen to know about permit no such assumption.

Contemporary documents and printed matter reveal the rather inaccurate language used at this time to define Far Eastern objects or the activities of their makers. As late as 1680, authors Stalker and Parker state on the title page of their *Treatise on Japanning* that they are providing "patterns for Japan work in imitation of the Indians." At that time *japanning* was simply the technical term used for lacquerwork and *Indian* indicated anything exotic, mostly Chinese. In 1702 a German traveler inspecting the palace of Rastatt reported rather vaguely that he saw "a lacquered Chinese paneling of a cabinet made by an Englishman who had been in India."[26]

The same indecisive language held true in France, as we learn from the brilliant study of the taste for the Chinese published by Madame Belevitch-Stankevitch. Here early data on lacquer are compiled from the period preceding that of Louis XIV.[27] We find that in 1560 the curio collection of Francis I had among its treasures *une petite boîte façon des Indes*, possibly a piece of lacquer. At this time the word *façon* meant no more than that the piece was of Oriental origin. A century later the *Inventaire général* of the furnishings at the court of Louis XIV mentions the following: "No. 205, *table vernie de la Chine*," decorated with engraved pieces of silver showing leafwork on a stand, formed by female terms, holding festoons, and "No. 207, *cabinet aussy de verny, façon de la Chine*." This cabinet was also enriched with engraved silver plates and with figures of children and female terms. The quotations show that in one case the word *façon* is used to define an Oriental item and in the other it stands for a French piece in the Oriental fashion. To add to the confusion the word *aussi* is joined; it must mean that for the preceding entry called merely *vernie de la Chine* the word *façon* would also be appropriate.

References of this kind, which can be multiplied, suggest that allusions to exotic products and countries were dealt with in an arbitrary way, making it extremely difficult to interpret them correctly. Unfortunately, just such "documentary evidence" has been used to prove that the beginnings of European lacquer were based on prototypes from the Far East and that these patterns were copied immediately after their introduction into Europe about 1600. The truth is that from the early period we know of hardly any *chinoiserie* and between (roughly) 1630 and 1670 we know no European lacquer of any consequence.

One letter, written by an expert on lacquer in 1616, is not very helpful. William Smith, an English lacquermaster, was plying his trade in Rome when he applied for a position with Thomas Howard, Lord of Arundel.[28] He reported that he had spent seven years traveling in France, Germany, and Italy "for the betternisse" of his knowledge. At present he was employed by "Cardinales and other Princes in works after the Chinese fashion which is much affected here." Circumstances speak against the possibility that the word *Chinese* means what it seems to mean; there is every chance that Smith was doing work in the Venetian style and that what he meant was lacquerwork in general.

Another fragment is reported by the Polish historiographer Stephan Pac who accompanied the Polish crown prince Ladislaus to Rome in 1624. At a banquet, as was the custom, the pope sat at a table by himself, while the prince sat at another on "a simple though painted armchair."[29] Considering the setting and the circumstances, this could hardly have been anything but a lacquered chair held to be precious. It would indicate that lacquer furniture was in use in Rome and might indicate the sort of ware provided by William Smith. It is quite unlikely that the armchair was imported from the Far East, nor is it likely that it was a piece of *chinoiserie*. Early in the seventeenth century, those few imports from the Far East that did turn up in Europe were not admired for their artistic value but rather for their strange and exotic character, in short as curios. It would be pointless to copy a curio, since only the rare import was in demand. There can be little doubt that the prince's armchair was an Italian original lacquered and decorated somewhat in the fashion described earlier.

A hundred years later the story would be quite different. By that time, Far Eastern lacquer was no longer of extreme value and the pride of its owner. Indeed, it had become the fashion to copy and adapt the style to suit the decorative needs of the day. The individuality of the copyist did not matter, and any *chinoiserie* as such was most acceptable.

The Netherlands would seem a logical place to search for early European lacquer, since the first lacquer products from China reached the Netherlands around 1600. They came by way of the first Dutch settlement in Indonesia, the village of Bantam on the isle of Java. In 1610 a cargo with nine cases of lacquerware arrived from Japan. Regular commercial relations began in 1639, but even before 1610 a guild of lacquerworkers was formed in Amsterdam. A prominent member of the guild was William Kick, whose workshop was a showplace for travelers.[30] When one Ernest Brinck called on Kick some time between 1615 and 1630, he had this to say about the lacquermaster's work: "In the house at the sign of East India I saw all sorts of lacquerware after the fashion of China, i. e., buffets, beds, chests, etc., and it is worthwhile to be seen." From existing account books it is known that in 1609 Kick made such lacquerware as chests, cabinets, salvers, and fruit trays. In 1612, when the States General presented gifts to Sultan Achmed Khan of Turkey, the ruler was given a genuine chest from the Far East and another matched by Kick, for which Kick charged 150 guilders.

In the following year Kick again produced a chest which the government presented to the Countess Palatine, the unfortunate queen of Bohemia. Kick is known to have invented in 1619 a kind of lacquer with which to treat tin, and he also knew how to lacquer leather. These details leave no doubt that Kick was an expert in his trade. As not one piece of his is known, nor pieces by his contemporaries, we can only guess what his work may have been like. There is, for example, a box with a domed lid generally considered as having been made in the Netherlands at the time of Kick (pl. 45). Another box, at the Palazzo Doria-Pamphilij in Rome (pl. 46), and a wooden plate (pl. 47), at the museum in Geneva, may be related. Typical is the decoration mingling Japanese floral motifs with such European elements as the classic border. Yet wherever these objects originated, they all seem to be closer to the early *chinoiserie* period (before 1700) than to a style characteristic of the early seventeenth century.

The evidence that suggests that Kick did copy Chinese lacquerwork should not be considered sufficient proof that in his time there was something like a general *chinoiserie* fashion either in the Netherlands or elsewhere. With the steady flow of Eastern imports into Amsterdam, it must be expected that attempts would be made to copy such objects. But in other European cities there were far fewer examples of this kind of merchandise and certainly there was not sufficient demand for copies of lacquer objects to create a fashion.

In the seventeenth century there happened to be very close commercial relations between the Netherlands and England, as was so clearly demonstrated by the exhibition entitled "The Orange and the Rose" held in London in 1964.[31] While this relationship was especially close in such craft work as cabinetmaking, the two countries do not seem to have much in common in the way of lacquerwork. The ballot box (pl. 38), for example, cannot be confronted with any objects definitely known to be of Dutch origin.

The French interest in early lacquerwork has been discussed, as has the fact that Ducerceau helped to spread the fashion for Moresque ornament to other European countries. In France, as was mentioned earlier, small frames and a certain type of cabinet must have been among the earliest copies of Venetian prototypes, shortly after the middle of the sixteenth century. Undoubtedly there also must have been such items as toilette boxes and other trinkets of that kind, although so far none has been recovered. Only some weapons are known, though of later date. One of these is a carbine dated around 1630 which belonged to Louis XIII and is now at the Metropolitan Museum (pl. 52). The shaft is finely lacquered and decorated with a Moresque pattern painted in gold. A few other objects of similar character can be recognized in other collections.

In Germany information about lacquer in the seventeenth century is so rare that we can be sure that lacquer was not in favor at that time. A reference tells us that one Paul Kick, who may have been related to the Dutch master, was active in Nuremberg in the 1630s. In 1648 he is mentioned as a "painter of Indian lacquer." Of greater interest, however, is a lacquer panel, dated 1628, showing a battle scene between horsemen with a surrounding border in a stylized floral motif (pl. 51). This piece has been attributed to a follower of the Augsburg painter Johann König, a pupil of the Roman painter Antonio Tempesta, who dedicated some of his prints and drawings of battle scenes to König. Prints of this kind were probably used for this panel, the painting of which seems mediocre. Technically it is well-executed. Its border reflects the Venetian style of lacquer ornaments.

Another product of Augsburg are two boxes of very thin fir wood ordered by the collector and erudite curio dealer Philipp Hainhofer (pls. 49, 50). The boxes were placed in a cabinet Hainhofer prepared for the city in 1632, but then Gustavus Adolphus, the victorious king of Sweden, suggested it be given to him.[32] Hainhofer was famous for the cabinets he fitted out with collections of objects intended to reflect in microcosm all human knowledge and experience. In this case Hainhofer added some lacquered plates imported from Goa (pl. 48). From these plates the decorator of the boxes took his cue, but he changed the design in crude fashion when he lacquered the boxes gold on black and colored the interior in red. These simple pieces used as containers for small artifacts were probably of no consequence, but they suggest that the craft of lacquer was at home in Augsburg at an early date.

The meager assembly of lacquer produced in Germany in the seventeenth century certainly held little promise for the future, and yet when toward the end of the century a new incentive for the production of lacquer came from the Far East the artisans of Germany produced lacquerwork of considerable importance. But before this could happen many decades were to pass.

Toward the middle of the seventeenth century all traces of European lacquer production vanish, as if the craft had subsided for awhile, and yet in the same period a number of books and reports on journeys to the Far East were published. Descriptions of strange peoples and even stranger customs whetted European appetites for more information about this far-off, alien world. At the same time the arrival of cargoes of oriental goods added to the growing interest. In 1644 John Evelyn went abroad and in Dieppe marveled at the treasures being unloaded: "Whatever the East Indies affords of cabinets, porcelain, natural and exotic rarities, are here to be had with abundant choice."[33] And in 1664 a Jesuit showed Evelyn an enormous collection of Eastern treasures which Evelyn took pains to list in his diary. Evelyn not only admired these treasures from the Far East but took part in efforts to learn more about them. In 1662, for example, he translated a report on China written by a Dutch scholar, although he rather doubted it would be worthy of publication since so many similar books had appeared. As the author of *Sylva* he was interested in all forest products, and this interest may have impelled his letter to Robert Boyle, written in 1661, transmitting a recipe for varnish he had received from a "curious person" who swore it would be found satisfactory. Since we know that Boyle was interested in learning about Far Eastern lacquer, it is possible that Evelyn's recipe had something to do with experiments to unlock the secret of the superior lacquer of the East.

1. Giuseppe Morazzoni, *Mobili Veneziani Laccati*, 2 vols. (Milan, 1954), 1:9–55; Agostino Sagredo, *Sulle consorterie delle arti edificativi in Venezia* (Venice, 1859).
2. G. Berchet, *La repùblica di Venezia e la Persia* (Turin, 1865), p. 63; Wilhelm von Heyd, *Histoire du commerce du Levant au moyen âge* (Leipzig, 1886).
3. The terms *ageminius* and *agemina* (Venetian dialect: *azzimina*) are derived from the Arabic, *al agem*, which means a faraway country, in some instances more specifically Persia. The terms were used to define damascened work made in Italy since the Renaissance. The source for information on Paulus Ageminius is Leonardo Fioravanti, *Specchio Universale*, 2d ed. (Venice, 1572), p. 67. Unfortunately, these terms have contributed to the perpetuation of a long-standing error in the literature on damascening as carried out in the Near East and in Venice. It is wrong to assume that Moslems were employed in Venice as artisans either singly or as members of guilds. This belief rests solely on a hypothesis first advanced by Henri Lavoix ("Les Azziministes," in *Gazette des Beaux Arts* 3 [1862]: 64–74; 16 [1877]: 28; 18 [1878]: 783). I have refuted this theory in "Sarazenen in Venedig?" in *Festschrift für Heinz Ladendorf* (Cologne, 1970), pp. 38–44. It seems important to call attention to this problem to avoid further speculation that lacquerwork in Venice was in any way stimulated by the presence of Moslem craftsmen.
4. Richard Ettinghausen, "Near Eastern Book Covers and Their Influence on European Bindings," in *Ars Orientalis* 3 (1959): 114–31; Filippo Rossi, "Le legature italiane del'500," in *Dedalo* 3 (1922/23): 373–96.
5. Rudolf Berliner, *Ornamentale Vorlegeblätter* Leipzig, 1926), pls. 83–90, 96; Joan Evans, *Pattern in Western Europe*, 2 vols. (Oxford, 1931), 1:225.
6. Julius von Schlosser, *Kunst- und Wunderkammern der Spätrenaissance* (Leipzig, 1908), p. 64 (fig. 88). The London table was exhibited at the Burlington Fine Arts Club, January 1936, no. 89, and published as Italian, seventeenth century, by H. Clifford Smith in the *Burlington Magazine* 29 (1936), 153.
7. Leonardo Fioravanti, *Livre des Secrets* (Paris, 1582), bk. 3, chap. 68. An Italian edition, *Compendio di secreti rationali*, was published in Venice in 1562.
8. Gustav Ludwig, "Restello, Spiegel und Toiletten-Utensilien in Venedig zur Zeit der Renaissance," in *Italienische Forschungen I* (Berlin, 1906), pp. 169–362.
9. Antonio Doni, *I Marmi* (Venice, 1552), p. 78.
10. Ludwig, "Restello, Spiegel...", p. 302.
11. Another cabinet without doors is illustrated in Carlo Rava, *Il mobile d'arte* (Milan, 1956), fig. 85. A small corner cabinet was owned in 1967 by Michael Hall, Inc., New York City.
12. Ludwig, "Restello, Spiegel...", p. 314.
13. Details of some caskets of a similar general character are given below:

    a) Museu Nacional de Arte Antiga, Lisbon, pl. 24 (length 96 cm). The casket was received from the Monastery de la Graça in Lisbon. Its earlier history is told in Sousa Viterbo, *Notes au catalogue de l'exposition d'art ornamental* (Lisbon, 1882). Viterbo follows Fr. Augustin de Sainte Marie, *L'histoire de la fondation du Couvent Royal de Sainte Monique dans la cité de Goa* (n. d.).

    According to this source, the casket had been purchased at a time unknown by a king of Ormuz from Venetian artisans for 50,000 pardaos (the pardao is a gold coin, the half rupia of Portuguese India, valued at approximately two shillings and threepence in the seventeenth century). The casket was later owned by a "Moor" who presented it to Dom Fr. Aleixio de Meneses, Primaz of the Church of the Indies residing at Goa in the period 1606–09. Dom Aleixio donated the casket to the Monastery de la Graça. Then King Philip III of Spain wished to obtain the casket as a gift for the queen but did not succeed. If the theory concerning the Mouchy casket advanced here is correct, the queen at this time must have owned a similar casket presented to her by the pope in 1601.

b) City Art Museum, St. Louis, pls. I, 26 (length 73 cm). Purchased on the art market, history unknown, in 1958.

c) The Honorable Gavin Astor, Hever Castle (Kent), (length 70 cm). Connected with this piece is the tradition that, containing baby linen for the Dauphin, Louis XIII, it was a gift by the Venetian Republic to Queen Marie de Medici in 1601. There is no supporting evidence for this story, but it is very similar to the tradition surrounding the Mouchy casket.

d) S. A. Le Duc de Mouchy, Paris, pl. 23 (length 66 cm). Reproduced in *L'art pour Tous* (1873), no. 323, p. 1291. This casket came into the family of the present owner with marriage of an heiress of the House of Beauvau-Craon in the early eighteenth century. According to family tradition the casket once contained the baby linen of Henri IV.

e) Hearst State Historical Monument, San Simeon, California (length 61 cm). Woodwork unlacquered; rock crystal; bronze plaques with figures in the Fountainebleau style; floor of silver-gilt, set with stones in varying colors. Formerly in Sale Heilbronner, third sale, 1922, Paris, no. 75. Illustrated.

f) Sale Alfred de Rothschild, London, 1884, no. 189 (height 30 cm, length possibly 40 cm). Illustrated.

g) Baron Alexis de Redé, Paris (length 39 cm). Formerly owned by M. Arturo Lopez, Paris, purchased on the London art market.

h) Sale Robiony, Nice, 15 February 1965, no. 157, pl. 25 (length 28 cm). Illustrated. Perhaps the same as the casket offered at the sale Comte R. de Ch.(ambrun), Paris, 12 March 1866 or May 1869, since both caskets seem to be of the same period and have sixteen columns. R. de Ch.'s casket was supposed to have been a gift of King Sigismund of Poland to his mother Bona. Details are incorrect, since Bona Sforza was the wife of Sigismund I (1466–1548) and unrelated to King Sigismund III (1566–1632) during whose reign the casket must have been made.

i) Baron and Baroness Elie de Rothschild (length 24 cm). Owned by the family since about 1850.

The library of the Bibliothèque des Arts Décoratifs in Paris owns photographs of a number of caskets that were probably on the art market; some may be the caskets previously mentioned. One photograph shows a drawing of a casket clipped from the catalogue of an Italian jewelry exhibition about 1900. The caption reads: Fig. 246. *Vecchio disegno di una cassetta lavorata in Venezia prima del 1587.* The drawing is poor and not of the period, but it may point to a dated casket, now unknown.

14. Francesco Sansovino, *Venezia, città nobilissima* (Venice, 1591), p. 134 verso. See also Pompeo Molmenti, *La storia di Venezia nella vita privata,* 3 vols. (Bergamo, 1910), 2:174.
15. The later version of Titian's Lavinia has been called *La cassette.* It was once in the collection of Lord Cowper at Panshanger; its present location is unknown. It is here reproduced from an engraving of the early eighteenth century when the portrait was owned by the Régent Duc Philippe d'Orléans.
16. Joseph Braun, *Die Reliquiare des christlichen Kultes und ihre Entwicklung* (Freiburg, 1940); Erich Meyer, "Reliquie und Reliquiar im Mittelalter," in *Festschrift für Carl Heyse* (Berlin, 1950), pp. 55–56.
17. Henry Havard, *Dictionnaire de l'ameublement,* 4 vols. (Paris, 1887), 1 (fig. 758). Here illustrated is a casket, but no text is given; probably it is a drawing of the Mouchy casket. Under the entry *langes* there are quotations from the *Mercure galant* and the *Gazette de France* about the papal gifts. Gaetano Moroni, *Dizionario de erudizione storico-ecclesiastico,* 108 vols. (Venice, 1844), 23. See *fascie* and various other *loci* there indicated. This report is not complete concerning all gifts. It describes some but not those of 1601, nor any caskets here mentioned. Patrick Marquis MacSwiney de Mashanaglass, *Le Portugal et le Saint Siège,* 2 vols. (Paris, 1899), 2. This rare volume, its paper now crumbling, is in the Law Library at Harvard University. The title hides the fact that it contains a history of the custom of the *fascie* but has nothing to say of the caskets or their nature. *Manuscript, Vatican Library* (Vat. Lit. 12228). This slim volume contains a collection of scattered papers, dated from the seventeenth century, concerning papal gifts. One list enumerates the sums spent on six *fascie* between 1640 and 1683; these vary between scudi 6,636,87 and 10,960,23. Another paper mentions that the gift of 1601 to Henri IV of France was composed of *una cassa, nella quale erano le fascie, una croce piena di reliquie e molte altre galanterie; il tutto pero con la Benedizione Pontifica et Indulgenza* (a case with the *fascie,* a cross containing relics and many other niceties, all of this accompanied by the papal benediction and indulgence). This passage confirms that a casket holding the gifts formed part of the present; the same is indicated by the considerable sums spent for the *fascie.*

The splendor of the sets becomes apparent from notations found in the *Gazette de France* of July

1639 in which the *fascie* sent to Louis XIII in honor of the future Louis XIV is described (see Havard 3:223). Some of the eighteenth-century *fascie* were decorated with paintings showing St. John baptizing Christ. The painter Clementina Subleyras executed such a subject in 1781 (Moroni, *op. cit.*, p. 229). When in 1725 the Pretender Charles Edward received his gift in Rome it was placed inside two cases covered with crimson velvet to which was attached the coat of arms of Clement XI embroidered in gold. Inside the case were two coffers (*due casse ... dentro a tali casse ... due cofani*) (Moroni, *op. cit.*, p. 228).

18. *Archivio secreto Vaticano, Rome: Francia*, 50: fol. 21′–22′; *Miscellanea Arm.*, 2:133, fol. 28′–29′; *B. Barbiche, Correspondance du Nonce en France Innocenzo del Bufalo* (Rome-Paris, 1964), pp. 47, 218.

19. Jules Guiffrey, *Inventaire général* (Paris, 1885/86). Volume I lists two caskets (pp. 224, 252): no. 37, *Un cabinet enchassé de cristal de roche garni de dix-huit colonnes aussy de cristal, le corps de bois doré* and no. 287 (the casket sent to Siam in 1702), *Un cabinet composé de sept grandes glaces ovales et seize colonnes, dont quatorze torses et deux lisses, le tout de cristal de roche ensemble de cent soixante et douze autres petites pièces de cristal enchassées dans un bois doré à la damasquine, long de 15 pouces* [about 38 cm], *large de 11 pouces sur 11 pouces de hault.* The description given for no. 37 does not conform to that of the Mouchy casket, since it mentions only eighteen columns instead of the twenty-four to be seen. This may be a scribal error; in any case, the description is much more general than that for no. 287. Be that as it may, the whereabouts of no. 37 is unknown, but the Mouchy casket is still in the possession of the family which inherited it in the eighteenth century.

20. Another casket is illustrated in J. F. Hayward "The Mannerist Goldsmiths: France and the School at Fontainebleau," in *Connoisseur* (May 1963), p. 12. The piece is described as made of silver following Italian precedent but using certain forms of design inspired by Ducerceau. It is not impossible that the "Italian precedent" might have been the casket given by the pope in 1601. If this is true, the casket discussed in the article would have to be dated a quarter of a century earlier.

21. *Le triomphe du manierisme européen*, Amsterdam Exhibition, 1955, no. 503.

22. Data kindly communicated by Mr. Gudmund Boesen, Curator of Rosenborg Palace, Copenhagen, November 1962.

23. Ralph Edwards, "The Master of the Saddlers' Ballot Box," in *Burlington Magazine*, 68 (1936), 232–35; Hugh Honour, *Chinoiserie* (London, 1961), p. 45; Günther Schiedlausky, "Über den flachen Holzteller," in *Anzeiger des Germanischen Museums* (1954–59), pp. 170–91.

24. Ralph Edwards, *The Shorter Dictionary of English Furniture*, (London, 1954), p. 224.

25. Louis Battifol, *Marie de Medici* (London, 1908), p. 250; Louis Battifol, *Le Louvre* (Paris, 1930), pp. 32, 35.

26. Gerhard Peters, *Das Rastatter Schloss* (Karlsruhe, 1925), p. 66.

27. H. Belevitch-Stankevitch, *Le goût Chinois en France* (Paris, 1910), pp. xxxiii, 132.

28. Edwards, *Shorter Dictionary*, p. 224.

29. Stefan Pac's report, published in Polish at Breslau in 1854, is quoted in Casimir von Chledowsky, *Rom* (Munich, 1921), p. 118.

30. Information about William Kick I owe to Theodor Lunsingh Scheuerleer and to his study "An besteding en verspreiding van Japansch lakwerk door de Nederlanders in de 17[te] eeuw," in *Oudheidkundig Genootschap Jaarverslagen*, 82–83 (1939–41), 54–74.

31. Theodor Lunsingh Scheuerleer, "The Decorative Arts," in *Catalogue of the Exhibition "The Orange and the Rose,"* Victoria and Albert Museum (London, 1964), p. 25.

32. John Boettiger, *Philipp Hainhofer und der Kunstschrank Gustav Adolfs in Upsala*, 4 vols. (Stockholm, 1905/10), 4: pls. 69, 84.

33. John Evelyn, *Diary*, ed. Bray, 4 vols. (London, 1889), 1:64, 402; 3:133, 137; John Evelyn, *Sylva* (London, 1670), p. 123.

CHAPTER II LACQUER IN THE EIGHTEENTH CENTURY

> We fetch our models from the wise Chinese,
> European artists are too cool and chaste
> JAMES CAWTHORN, 1756

The fashion for early European lacquer lost its impetus around 1630. Certainly its simplicity and the lack of imagination shown in its decoration compared unfavorably with the striking colors, novel shapes, and sparkling luster of the lacquerware arriving from the Far East. As the century progressed, imported lacquer came in such quantity that it was fast losing its value as a rarity and a curiosity. By the middle of the seventeenth century, the China trade had become a thriving business as the result of trading posts established by European seafarers in the Orient.[1] First to gain a foothold in China (Macao, 1557) and in Japan (Kyushu, 1542) were the Portuguese, who lost out when Portugal came under the domination of Spain in 1581. The Portuguese colonies ceased to be particularly prosperous as Spain usurped colonial trade and controlled the sea lanes across the Pacific by way of the Philippines, even using its American colonies as intermediate trading posts.

The Spanish were not the sole threat to Portuguese traders; in time they also met sharp competition from the Dutch who formed a Far Eastern trading company and established themselves in 1609 on the island of Hirado Shima, where somewhat earlier the Portuguese had set up a trading post. In 1639, when the Portuguese were expelled from Japan, the only Europeans remaining to trade with the Japanese were the Dutch from a trading post established on an artificial island called Deshima in the Bay of Nagasaki.

In India, too, at the same time, the Dutch carried on a considerable trade with Bengal, where goods were produced for the European market. Particularly of note was lacquered furniture from Cambaye and Chaul in South India. By the middle of the seventeenth century the Dutch had become masters of the trade with the Orient and for the remainder of the century reaped huge profits. For example, by 1653 the Dutch company had made a profit of 51,000,000 livres, increased to 100,000,000 livres by 1693, and this in spite of the extremely long and hazardous voyages of from two to three years in ships carrying a cargo of only 300 tons. And yet by 1730 a large deficit had developed, due in part to mismanagemen but more directly to strong competition from the English. In addition, in 1737 the imperial government of China put restrictions on trade and confined European merchantment to the harbor at Canton, where they were only permitted to unload their vessels and pick up new cargo. This restriction remained in force until 1842 when the Chinese were required to open the four so-called treaty ports of Amoy, Fu-chow, Ningpo, and Shanghai.

The English made their first effort to establish trade with the Orient in 1596 when Queen Elizabeth invited the emperor of China to engage in business transactions for their mutual benefit. The East India Company was established in 1599. As long as the Dutch controlled the China trade, these efforts were unsuccessful, but during the reign of Charles II, and after the reorganization of the East India Company in 1698, English trade became more prosperous.

The French, who began trade with the Far East in 1664 through their *Compagnie des Indes Orientales*, were never equal to competition with the Dutch or the English. Of an estimated 20,000 European ships in 1660, only 600 were French and some 16,000 were Dutch. Although the French were not successful commercially, they had important ties in the Far East – since 1582, many of the Jesuit missions in Pekin and throughout China were of French origin. Reports from these missions, often translated into other languages, provided a good deal of knowledge about Chinese techniques in the arts and crafts, yet the bulk of information about the Orient came from reports by Dutch legations and from travelers. Actually oriental objects had been known in Europe before the sixteenth century. For instance, in the treasury of San Marco in Venice is a Chinese *Ting yao* vase dating from about 1250 which may have been brought back by Marco Polo. Occasionally in the fourteenth and fifteenth centuries silks and other goods found their way into the treasure houses of Europe. There is, for example, a Chinese celadon bowl of the Ming period, in a rich silver-gilt mounting, once owned by the counts of Katzenellenbogen and now in a museum in Kassel.[2] Such incunabula usually became part of a church or court collection and disappeared from public view. During the sixteenth century, Eastern wares which today we would consider objects of art became more frequent in the cargoes of Spanish and Portuguese merchantmen. These too were absorbed into the collections of the great and the wealthy. By the middle of the seventeenth century, when the Dutch controlled the Eastern trade, large cargoes arriving regularly in Amsterdam established that city as a world market and attracted buyers and court agents from all over Europe. Merchandise purchased at the docks in Amsterdam was immediately sent to other continental markets. In Paris, as early as 1610, Portuguese merchants traded oriental wares at the annual fair of St.-Germain. In spite of the enormous quantity of Eastern lacquer and porcelain brought to Europe, the demand continued to increase, thus creating a favorable market for European competition.

Dutch traders of the seventeenth century called both oriental products and European imitations *lac-werk*, the English referred to their imitations as *Japan work*, though copied from the "Indians," and the French used the terms *vernis de la chine* or *lachinage* for both oriental wares and European imitations, although the latter were often referred to as *vernis*. In Germany and occasionally in Holland, the term *Indianish werk* was applied with no great distinction made between products of the Orient and those of Europe. Technically, the Dutch term *lac-werk* for Eastern goods is misleading because it is derived from shellac, an ingredient never used in the Far East. A product of India, shellac takes its name from the Sanskrit *lac* or *lakh*, meaning 100,000. This figure, a symbol for "innumerable," has reference to the enormous number of shell lice which deposit a secretion on the branches of certain trees and, in combination with an exudation from the tree itself, produces a gum or resin from which shellac can be distilled. In raw shape, it is *sticklac*, since the gum settles on twigs; in purified form, it is *seed lac*, in the shape of grain. This shellac, also called *gomma lacca* or simply *lacca* in India, had been traded to Persians, Arabs, and Turks centuries before European lacquermaking began.

In China and Japan, only the resin from the *rhus vernicifera* (Chinese, *Chi'ichou*; Japanese, *Urishi-no ki*), a variety of the sumac family often called Tsi, Ci, or Chiaram in eighteenth-century European tracts, was used in making lacquer, for only this resin gave a brilliant and lustrous finish and was amazingly durable. That this resin, most irritating to the skin, was the basic ingredient of Chinese lacquer was unknown in Europe until the middle of the seventeenth century, half a century after oriental lacquer had begun to arrive with any regularity and when already various efforts had been made to copy the technique.

Today it is difficult to imagine the extraordinary impact Eastern lacquer made on Europeans. These shiny objects of an apparently very durable material, shaped and decorated in a way entirely new, fitted into no European category. Yet the very strangeness and scarcity of these items prompted the desire to find out how they were made.[3] At the same time, the high asking price stimulated the desire to find a way of imitating "lacquer" to allow European craftsmen to compete with the foreign product.

Throughout most of the seventeenth century European scholars believed that Indian shellac formed the basis of all Eastern lacquerwork. The ground for this belief was a confused report published by a Dutch traveler, Jan Huygen van Linschoten, in an account of his travels in India (*Navigatio ac itinerarium*, Leyden, 1595/96). According to Linschoten, the lacquer produced in India, China, and Japan required shellac. He also remarked that the best work of this kind came from China: "Desks, targets, tables, Cubbordes, Boxes, and a thousand such like thinges that are all covered and wrought with lac of all colours and fashions; so that it maketh men to wonder at the beautie and brightness of the colour, which is altogether lac."[4]

Among Englishmen interested in the lacquer process, the most eminent was the scientist Robert Boyle (1627–1691). Boyle accepted Linschoten's erroneous statement that shellac was the basis of Chinese and Japanese lacquer but confused the issue by omitting Linschoten's reference to India, where indeed shellac was used.[5] Some time after the founding in 1663 of the Royal Society for Improving Natural Knowledge, an outgrowth of the "invisible college" of Boyle and his friends, some samples of oriental lacquer were sent to the society for analysis and promptly forwarded to Gresham College with the idea that "the curious, or those who desire to improve the art of varnishing may use the several substances made use of in China for these purposes."[6] The examination proved fruitless; the learned men of the college were unable to provide any additional information. Once again one must mention the ubiquitous John Evelyn, who also had become interested in lacquer; he must have had considerable practical knowledge of varnish as a result of the studies he made for his report on the depletion of standing timber in England. Here much useful information was included on the production and use of varnish.

Like the English, the French were eager to learn the secret of Eastern lacquer and commissioned members of the Académie des Sciences to examine specimens, only to be informed of their failure.[7] Meanwhile, in 1655, a notice had been published by the Jesuit father Martin Martinius in his *Novus Atlas Sinensis* which apparently eluded the scientists seeking to learn the riddle of lacquer. Martinius mentioned that in the Chinese province of Che chiang there were trees exuding a substance which was used to prepare a liquid with which to cover the elegant wares so much admired in Europe. Here at last was a statement by a European writer establishing some of the details of oriental lacquermaking. It should have been followed up by an examination of this substance brought back from China, but this was not to happen until the last decade of the century when the erudite Jesuit, Father Filippo Bonanni, who became an expert on lacquer, was given the opportunity.

Around 1690 the grand duke of Tuscany, Cosimo III (1642–1723), himself interested in scientific studies, received specimens reported to be the resin used in China together with some oil in which to dissolve it. He ordered Joseph del Papa, the court physician of Cardinal Medici, to analyze the material, and the doctor commissioned one Signor Ignatio to deal with the substance. Unaware that the resin was irritating to the skin, both the worthy signor and his maidservant were infected with a painful inflammation and reportedly had difficulty in breathing. In addition, all efforts to dissolve the substance in liquid were in vain, and no conclusions could be drawn as to its properties. And yet before del Papa gave up, he did draw the correct conclusion that the resin might have been derived from the gum or juice of some resinous herb or tree – but not quite willing to be content with his observation, he added, unfortunately, that it might well be "the fat of an animal."

The doctor remained ignorant of the properties of oriental resin, but there was another man who had access to the court who was eager to experiment. This ardent investigator was Father Filippo Bonanni, who procured some specimens from the grand duke as well as some of the oil sent from China and published a report on his experiments in Rome in 1720 under the title *Trattato sopra la Vernice*.[8] Unlike others who had examined the variety of substances sent from China, Bonanni was not only skilled in chemical analysis and experimentation but also familiar with the early publications on the nature of lacquer. Some of Bonanni's knowledge came from information provided by another Jesuit, Father Eustache Jamart, in his *China monumentis illustrata* (Amsterdam, 1667), published by Father Athanasius Kircher, and from studies made by Father Johannes Zahn of Würzburg and published as *Ocular Artificialis* (Würzburg, 1685), a treatise on optics in which lacquer was recommended as a cover for tin in the construction of optical instruments – probably the first time that the possibility of combining lacquer and metal is mentioned in the literature. Valuable information on China also came to Bonanni through Father Louis le Comte's *Memoirs*, published in Paris in 1696. As a result of his studies conducted in Florence between 1690 and 1700, Bonanni was the first to publish an accurate and authoritative report on Chinese lacquer and the adaptation of lacquer techniques in Europe. He concluded that Europeans would have to be satisfied with substitutes for the Chinese resin he called *Chiaram*, since it could neither be shipped to Europe nor could the *Tsi* tree be cultivated in the western hemisphere. As substitutes Bonanni recommended the most obvious: varnish or shellac and certain other ingredients of similar character already used by European lacquermasters.

The importance of Bonanni's booklet as a scholarly tract as well as a sound guide was immediately recognized. It was translated into French in 1723 by the well-known writer on French art, Dézailler d'Argenville, who even took the trouble to interview Bonanni in Rome in order to achieve a correct translation. Other translations followed up to 1780.

I. Casket, Venice, about 1600

II. Shield, Venice, end of sixteenth century

While Bonanni's findings must be considered a milestone in the history of European lacquer because they ended the era of uncertainty about the differences between oriental and occidental ingredients, there is certainly no reason to believe that contemporary lacquermasters were much impressed or indeed interested in his results. After all, these artisans had been dealing with the problem of producing lacquer for more than a hundred years, and had achieved results which, within reason, made some of their work comparable to oriental wares. The question then arises, where did these early masters discover the methods they used in their craft? The answer will be found if we turn to those age-old books containing an extraordinary variety of recipes for almost everything, from the treatment of diseases and matters of husbandry to the ingredients necessary for paints and varnishes. One of the oldest of these written, and later printed, texts, some worthless, others valuable, was the famous work *De coloribus et artibus Romanorum* which concentrated on painting. Compiled around the tenth century in Byzantium, it was based on older collections of recipes by a man who gave his name as Heraclius (eighth century). In the twelfth century, the German Theophilus Presbyter was the leading authority in the field on the basis of his book, *Schedula Diversorum Artium*. Later, in 1390, the painter Cenno Cennini of Florence provided the first technical knowledge about the paintings of his age in *Trattato de la Pittura*. Similar books continued to appear as late as the sixteenth century. One, with the appealing title, *Secreti*, was published anonymously by Don Alessio Piemontese at Venice in 1556.[9] Another compendium of secret recipes was written by Leonardo Fioravanti in 1562. Both are quoted frequently in Bonanni's tract, which includes Fioravanti's references (mentioned earlier) to the lacquering of Turkish bows and arrows.

Toward the end of the seventeenth century, when interest in painting and lacquering *à la Chine* became popular, a number of tracts were published which specialized in advice on lacquering or japanning. Possibly a French collection of recipes by Antoni d'Emery, *Recueil de Curiosités Rares et Nouvelles* (Paris, 1674), may have been the first book of the new type to be printed. In the same year in which an English translation of d'Emery's book appeared, William Salmon published a work on the subject to which he gave the abstruse title *Polygraphice* (London, 1685). Shortly after, one "C. B." published a *Traité de mignature, les secrets de faire le verniz de la chine* (The Hague, 1688). Salmon's book was reprinted frequently, but by far the more widely read was *A Treatise on Japanning and Varnishing*, published by John Stalker and George Parker in London in 1688 (most recently reprinted by Tiranti, London, 1960). In a preface the authors state that a definite need for the book exists because there are "so many who tried to exercise the new art but did not know how to practice it." In fact, the authors found it nothing short of scandalous the way "stuff and trash" purporting to be japanwork was foisted off on customers. Their aim was to show the gentry how to distinguish between "good work and rubbish, between an ignorant knave and an Artist, and put a stop to all the cheat and cousenage of those whiffling, impotent fellows who pretend to teach young ladies that art in which they themselves have not been instructed, and to the disgrace of the Title, Lurk and shelter themselves under the notion of Japanners, Painters, Gilders, etc." The treatise was arranged in a practical way, combining recipes with valuable instructions and including novel patterns for decorations in the Eastern style. Strangely crude illustrations nevertheless give a good idea of the decoration which was applied to furniture, powder boxes, patch boxes, trays, comb cases, brushes, mirror frames, candlesticks, and other articles.

Because Stalker and Parker's book was a large tome not always within the reach of those dealing with lacquer either as professionals or as dilettantes, there were many smaller volumes published in England as well as abroad giving instructions in lacquer painting. Although Bonanni's book of 1720 had been written by a scholar, it contained much practical advice and remained in use throughout most of the eighteenth century until replaced by a systematic volume that became the gospel of Europe's lacquerworkers, Sieur Watin's *Le peintre Doreur et Vernisseur* (Paris, 1772). Jean Felix Watin was an experienced and learned craftsman as well as a purveyor to the court of Louis XVI. As a supplement to his book, Watin included the excellent report on Eastern methods of lacquer making which Father d'Incarville had sent back to Europe. First published in the Memoirs of the French Royal Academy (vol. xv, 1760), this report was especially valuable because d'Incarville had made a close study of Eastern lacquer workshops and had experimented himself. A valuable addition to Watin's treatise is the list he gives of lacquer ingredients and the tools he had for sale. Following Watin, many books of lesser importance, albeit advising on new methods developed, were published well into the nineteenth century.

Undoubtedly the study of old recipes is of interest to the historian of chemistry, but it does little to advance connoisseurship in matters of lacquer. While there is nothing difficult to understand in the general processing of lacquer, it is rather irksome to interpret old recipes, for in the seventeenth century no effort was made at clear formulation and frequently the terms used are confusing because they do not always have the same meaning. For example, there was shellac, a resin and a true lacquer ingredient, which was also called *gomma lacca* or *lacca*. Since shellac contains a red pigment which could only be eliminated by a process discovered after 1770, *lacca* frequently stands for "red color."

What one should realize is that European lacquer techniques developed quite independently of those of the Far East for the very reason that Eastern resin was not available. Lacking this, Europeans used the next best thing, varnish, with which they had been familiar for centuries. Varnish (*vernis, fernis, firnis*) as it was used in the seventeenth century was a solution made of an oil combined with a hardening and drying ingredient, today called a siccative. The application of several coats of varnish, clear or pigmented, gave an object something of the appearance of having been lacquered in the oriental manner. This was especially so when seen by a European eye not so aware of what was missing of the delicacy and subtle quality of an oriental piece, to say nothing of the loss in durability.

A good deal closer to the Eastern ideal was the method of covering a piece with a European lacquer based on a resin such as shellac. This was made up with spirits of wine used as a thinner and combined with a siccative or catalyst (litharge, cobalt, manganese). For a long time shellac was the most common resin used in making European lacquer, but as time went on other resins were also recognized as being suitable – copal, sandarac, *sanguis draconis, pix greca, amber* (also called *bernstein, agtstein, succinic*), and others. Unlike Eastern lacquer techniques, the use of shellac left much to be desired in the way of brilliance, smoothness, and durability. Shellac does not contain the infinitesimally small bodies of the *Tsi* resin which give lacquer intense luster and make it practically impervious to scarring. In addition, Europeans did not devote the same painstaking care that the Far Eastern craftsmen would give to a piece. This goal of absolute perfection in the production of an object is one of the main factors distinguishing an oriental piece from its European equivalent. Indeed, general routine and a few technical tricks were not nearly so decisive in explaining the discrepancy than were the differences in the character and philosophy of the workers involved. One can fathom what this means if one imagines a master of Zen philosophy at work on a piece of lacquer and then thinks of a European craftsman obeying the whims of a prince in fashioning a China cabinet *à la mode*.

In spite of these severe limitations, the achievements of European lacquerworkers were quite remarkable as they gained experience in their techniques and began to develop a style of their own. As they experimented with lacquer, they found a solution to each new problem. For example, the process called polymerization today was discovered in the seventeenth century: linseed oil, known as *fat-oil* or *stand-oil*, was used to bind like molecules together in a compound having the same elements in the same proportions but a higher molecular weight and different physical properties, including greater durability. To harden the solution, artisans resorted to a slow combustion process by exposing the substance to air; then it was discovered that this process could be accelerated by drying the solution in specially constructed ovens, if certain precautions were taken.

Until well into the first half of the eighteenth century the carrier for most lacquer was wood – generally only custom-made works, with some few exceptions. In places like Venice or Spa, the fashionable health resort in Belgium, small lacquer pieces were carried in stock, since there was a ready market for such bric-a-brac as sets of toiletry boxes, trays, mirrors, and frames. Such exceptions are to be noted because it was this kind of "seasonal selling" that marked the beginning of the industrialization of lacquer. In England during the same period "lacquer" was still a synonym for objects of lacquered wood, but already artisans were looking for other basic materials that might be lacquered, and this too pointed toward industrialization. In Italy, as the Jesuit Johannes Zahn pointed out, there had been some early experiments in lacquering small metal objects of bronze or copper, notably lamps and optical instruments.[10]

If iron could be rolled into thin sheets and then shaped and lacquered, it might lead to the manufacture of pots, boxes, trays, and other items at prices with which no craftsman could compete, even if each piece were painted by hand. This search for new materials and new methods was a trend of the period and had already proved successful with such one-time handicrafts as spinning and weaving. At Pontypool (Wales) in the second quarter of the eighteenth century, after many years of experimentation, it was at last possible to produce cheap lacquered tinware for household use. How this was done and the consequences thereof will be discussed in the last chapter.

Another substitute for wood was papier-mâché which had been used earlier in Europe as a substitute for stucco ornaments in the building trade. Now it began to be used in the making of snuffboxes and similar objects which were to be lacquered. Papier-mâché, like tin, proved an ideal material when lacquermaking became an industry.

For the lacquermaker the technique itself did not offer any particular difficulties, although it did demand the hand of a master skilled in the art of decorative painting. Often the wood was first covered with muslin, either completely or where there was a joint or some unevenness or imperfection in the wood, and then the gesso ground was applied. If desired, certain motifs – rocks, clouds, or figures – were modeled in relief. The piece was then painted with tempera colors, usually black, red, or blue, and finally the painted surface was covered either by a clear or pigmented lacquer. Then came a thorough drying and polishing of the ground. The process of lacquering and drying was repeated up to as many as twenty times, according to the intended preciousness of the piece. Before the last clear coat of lacquer was applied, decorations in gold or silver were added. Black lacquer pieces were in great demand in Europe since black was the color of the majority of pieces imported from the Orient; red or coral was the next most desirable color. Yellow, green, and white were used more rarely, and today many of these pieces present a very different appearance since the varnish has turned from white to yellow or from blue to green.[11] A great number of recipes for marbelizing and especially for giving a tortoiseshell appearance testifies to the popularity of these kind of decorations, especially in the seventeenth century.

Another technique required carving into the lacquer, as deep as the gesso ground, though not into the wood itself. The design, embedded in the lacquer like a relief in reverse, was then colored and coated again with clear varnish. This technique was not in great favor, and in 1688 Stalker and Parker insisted that this so-called Bantam work was outmoded: in being "torn and hacked to join a new fancie, you may observe the finest hodgepodge and meddly of men and trees turned topsie turvie... men instead of marching by land you shall see them taking journeys through the Air as if they had found out Doctor Wilkins way of traveling to the moon."[12] Original Bantam work was lacquerware collected for resale at the Dutch trading post of Bantam in Java and also on the Coromandel coast in southwestern India – hence also "Coromandel" lacquer – for shipment to Europe. The region where these lacquers were made during the K'ang Hsi period (1662–1722) was the province of Honan in China. European craftsmen were not greatly interested in copying this ware because of the rich supply shipped to Europe in the form of ornamental screens that were easy enough to take apart and cut to measure for cabinet doors or wall paneling.

To an oriental artisan, the European process would have seemed a rather careless and shoddy one. The precious Japanese *Guri* lacquer, for example, required forty or more polishings. In the Orient, the lacquerworker wore as few clothes as possible to avoid dust that might settle on the lacquer as it dried. He sealed his workshop door so that no draft might stir up dust. In doing particularly fine work, he might even arrange to go to sea so that no particle of any kind might settle on the surface before it dried and interfere with the perfection of the lacquer. That Europeans did not have either understanding or appreciation of the differences that distinguished the quality of lacquer was well known in the Orient and consequently those pieces shipped to Europe were often of lower quality than those offered for domestic sale. It is only by chance that pieces of first quality reached Europe.

Here an incident should be mentioned that will be reported later in more detail. It remains unique in the history of the development of European lacquer techniques. Two sculptors, Marcel Wolfers and Jean Dunand, working independently in the wake of the *style nouveau* movement, became interested in creating lacquerwork. It was their aim to use the Far Eastern ingredient *rhus vernicifera* and follow all the painstaking steps of oriental techniques but without making concessions to oriental style. In an interview Dunand once explained his way of working: "At the bottom the first layer of lacquer, then comes the second and at the top the twentieth. So you have to varnish or lacquer twenty times – or rather forty, as the job has to be repeated on the other side to keep the wood from warping: otherwise it would crack, for you wouldn't believe how easily the lacquer can twist even the hardest wood into a semicircle. Actually not forty but as many as a hundred preparations are required since after each varnishing you have to polish and before each varnishing there have to be twenty seasonings, each lasting four days . . . [they] . . . require damp conditioning, and a dark room where water flows continuously, and that success is more certain at the full moon."[13]

A real difficulty for a craftsman of the seventeenth century working in some remote court of a small princedom was the problem of finding suitable patterns wherewith to decorate his lacquer. At a court where there was a large collection of oriental porcelain or at least some blue and white Dutch or German pottery copied from Eastern models, the worker found a welcome source for needed patterns, but all too often the lacquerworker had to be content to copy details of engravings in books.[14] After Martin Martinius published his atlas in 1655, other illustrated descriptions of China were published. Perhaps the most popular was a report by John Nieuhoff, who had been a member of a legation sent to China: *Het Gezantschap der Neerlandtsche Oost-Indische Compagnie* (Leyden, 1665). The next book of consequence was by Athanasius Kircher; his big tome on China, *China Monumentis Illustrata* (Amsterdam, 1667), was based primarily on extensive information received from Jesuit missionaries. Dr. Olfert Dapper, a tireless explorer, published his travel account, *Gedenkwaerdig Bedryf . . .*, in Amsterdam in 1670. Dr. Engelbrecht Kämpfer (1651–1716) was an indefatigable traveler to the Middle and Far East who only published one book *Amoenitatum Exoticarum Fasciculi* (Lemgo, 1712). From his manuscripts, owned by the British Museum, some books were published in the eighteenth century, others quite recently. All of these books contained illustrations from sketches made by travelers or drawn from memory – or perhaps were sheer fantasy. These accounts were constantly pilfered, adapted, and rehashed by other writers who had never been in the Orient but were intent on satisfying Europe's interest in that unknown region. Such compilations were brought out by Erasmus Franciscus, *Neupolierter . . . Spiegel ausländischer Völker* (Nuremberg, 1670); Arnold Montanus, *Denkwürdige Gesandschaften* (Amsterdam, 1669); and others. Inspired by the travel book, and only rarely by original prints or watercolors (pl. 6 a), European printers and engravers were not long in providing prints (pl. 5 a) purporting to depict oriental scenes.[15] A very popular early series of twelve prints, *Picturae Sinicae* (fig. 6 d), was engraved in 1702 by Peter Schenk, Sr. (1660–1718/19 of Amsterdam. It is more than likely that these prints were copied from Chinese sepia paintings, since the Chinese titles given are correct. Later, Schenk and his son Peter (bef. 1698–1775) produced other prints (figs. 5 b, 6 b–e), some of them astonishingly like their Far Eastern prototypes. Pieter van der Aa (d. ca. 1730) was another Dutch engraver who published prints (figs. 5 d, 5 e) showing Far Eastern subjects. Many of these prints were copied by the versatile Leipzig publisher and engraver, Johann Christoph Weigel (1654–1725), who brought out many series of Chinese designs under his own name, some of them based on early book illustrations which he then treated in his own way (figs. 5 c, 5 d, 5 e, f, g).

Augsburg, the foremost center of German printmaking, had a close rival in Nürnberg as a source of pattern sheets which soon spread throughout Europe. For this purpose, Martin Engelbrecht (d. 1756) and Elias Baeck (1675–1777), among others, produced a great variety of *chinoiserie* prints. Designers of greater quality were Paul Decker (1677 – after 1727), who published a series of designs for lacquerwork (fig. 10), and Johann Esaias Nilson (1727–1788) whose "Chinese" designs, done in the graceful South German rococo style, rival in spirit certain French creations. Augsburg and Nürnberg printers were quick to republish engravings from France, England, and elsewhere, usually in series which found a ready market in Europe. The steadily growing number of English *chinoiserie* engravings printed toward the middle of the eighteenth century indicate the increasing demand. William and John Halfpenny published *New Designs* between 1750 and 1752, Edward Edwards and Mathias Darly brought out their *New Book of Chinese Designs* in 1754, and Paul Decker his *Chinese Architecture* in 1759. William Chambers (1726–1796) should also be mentioned here as the author of *Designs of Chinese Buildings* (1757).

In France, Daniel Marot (1661–1718) was the first to use Chinese motifs in his designs and in the room interiors he executed in Holland between 1702 and 1712. From 1735, drawings with Chinese motifs made by Antoine Watteau (1674–1721) were known from the engravings made of them (fig. 12). In the same period, Jacques Gabriel Hucquier (1695–1772), François Boucher (1735–1782), Jean Antoine Fraisse (active 1733–1740), Christophe Huet (1745–1811), A. Peyrotte (d. 1762), and above all Jean Baptiste Pillement (1728–1808) produced their widely acclaimed engravings utilizing Chinese motifs. In Italy it was the firm of Giovanni Antonio Remondini (1634–1711) and his followers in Bassano who for three generations had been furnishing prints to Venetian japanners (fig. 13). Catalogues of the firm were published from 1751 to as late as 1817. Among many other items were announced "engravings with Chinese subjects on fine thin paper to cut out and use for fruit platters, boxes, and cabinets." Besides the Remondini there were in Venice Theodoro Viero and Giuseppe Wagner (from 1754) and others who kept prints in stock for japanners. By borrowing from many of the artists mentioned and adding a few original designs, the London publisher Robert Sayer (1725–1794) was able to publish a volume which he called *The Ladies Amusement or the Whole Art of Japanning Made Easy*, issued in at least two editions between 1758 and 1762. This publication, containing fifteen hundred designs of *chinoiserie*, must have been the lacquerworker's delight. Like Sieur Watin, Sayer carried artists' supplies and published an interesting list in his book. He also offered liberal advice on the selection of illustrations and how to employ them for lacquerwork. According to Sayer, great liberties could be taken with Indian and

Chinese subjects, "because luxuriance of Fancy recommends these Productions more than Propriety . . . in them is often seen a butterfly supporting an elephant or things equally absurd; yet from their gay coloring and amusing disposition they seldom fail to please. The grotesque is a taste which at present prevails and seems particularly calculated for this work which consists in a wild connection of beasts with flowers and shells with birds." The types of lithographs which were used around 1830 to replace handpainted decorations may be seen in the extremely rare tract by Achille Robin, fils, *Traité de peinture* (Paris, 1833). A number of original lithographs in color illustrate the text.

Throughout the eighteenth century and into the nineteenth century, *chinoiserie* patterns were in use, although varying in popularity and varying greatly in the style in which the Chinese subjects were treated. Without consideration of these fluctuations it is impossible to establish the chronological sequence of European lacquer. To a great extent, the evolution in style resulted from changing attitudes adopted toward the Orient. It should be added that from the second quarter of the eighteenth century *chinoiserie* patterns ceased to dominate lacquer decoration.

The early period of *chinoiserie* – up to 1700 – was defined by decoration and shapes closely imitative of oriental patterns (fig. 6 d, pl. XI). It would be tempting to assume that oriental patterns were believed worthy of imitation because China, the country of Confucius, was held to be the seat of eternal wisdom and deeply rooted civilization and therefore eminently suited to be the progenitor of intellectual and spiritual patterns for Europe. In this vein the renowned scholar Gottfried Leibniz seriously considered promoting Chinese as a world language. Indeed, quite generally China was recognized as a country of high philosophical standards in which the arts and crafts were cultivated diligently (fig. 6 c, pl. 191). This belief was disseminated by the Jesuits who were concerned in maintaining a favorable opinion of China. In 1704 a decisive blow was dealt such belief by a papal bull concerning the Rites controversy. The bull strenuously condemned the positive moral implications the Jesuits had attributed to the ideas of Confucius. Thereafter moralists found little reason to interpret Chinese ideas in a favorable light, and any illusion about China, if such still remained, was eradicated by the English who recounted innumerable stories of their unfortunate dealings with the Chinese and told of strange and ridiculous Chinese customs. This change of opinion and the increasing belief that conditions in the Orient were probably no better than those in the rest of the world gradually began to be reflected in European-designed *chinoiserie* during the first quarter of the eighteenth century. Since dignity was no longer regarded as a characteristic of the Chinese, designers went to great lengths to depict the Chinese in every sort of comic situation – and sometimes substituted monkeys in oriental costumes performing like human figures. Thus the *singerie* motif was adopted by Gillot and Watteau and popularized in ornamental prints (fig. 12). In unending variety, the Chinese or monkeys or both together were seen cavorting in droll fashion around and within decorative elements of balusters, cupolas, fretwork, and draperies.

Toward the end of the third decade of the eighteenth century, ornamentalists ceased to imitate the Chinese; instead, Chinese motifs were absorbed into decorative schemes in the European style (pl. VIII). Arbiters of fashion tired of *chinoiserie* and the somewhat scurrilous interpretation of the Chinese and their world and lacquer products began to appear no longer decorated *à la Chinoise* but bedecked with rocaille ornaments and European flowers (pl. 112).

Around the middle of the eighteenth century, coinciding with regained interest in lacquer, a new theme in decoration emerged. It was *chinoiserie*, but with a difference: images of a fanciful pastoral life as seen in the engravings by Boucher and Pillement and the numerous pastiches of their work. Used as patterns for many different crafts, these prints make no pretense at realism, nor are they caricatures or even an interpretation of some supposedly philosophic idea out of China. What they depict is a fairyland peopled by charming beings – beautiful women, happy children, busy fishermen – all playing in a pleasant landscape dotted with graceful pavillions and delicately arched bridges above whirling waters shaded by slender and elegantly curved trees (fig. 5c). Admittedly such representations were totally unlike the scenes on the lacquered panels still being imported or occasionally copied, and yet the serene atmosphere and the novel interpretation conveyed by the new style were somehow akin to the oriental scene. What a contrast there was between China, apparently so remote from worldly strife, and impoverished, war-ridden Europe! The impression remained that China was a country of grace and eternal bliss where men might live in peace, with joy accompanying all of their doings.

When William Chambers visited China in 1750 he may have carried along just such preconceived ideas and so very likely did experience some such evanescent landscapes as we see represented on screens and furniture panels. He may also have transferred such impressions into the designs he published in 1757. These views, real or imagined, prepared the public for the impression the Chinese world was to make upon Europe toward the end of the eighteenth century. In this period of sentiment and the romantic spirit combined with the quest for the exotic, China was again hailed as an exemplary country untrammeled by the vicissitudes of modern civilization (pl. 72). When, occasionally, the nineteenth century returned to the Chinese style, the interest was short-lived and of little consequence, materializing one year and disappearing the next.

It is unfortunate that we know almost nothing about the masters who created the lacquered objects with which we deal today. On the other hand, we do find the names of a number of craftsmen mentioned and often praised in documents of the seventeenth and eighteenth centuries – and yet we fail to identify their work. Considering this lack of information, it is gratifying to find at least one master, and his disciples, about whom, by great good chance, we find it possible to establish provenance. His life provides us with a picture of a court lacquermaster, and he may very well be typical of others in similar positions. The master, to be discussed later, was Gérard Dagly (1657–1726), who worked for the Prussian court, mainly in Berlin, around 1700. A former apprentice, Martin Schnell, went to Dresden and was there employed by the court of Saxony. In England we know of a chairmaker, Giles Grendey (1693–1780), who produced lacquer chairs, but we know nothing of the master he probably commissioned to execute the lacquer. Although we have learned much about eighteenth-century French furniture, we know virtually nothing of those who created the lacquer used so frequently by great cabinetmakers and joiners. The exception is a family named Martin in Paris who produced an enormous amount of lacquer. Even so, we have yet to recognize a single piece definitely documented as their work. Their so-called *vernis Martin* has become a trademark of great renown, and undoubtedly many a fine piece of first quality will be considered a product of their shop, but how far one may go in attributing pieces of lesser quality to the Martins is not yet determined. Strangely enough, the only two rooms which we know to have been lacquered and decorated by a member of that family are to be seen in the Potsdam palaces of Frederick the Great (pl. 181).

In some cities lacquermasters joined guilds such as the "Patentees for Lacquering after the manner of Japan" in London, the *verlakkers* in Amsterdam, and the *depentores* of Venice. Unfortunately, the archives of these guilds provide scarcely any information about their members. Most of the craftsmen we do learn about were the itinerant workers who were commissioned by some prince or nobleman to decorate an "Indian room" or a set of furniture. While we may know their names, in the cases where names are associated with their creations, we rarely learn from whence they came and whither they went.

In addition to the professional craftsmen in the lacquer trade, there were a number of dilettantes, most of whom moved in fashionable circles. Because their work varied greatly in quality, technique, and style, it is difficult to date certain pieces of lacquer, since an amateur might well have used a piece of old furniture on which to practice his skill. Much of the charm of Stalker and Parker's fascinating book stems from the way the authors try to tutor the dilettante.[16] It seems that Lady Walpole was among the ladies who indulged in the polite accomplishment of lacquering. This hobby cannot have been to the liking of Sir Horace, who once expressed his disgust for "Two vile jars that look like the modern Japanning by ladies."[17]

An easy way for both the professional and the amateur to decorate furniture was to use motifs cut from prints especially prepared for this purpose. Professionally, much of such work was done in Venice from prints made by the firm of Remondini in nearby Bassano. But amateurs throughout Europe dabbled in this kind of "lacquer," which was contemptuously dubbed *lacca povera* or *lacca contrafatta*. In France, such work, called *découpure*, must have become fashionable about 1720. In 1727, one Sieur Crépy, fils, advertised engravings done after a screen painted by Watteau, with compositions *très galantes*, suitable *aux découpures dont les dames font aujord'hui de si jolies meubles*. Even as late as 1740 this kind of entertaining hobby must have been still in vogue, since a comedy by Boissy given in Paris in that year mentions as one of the fashionable customs *chez le petit marquis découper des oiseaux*.[18] Motifs – a battle scene or a goddess of victory – were cut out of a printed sheet and arranged together with a wreath or some other emblem to form a splendid decoration. Once pasted on furniture, the motifs were painted in suitable colors and covered with a few coats of heavy lacquer. Some amateurs, of course, had neither an artistic eye nor clever hands. Complaints from one lacquermaster at the Prussian court have come down to us: each time Queen Sophia Dorothea attempted to decorate a piece of furniture, she muddled the whole job, and the good man had to put her work in order.[19] In Regensburg, a fashionable center in the days when the Diet of the Holy Roman Empire convened there, a master turner wrote a pamphlet on the subject of japanning and listed as his subscribers ladies and gentlemen of society who were training on his premises. It was understood that the master would "rearrange" the handiwork of their excellencies after they left for the day.[20] In England, in 1689, a young lady who wished to pass her leisure hours in japanning asked permission of her father to join a class at her school in Great Chelsey, and he responded: "I find you have a desire to learn Jappan as you call it, and I approve it... for I admire all accomplishments that will render you considerable and Lovely... to learn the art costs a Guinea entrance and some 40/2 more to buy materials to work upon."[21]

Although the dilettante may have been responsible for some of the poorer pieces of lacquer that survive, his far uglier counterpart is the faker producing "antiques." In the years following World War I, years of great social and financial unrest, much valuable furniture which had come down through the centuries in the houses for which it had been made was to be found on the market. Lacquer objects, particularly English lacquer, were greatly in demand. Information about lacquer and *chinoiserie* was beginning to be known; between 1910 and 1914, and again in the twenties, Herbert Cescinsky and R. W. Symonds published detailed studies of English lacquer.[22] Henri Cordier (1910), J. Guerin (1911), and above all Madame H. Belevitch-Stankevitch (1910) treated the subject of *chinoiserie* in France.[23] In Germany, Adolf Reichwein (1923) and Otto Pelka (1924) dealt more generally with the relations between China and Europe in the eighteenth century. All of these publications stimulated interest in lacquer and invited the attention of collectors. American buyers seem to have been equally attracted by English and Venetian lacquer. The result was obvious: if R. W. Symonds' estimate is correct, in the twenties two-thirds of the lacquer objects on the market were fakes.[24]

The situation was somewhat different in France. Lacquer pieces produced up until the middle of the eighteenth century had been so decimated that there was practically none to be had. To copy and fake extremely ornate Louis XV commodes would have been a complicated undertaking, well beyond the skill and the pocketbook of the average interior decorator. And yet André Mailfert, the ubiquitous faker of Tours whose *belle epoque* was 1919–29, must have created at least a few Louis XV lacquered commodes; he includes a photograph of one in his memoirs, first published in 1935.[25] Although he was extremely proud of his work, his style, never altogether convincing, his poorly faked signatures, and certain set ways of aging "antiques" make his products less acceptable today when they are certain to be more carefully examined than was the custom in the past. Catering to the preferences of the buyers, fakers of English furniture produced cabinets on stands, bureaus with bookcases, chairs, card tables and tea tables, and toilette mirrors. In Venice, bureaus, commodes, chairs, settees, toilette mirrors, boxes, and other small knicknacks were "multiplied" to satisfy the demand.

No one has studied fake antiques with more knowledge and experience than R. W. Symonds. Symonds distinguishes between the commercial imitator who provides reproductions for persons of middle income and the skilled faker who spares no cost and demands the highest price for his ingenious deceits. The imitator is guilty of shoddy workmanship and improper materials – the use of bronze powder instead of gold leaf, varnish instead of true lacquer – with the result that the pieces do not wear well. The faker, on the other hand, tries to observe all the rules of the craft and often offers a sound piece of workmanship, even if inauthentic. One problem in "faking" lacquer is to produce a surface covered with fine, hair-like cracks, a process that may evolve over many years in an authentic piece of lacquer.

How a piece wears is important in judging its authenticity. A fake may be exposed when a hinge is removed, to discover that the color beneath is not as bright as it ought to be in view of the fact that supposedly it has been protected for a long time. The basic structure of faked lacquer cabinets may be old, but stripped of their original veneer, which has been used elsewhere. Chairs and tables are usually of new construction, since old tables and chairs, unlacquered, are too valuable or too rare to be used in this fashion. Wooden chests are a different story. Old chests are more easily obtained than tables and chairs. Among the popular "antiques" is the long-case clock. One often finds a mahogany case treated with lacquer, since so many mahogany cases were made throughout the eighteenth century. Finally, many authentic wall mirrors have been given a base with drawer stands and then lacquered to make them appear as a more important piece.

Much of what we know of Italian lacquer comes from the writing of Giulio Lorenzetti and Giuseppe Morazzoni, and yet they have nothing to say about the practice of faking lacquer.[26] Considering the great skill with which Italian craftsmen are able to duplicate traditional styles and techniques, surely many copies and fakes have reached the market. Here the borderline between lacquered furniture and painted and varnished furniture is very slim, and it is often difficult to distinguish between them. Haphazard workmanship is not necessarily proof of recent origin, nor does the use of *lacca povera* techniques and old prints necessarily indicate great age.

While the usual custom in examining cabinetwork must be observed, special attention should be given to the decoration, particularly the style of the rocaille ornaments and flower arrangements. All too often the style is "wrong" – the flowers suggest impressionism or even a kind of realistic treatment alien to the eighteenth century.

Following the trends of the eighteenth century, lacquer continued to be popular for at least another half-century, though the basic trends of the craft changed greatly. The impoverishment of Europe following the French Revolution and the Napoleonic wars did not favor the crafts that once had catered to brilliant courts and wealthy individuals. During these years guilds were disbanded and craftsmen dealing in luxury goods hard-pressed to make a living. Certainly it became difficult for self-employed lacquerworkers to continue their trade. But tin production at Pontypool and Usk and the papier-mâché industry at Birmingham, at Brunswick, in Russia, and in a number of smaller industrial centers saved the lacquer trade for another few decades. At mid-century, tin was supplanted by papier-mâché as a surface for lacquer. This marked the beginning of the era when the craft of lacquer became an industry. In time, unfortunately, the new industry, building on no solid basis, overreached itself. How this happened, and how once enthusiastic collectors lost their taste for lacquer, will be related in the final chapter.

1. A. Reichwein, *China and Europe, Intellectual and Artistic Contacts in the Eighteenth Century* (New York, 1925); Chisaburo Yamada, *Die Chinamode des Spätbarock* (Berlin, 1935); William W. Appleton, *A Cycle of Cathay* (New York, 1951); F. Gibbs, "Historical Survey of the Japanning Trade. I. Eastern and Western Lacquer," in *Annals of Science*, 7 (1951): 401–16; "II. Early British Japanning," 9 (1953): 88–95; "III. Pontypool and Usk," 9 (1953): 197–213; "IV. The Midlands," 10 (1953): 214–32; John Irwin, "A Jacobean Vogue for Oriental Lacquer-ware," in *Burlington Magazine*, 95 (1953): 193; Erich Köllmann, "Chinoiserie," in *Reallexikon zur Deutschen Kunstgeschichte*, 3 (1952): 439–82; Hans Huth, *Europäische Lackarbeiten, 1650–1850* (Darmstadt, 1955); Walter Holzhausen, *Lackkunst in Europa* (Braunschweig, 1958); Gertrude Z. Thomas, "Lacquer," in *Antiques*, 79 (1961): 572–75; Hugh Honour, *Chinoiserie, the Vision of Cathay* (London, 1961); Giovanni Mariacher, "Lacquer," in *Encyclopedia of World Art*, 8 (New York, 1963): 1063.
2. F. H. Hofmann, *Das Porzellan* (Berlin, 1932), figs. 1, 3; J. von Schlosser, *Die Kunst- und Wunderkammern der Spätrenaissance* (Leipzig, 1908), fig. 54.
3. Sources for the history of lacquer recipes: Fritz Hellwag, *Die Geschichte des deutschen Tischlerhandwerks* (Berlin, 1924), pp. 485–503; Paul Debo, *Aus der Geschichte einer Curiösen Kunst* (Wiesbaden, 1937); Walter Holzhausen, *Lackkunst in Europa* (Braunschweig, 1958), pp. 252, 256; Gibbs, "Japanning Trade," *Annals of Science*, 7 (1951): *passim;* Paul Baur, "Aus der Chronik von Lack...," in *Farbe und Lack*, no. 1 (Cologne, 1963): 3–11; Paul Baur, "Rezepte und Arbeits-Anweisungen von 1650–1850," in *Farbe und Lack*, no. 1 (Cologne, 1964): 5–16.
4. Gibbs, "Japanning Trade," pp. 404 ff.
5. Gibbs, "Japanning Trade," pp. 403–07.
6. Gibbs, "Japanning Trade," p. 406.
7. Gibbs, "Japanning Trade," p. 407.
8. Bonanni's book was republished in Italian in 1723, 1750, and 1786; in German in 1727 (5th ed., 1746); in French in 1723 (last edition, 1780). I quote from the French edition, *Traité des Vernis* (Paris, 1723).
9. It was once believed that Girolamo Ruscelli of Florence was the author; this attribution has been discredited. More than fifty editions, revised and enlarged, were published in many languages throughout the sixteenth century and early seventeenth century. See John Ferguson, *Bibliotheca Chemica* (London, 1954). Among many other books, Leonardo Fioravanti published *Compendio dei secreti . . . libri cinque* (Venice, 1564; French edition, 1582). Also important on the subject of lacquer is his *Dello Specchio di scientia universale* (Venice, 1567; 2d French edition, Paris, 1582).
10. Bonanni reports that "on porte à Rome la nuit dans les rues des petites lanternes sourdes, qui sont noires... dont toute la monture qui est de fer, est couverte de ce vernis" (French edition, 1723, p. 77 n.). The reference is to the varnish used by the Turks to treat their arrows mentioned by Fioravanti (Ch. I, n. 7). In this connection one might refer to certain night lamps or *brûle parfums* of the sixteenth century, made of bronze and lacquered, such as the one in the Museo del Bargello (illustrated in the catalogue of the Detroit Renaissance Exhibition, 1959, fig. 17).
11. This change of color from white to yellow is seen most clearly in the tables made by Bernard van Risenburgh. One is to be seen in the J. Paul Getty Museum at Malibu, California (pl. 231); another is in the collection of the Louvre (illustrated in color on the cover of Pierre Verlet's *Les meubles du XVIIIe siècle, II. Ebénisterie* [Paris, 1956]). See also the table by Roger de Lacroix in the Camondo Collection of the Louvre (illustrated in color in the same volume by Verlet, pl. VIII). A lacquer commode from the chambers of Madame Adelaide, acquired by the Château de Versailles in 1965, shows the same change from white to yellow (illustrated in color in Sotheby's catalogue, 29/30 April 1965, no. 188, here light celadon green; also illustrated in *Connaissance des Arts* [April, 1965], p. 68, no. 158, here light yellow to orange). According to the Sotheby catalogue, the commode is mentioned as follows in the old inventory of Versailles (no. 1965): ". . . vernier de Martin . . . fond blanc à fleurs et filets rougeir." As far as one can tell from the reproductions, the present flower decoration seems mediocre. If it is indeed the original decoration, it would indicate that the Martins' work varied in quality or that, once more, the name "Martin" was used as a generic one. Splendid pieces which have kept their white color are those by Gérard Dagly and the Schnell Shop (pls. 159, 161, 200, 201, X, XI).
12. John Stalker and George Parker, *A Treatise on Japanning* (London, 1688). I quote from the reprint edition, 1960, p. 37.
13. René Gimpel, *Diary of an Art Dealer* (New York, 1966), p. 137.
14. Some illustrations from travel accounts are reproduced in Otto Pelka's *Ostasiatische Reisebilder im Kunstgewerbe des 18. Jahrhunderts* (Leipzig, 1924).
15. The large number of *chinoiserie* prints in the State Art Library in West Berlin is catalogued in *Katalog der Ornamentstich-Sammlung der Staatlichen Kunstbibliothek* (Berlin, 1939), nos. 4188–97. A number of these are illustrated in Chisaburo Yamada's *Die Chinamode des Spät-*

barock. More than one hundred *chinoiserie* prints dating from the period 1700–1845 by Peter Schenk & Son, Pieter van der Aa, Joh. Christoph Weigel, and others are held by the University Library, Göttingen. They were once owned by Johann Friedrich von Uffenbach (1687–1769), a Frankfurt collector. Georg Schulze, "Augsburger Chinoiserien," illustrations by E. Baeck, in *Schwäbisches Museum*, 2 (1926): 190 ff.; 4 (1928): 121 ff. See also Köllmann, "Chinoiserie," in *Reallexikon zur Deutschen Kunstgeschichte*, 3 (1952), and Honour, *Chinoiserie* (London, 1961). A. L. den Blaawen, "Ceramiek met chinoiserieen naar prenten van Petrus Schenk jr.," and J. Fontein and A. L. den Blaawen, "Picturae Sinicae ac Surattenae van Petrus Schenk sr.," both in *Bulletein van het Rijksmuseum*, 2 (Amsterdam, 1964): 35–49, 3–4, 91–101.

16. Stalker and Parker, *A Treatise on Japanning*, p. xvi.
17. James Rambo, "French and English *Tôle*," in *Chronicle of the Museum For the Art and Decoration of the Cooper Union*, 2 (New York, 1951): no. 2, pp. 67–86.
18. Henri Havard, *Dictionnaire de l'ameublement*, 2 (Paris, 1887): 51; Tove Clemmensen, *Möbler* (Copenhagen, 1946), pp. 33, n. 88, 202.
19. Walter Stengel, *Alte Wohnkultur in Berlin* (Berlin, 1958), p. 82.
20. Huth, *Europäische Lackarbeiten*, p. 11.
21. Percival Macquoid, *A History of English Furniture in the Age of Walnut* (London, 1925), p. 138.
22. Herbert Cescinsky, "Lacquerwork in England," in *Burlington Magazine*, 19 (1911): 294–99, 332–37; Herbert Cescinsky, *English Furniture of the Eighteenth Century*, 3 vols. (London, 1910/11). Compare also chap. iii, nn. 9, 24.
23. H. Belevitch-Stankevitch, *Le goût Chinois en France* (Paris, 1910); Henri Cordier, *La Chine en France au XVIIIe siècle* (Paris, 1910); J. Guerin, *La Chinoiserie en Europe au XVIIIe siècle* (Paris, 1911).
24. R. W. Symonds, *Old English Walnut and Lacquer Furniture* (New York, 1923); R. W. Symonds, "English Lacquer Cabinets," in *Old Furniture* (New York, 1928), pp. 138–50; Herbert Cescinsky, *The Gentle Art of Faking Furniture* (London, 1931).
25. André Mailfert, *Au pays des antiquaires, confidences d'un maquilleur* (2d ed.; Paris, 1955), plate following p. 142. On Mailfert see Hans Huth, "Über gefälschte Möbel," in *Kunst und Künstler*, 28 (1929): 105–08. Hans Huth, "The Gentle Art of Faking," in *Apollo*, I (1936): pp. 200–204. Pierre Verlet, *Les meubles du XVIIIe siècle*, 2: 71.
26. See chap. iv, n. 1.

CHAPTER III

LACQUER IN ENGLAND AND THE NORTH AMERICAN COLONIES

> ...if you find the matter of the book to be useful,
> and to answer the test of experience,
> you will easily overlook any imperfections.
> JOHN STALKER and GEORGE PARKER, 1688

Lacquer and color played a more important role in the history of English furniture and decoration than it did in other European countries. Apparently in England there was a ready disposition to use color in woodwork. As H. Clifford Smith points out, there are indications of a considerable amount of colorful wainscoting and oak furniture during the sixteenth century.[1] This was a taste contrary to that prevalent on the continent, where woodwork decorated with color was the exception rather than the rule, and this liking for color may have made lacquerwork more readily acceptable in England. Perhaps, considering this trend, it is more than chance that the first European lacquermaster about whom we have a few facts was an Englishman, William Smith, whose activities in Rome have been mentioned.

When lacquer once again came into fashion at the time of the Restoration, the English trade with China had grown to quite considerable proportions. Although England had established connection with China in 1612 and 1613, these ventures were never particularly prosperous and halted in 1637 when the Dutch gained exclusive right to the China trade. Cromwell, it is true, granted the East India Company a new charter in 1657, but the English no longer had direct access to the East and were forced to rely on the Dutch if they wished to important oriental goods. In 1672, after the Restoration, Charles II renewed the charter of the East India Company, and in 1688 Stalker and Parker refer to the Chinese fashion as an art "very much admired by us." There were those who differed in their opinion and with reason, as the author of *A Discourse of Trade, Coyn and Paper credits and of Ways and Means to Gain and Retain Riches* (1679)[2] sets forth with emphasis: "As ill Weeds grow apace so these manufactured goods from India met with such a kind reception that from the Greatest Gallants to the meanest Cook-maid nothing was thought so fit... to adorn... for the ornament of Chambers like Indian screens, Cabinets, Beds and Hangings; nor for closets, like China and Lacquer ware." The author goes on to lament the unfortunate consequences engendered by this kind of import. The fashion was carried to such an extent that English craftsmen had to provide "whole setts of Japan work," whereas earlier collectors had been content with single pieces. In spite of the enormous number of pieces of lacquer imported from the Far East during the last quarter of the seventeenth century, there was a constant demand for more and in time these were supplied by imitations, in the production of which England ranked first.

At this time it was proposed that English joiners be sent to the Far East, there to fashion cabinets which would be far superior to those produced by local workers; only the lacquering would be done by native workmen. In 1688 a Captain Dampier noted in a travel report that he knew a captain who not only had taken a joiner with him but had carried along deal boards "to make fashionable Commodities to be lacquered,"[3] and the records of the East India Company for 1672–73 mention that "several artificers were sent over to the east to teach the Indians how to manufacture goods to make them Vendible in England and the rest of the European markets."[4] At the same time, English cabinetwork was shipped to the Far East to be lacquered. On 16 September 1684 the factor of the East India Company in Tonkin (Indochina) received the following advice: "...we have Sent you to help fill up your Ship some quantity of Joiner ware to be lacquered there. We can give you no particular directions, we would have them all well done and Substantiall... Some plain black, but most to be adorned with birds, flowers or imagery." Shipping costs for outgoing goods were negligible because the weight served as ballast. As a result of this or some similar order, we read in the minutes of the East India Company for 31 August 1687: "The Committees are desired to view the general sorts of lacquered wares now brought home on the 'George' and the 'Rainbow' to give direction for... frames of chairs and other things ...to be sent... in the next ship for Tonquin to be lacquered...." But the workmanship in Tonkin was found to be shoddy, and after 1680 shipments were sent to Amoy and Canton.

With Eastern goods flooding the London market, many "Indian" shops were established to deal in the goods the East India Company auctioned at their sales. An examination of available figures will give an idea of the volume of imports. Toward the end of the seventeenth century, shipments of China goods on the "Sarah," the "Martha," and the "Dorothy" were valued at £150,000. Among them were the following items of lacquer work, value indicated in pounds:

Fans	38,557
Sticks for fans	13,470
Trunks, Execreters [spittoons], bowls, cups, and dishes . . .	10,500
Tables inlaid	189
Panels in frame painted and carved for rooms	47
Boards	178
Brushes	3,099
Tables not inlaid	277
Board for screens	174
Screens set in frames	54
Brass hinges in chests	(no price)

The tables mentioned in this list were probably inlaid with mother-of-pearl in the manner called in the trade *burgauté*. The carved panels were Coromandel screens, also known as Bantam work. It is worth noting that chests containing hinges appear in the list; obviously the hinges were to be used for cabinets and chests fashioned in London.

The London craftsmen making japanware in the Indian style (the term lacquerware was reserved to define objects other than those in the oriental style) had to compete with these enormous quantities of imports. Toward 1700, competition between importers and London joiners and japanners became so keen that the joiners found it necessary to present a memorandum to Parliament stating that "... Artificers, Members (of the Joyner's Company) have been bred up in the said Art or Mystery of making Cabinets, Scrutoirs [writing cabinets], Tables, Chests, and all other sorts of Cabinet work ... they have arrived to so great a Perfection as exceeds all Europe. But ... Merchants ... Trading to the East Indies have procured and sent over to the East Indies Patterns and Models of all sorts of Cabinet Goods; and have returned from there such Quantities of Cabinet Wares, manufactured there after the English fashion by our Models, that the said Trade in England is in great danger of being utterly ruined ... they also spoil the Exportation of the said Joyners and Cabinet makers." The joiners also maintained that within four years the following quantities of lacquer had been imported:

244 cabinets	589 looking glass frames
6,582 tea tables	655 tops for stands
428 chests	818 lacquered boards
70 trunks	597 sconces
52 screens	4,120 powder, comb, and dressing boxes.

In 1701, japanners who before 1695 established themselves as "Patentees for lacquering after the manner of Japan" made a similar appeal to Parliament. Probably they were already in straitened circumstances in 1695 when they advertised a lottery of "cabinets, execretors, tabletts, stands, looking glasses, tea tables, chimney pieces, etc." Another serious predicament faced the japanners when the East India Company forbade private trading in *gum lacca*, thus making it possible for the company to fix the price of the ingredient needed by the japanners for their trade. When the japanners asked Parliament to suppress imports, they argued "Many of the Artificers in the same Art and Mystery have brought it to so great a Perfection as to Exceed all manner of Indian lacquer, and to equal the right Japan [ware] itself, by enduring the fire in the Boyling of Liquors used for Japanning."

During these years the joiners and japanners were not the only English craftsmen to suffer because of the importations of the East India Company. The weavers endured even greater difficulties; not only were they threatened by imports but by the rapid industrialization of the craft, a threat which the japanners did not face until production began at Pontypool and Birmingham in the second half of the eighteenth century. In 1696 the weavers complained to Parliament, and as a result of this and other petitions Parliament in 1700 prohibited the importation of silks and calicoes and, in 1702, imposed higher duties on the import of lacquer.[5] The result was a considerable decrease in imports at a time when the English trade needed just such protection. The struggle of the joiners and japanners to lessen the competition of imported goods was complicated by the fact that to compensate for the decline in the English marketplace the East India Company had to seek foreign markets. This in turn created a problem for the exporters of English furniture, since a great deal of japanned furniture was sent to Spain and Portugal. In 1700, for example, the following items were shipped (value indicated in pounds and shillings):

III. Cabinet, Venice, about 1600

IV. Bureau-cabinet, English, about 1700

V. Cabinet, English, early eighteenth century

VI. Cabinet, English, about 1730

To Spain

Cabinets, etc.	£216	10s.
Chairs, etc.	642	7
Chests of drawers, etc.	104	5
Clockcases 25	73	14
Escrutores, etc. [Escritoires]	474	17
Looking glasses, etc.	311	11
Upholstery ware	426	—

To Portugal

Cabinets, Japanned	£67	7s.
Chairs, etc.	787	12
Chests of drawers	38	8
Clockcases	54	18
Escrutores [Escritoires]	148	6
Looking glasses, etc.	426	12
Upholstery ware	556	2

The goods sent to Portugal enjoyed special custom privileges in exchange for similar privileges for the Portuguese wine trade in which English interests were heavily involved.

The only craftsman whose name and whose furniture we know was Giles Grendey, of whom we will learn more later. He sold japanned furniture in quantity, much of it for export: looking glasses, chairs, day beds, folding tables. Another exporter who was also a japanner we only know through his trade card (fig. 14); this was Daniel Mills, active in the period 1768–77. Mills is also known to have japanned copper and leadware. Like Mills, John Belchier, active in the period 1735–53, is known by his trade card; in addition there exists a japanned secretary which bears his label.[6] From various pieces of evidence we know that many types of English furniture were sent to a number of foreign courts where the court cabinetmakers often tried to copy English styles. Even Venice, as we shall see, was touched by some of these English trends.

As we advance into the eighteenth century, English influence on the continent played an increasingly important role in cabinetmaking and such joiner work as chairmaking. In the Hague, cabinetmakers were expected to produce a cabinet "in the English style" as *chef-d'œuvre*, and one Dutch writer in 1758 criticized his countrymen for looking to England for the newest in fashion.[7] When David Roentgen settled in his birthplace of Neuwied on the Rhine in the 1760s, he advertised himself as an English cabinetmaker, although he had never been in England, in order to lend prestige to his work.

To the baroque mind which marks the style of interior decoration during the period of the Restoration, colorful elements such as exotic cabinets on elaborate stands were welcome as contrasting motifs against the Palladian elements of the decoration. The engravings of Marot indicate that in this period China cabinets – that is, rooms arranged in Oriental fashion – were designed in European style, relying on the inclusion of Chinese porcelain, lacquer, or hangings to introduce a foreign accent. Oriental rooms done entirely in the fashion of the Far East, including sets of lacquer furniture, were introduced only after the middle of the eighteenth century. For the present, color, exotic shapes, and the rich appearance of single pieces provided relief from the drab austerity of the Cromwellian era. According to Stalker and Parker, "Japan alone, has exceeded in beauty and magnificence all the pride of the Vatican at this time. Not that 'tis only strong and durable but delightful and ornamental beyond expression . . ."[8]

The bulk of English lacquer of the first period was produced until well into the 1730s. Because of the vulnerability of its surface, much of it has perished or has so changed in appearance that it is difficult today to realize how much of it must have been in existence. We can get some idea of the amount of japanned ware when we consider the sale in 1746 of furniture from the London town house of the Duke of Chandos, when 36 lots of walnut, 11 lots of mahogany, and 17 lots of "Japan lac" were offered.[9]

The greatest demand was for copies of Far Eastern cabinets, boxlike pieces with drawers concealed behind doors and usually decorated with raised lacquer. The earliest examples have gilt stands of European design decorated with cupids and richly carved, intertwined foliage (pls. 53, 54). The English stands of the period are very similar to Dutch pieces. The landscape decorations on early lacquer pieces are somewhat inconsistent, and often it is obvious that the japanner had difficulty building up his composition because he lacked suitable patterns. During the period of William and Mary the strongly curved and massive legs connected by curved stretchers were supplanted by more graceful legs in the manner of Marot (pls. IV, 55). These legs, shaped like pilasters, were usually connected by an arrangement of rather flatly curved ornaments which also might top the cabinet and surround a coat of arms or initials accompanied by a crown. All of the carving is gilt; more rarely it is covered with silver. Since there is such a close resemblance between stands of Dutch and English design, the origin of some cabinets is frequently in doubt, especially since we know that Dutch lacquermasters came to England following the Prince of Orange. A piece of undoubted English origin is the cabinet with a double hood as a top (pl. 56).

In the Queen Anne period, pilasters were replaced by cabriole legs either japanned or gilt or occasionally silvered. Cabinets were decorated with flat as well as raised lacquer and only rarely with incised lacquer in the style of Coromandel screens (pl. 54). It should be mentioned that when English cabinets were made of oak or deal the surface of the wood was often not deemed smooth enough to be japanned and so was veneered before the gesso was applied. It was fashionable in this period to display china objects on top of the cabinets (pl. 57). In his disputation on the China craze, Daniel Defoe tells us that "Queen Mary introduced the custom or humour as I may call it, of furnishing houses with Chinaware which increased to a strange degree afterwards, piling the China upon the Tops of Cabinets, scrutoires, and every Chymney piece . . . it became a grievance in the Expense of it and even injurious to their Families and Estates."[10]

Somewhat akin to the cabinet, especially in its later shape when it was placed on a chest of drawers instead of the earlier stand, was the lacquered bureau-cabinet which originated toward the end of the reign of Charles II. This was a successor to the much earlier, boxlike, often portable "escritoire" (Portuguese: scrutor) going back to the sixteenth century. The bureau was built in stages, with a chest of drawers or kneehole desk as a base, on which rested a writing compartment hiding small drawers and closed with a slanted lid which served as a writing board when open (pl. VI). The desk was topped by a tall, recessed, two-door case with shelves, an upright section, and pigeonholes for books, ledgers, and papers. The cornice was usually crowned by a broken and curved pediment, leaving space in the embrasure and at the outer ends for finials or for the china Defoe complained of. A pediment of an unusual serpentine shape decorated with china vases is seen on a bureau at the Palazzo Pallavicini in Rome (pl. 57). After 1700 we sometimes find double-hooded pediments (pl. 56), and toward the middle of the century triangular-shaped pediments, often broken, came into fashion. There were also lacquered bureaus on cabriole legs and with no bookcase on top, more like those used in France, but since today they are extremely rare we can hazard that they were not much in favor.

Even a cursory study of English lacquered bureaus suggests a comparison with similar furniture made in Italy, generally supposed to be of Venetian origin. There is more than one similarity – for example, the broken segment top, the general tripartite construction of chest, desk, and bookcase, and the disposition of the interior. Sometimes it is necessary to make a study of the wood and the joining in order to determine the origin of a specific piece of furniture. As far as the general type is concerned, it undoubtedly originated in England. In the history of Italian furniture the upright secretary has no antecedent, but since Venice was the meeting place of distinguished travelers a model of just such a bureau could quite well have been brought to the city where it was copied for export as well as for domestic sale. The presence of four English secretaries and a set of chairs in the Palazzo Pallavicini is proof that this kind of furniture was brought to Italy in the early eighteenth century (pls. 57, 58, 84). A feature apparently typical of export ware, probably in order to meet a continental fashion, was the custom of providing bureaus in pairs, something which was rarely done in England.

Very rare today are lacquered chests of drawers, called highboys in the North American colonies, which were fashioned as double or single chests on stands of tapered legs connected by stretchers. Two such pieces are illustrated in the *Dictionary of English Furniture*.[11] The tops of these chests of drawers are usually flat, more rarely double-hooded. When they were in fashion around 1690 as blanket chests and as typical pieces of bedroom furniture, they frequently became the targets of amateurs who ventured to decorate them. In the American colonies the highboy (pls. 90–95) was much favored and was often accompanied by a dressing table called a lowboy (pl. 96). Chests mounted on low stands rank among the early types of lacquer furniture but appear infrequently after the second decade of the eighteenth century (pl. 62). The chests were made with a flat top or were domed, with tapering or cabriole legs sometimes replaced by more sumptuous elements, perhaps a wivern – a two-legged creature like a cockatrice but having a dragon's head – as a final decorative touch. English-made chests were not in great demand, probably because chests from the Far East were in good supply since they were used as packing cases for other goods. Too, chests could easily be made of Coromandel screens.

Apparently one of the most capable japanners of the late seventeenth century was a Dutchman named Gerrit Jensen. In 1680 he made a "cabinet and frame table stand and glasse all of Japan worke" as a gift from Charles II to the emperor of Morocco.[12] Jensen was also employed at Chatsworth, the seat of the dukes of Devonshire, in 1683 when he was paid £41 for work on wainscoting of "hollow burnt Japan," meaning incised lacquer of the Bantam type, and in cutting such for a closet. The closet itself was dismantled in 1700, but it is likely that two of the chests now in the state drawing room at Chatsworth were made from salvaged panels. Today English Bantam work is extremely rare and little more than a dozen pieces are known. A few years ago, a chest or coffer of great elegance came to light as if to make possible the assertion that around 1710 there must have been some extremely skilful English craftsmen at work.[13] The stand, English in style with cabriole legs, shell ornaments, and a decorated frieze, is most convincingly adapted to the *chinoiserie* of the chest. A group of Bantam work, mixing those of Far Eastern and of English origin, is still *in situ* at Ham House in Surrey. Included is a cabinet on a carved and gilt stand made of imported Bantam work, composed so skilfully that its adaptation from large screen panels is scarcely noticeable—and thus in no way represents the "hodgepodge" mentioned by Stalker (pl. 54). In addition there is a large mirror with a curved frame of Far Eastern Bantam work (pl. 63). The curving was achieved by cutting the Bantam work very thin and bending it under heat. Set under the mirror is a table on S-scroll legs connected by stretchers which is completely covered with incised colored lacquer of the finest quality and of English make (pl. 64). The existence of these fine pieces of imported and English Bantam work belies Stalker and Parker's statement of 1688 that even in their day Bantam work was almost "obsolete, out of fashion, out of use and neglected."

One of the most essential pieces of furniture of the period was the screen which helped to conserve heat and prevent draft in large halls and bedrooms. For this purpose the Coromandel or Bantam screen was used. Many of the screens were made of pieces cut from imported panels and then fitted with English borders to make them the desired size. Because wooden screens were both heavy and cumbersome, they were sometimes replaced by japanned leather screens, a comparatively new craft in England although established for some years in Spain and the Netherlands. The making of leather hangings for wall decorations and in conjunction with japanning must have been introduced into England during the Restoration, probably around 1666 when one Hugh Robinson applied for permission to settle in London. He had learned his trade in Amsterdam and announced that he would produce leather "brighter than gold." In 1716 the *London Gazette* carried an advertisement from a leather gilder, Joseph Fletcher, who produced "leather hangings in the latest fashion of the Chinese style to cover walls, settees and screene."

Some of these craftsmen who worked into the 1780s had their workshops around St. Paul's churchyard. Of the many known leather screens, only a few have been found which carry signatures (pls. 68, 69). There is one signed by the maker "Holford," another marked "Coventry-London" (pl. 70), which may either refer to the place of manufacture or be the name of the person who made the piece.[14]

To make these hangings, the grain of calf or goatskin was used. It was first smoothed, then covered with silver leaf and burnished. Spanish leather hangings were sewn, but English hangings were glued and then coated with a yellow lacquer to give them the appearance of gilding. The design was applied in oil paint and after that the background might be tooled; finally, the leather was completely varnished. The majority of these screens date from the first half of the eighteenth century. Toward 1740, when the Chinese vogue was beginning to wane, Bantam screens as well as those made of leather were no longer fashionable and were replaced by handier ones either painted on paper or made of wallpaper.

Much favored as a japanned showpiece was the dressing table, today often erroneously identified as a desk. Seated at such a table, ladies would receive their friends or deal with members of the household staff. A fine example, purchased toward the end of the seventeenth century by Count Dohna, used to be at Schlobitten in East Prussia before the manor house was destroyed in 1945 (pl. 61).[15] The piece follows the typical shape, with chamfered and tapered legs connected by stretchers, the top equipped with drawers and japanned with raised lacquer in white, yellow, and blue on a black ground. (Another table, pl. 210, possibly of English or Dutch origin, will be mentioned later.)

A favored lacquer piece introduced early in the eighteenth century was the folding card table, often pictured in paintings called "conversation pieces" (pl. 65). These tables were usually fitted with cabriole legs and lacquered in black, only sparsely decorated with gold ornaments on the aprons and shoulders of the legs. Folding tables lent themselves to export; lavishly decorated in gold on scarlet lacquer, they were among the pieces exported by Grendey (pls. 66, 67).

For the dressing table the japanned mirror mounted on a stand with receptacles for toilet articles came into fashion around 1700 and, with changes occurring only in its style, remained much the same for the next fifty years. The earliest are squat; later they are narrower and even more elongated by a hood carved out of the board in silhouette style (pls. 76, 77).

In the third decade of the century lacquerwork began to change in character. Raised lacquer motifs were no longer used. This change considerably simplified the technique since less complicated gesso work was required; at the same time, the new method contributed to a change of design. Instead of bold figural motifs there was a preference for floral designs, foliage, and evanescent landscapes, allowing more free space and so resembling more closely Far Eastern patterns. For the next twenty years there was a lull in the demand for lacquer *à la Chine*, but when the fashion returned in the fifties what was sought was not a single piece of furniture, a tall bureau or a cabinet, but an entire ensemble, complete furnishings for a bedroom or a dressing room. Imported wall hangings provided an appropriate background for a set of lacquered furniture which was thought to summon up a vision of Cathay. The bedroom furnished for the fourth Duke of Beaufort at Badminton by Thomas Chippendale about 1755 was a perfect example of the new type of decoration. (The room was dismantled in 1929, and most of the pieces are now in the Victoria and Albert Museum; pl. 71.) The bed, related to a design published in Chippendale's Directory, is fitted with a pagoda-shaped tester resting on the bedposts. The tester is surmounted by a vase with acanthus foliage of gilt metal, and at each corner is a scroll turned upward and holding a gilt dragon carved of wood which at one time carried ivory bells. The back of the bed is fitted with paling like that decorating the chairs. The ensemble includes a commode, a kneehole dressing table, and four small open stands in which china might have been arranged, all japanned in red, black, and gold and once set against Chinese wallpaper.

From the scattered pieces of this bedroom we can only imagine what it must have been like when complete, but the Chinese bedroom at Nostell Priory in Yorkshire is still intact (pl. VII).[16] Just as the lacquer room in the palace of Turin gives us a notion of a well-appointed Italian room of the period, so the bedroom at Nostell Priory provides us with a paragon of Georgian elegance. This manor house, built in 1733, was enlarged by Robert Adam in the period 1760–70 for the owner, Roland Winn Lord Saint Oswald. According to the account books still in existence, Thomas Chippendale provided the furnishings. The arrangement of the Chinese bedroom has not been disturbed, and we can still enjoy a creation in which Chippendale presents a truly lavish incarnation of the "Chinese taste" as the eighteenth century conceived it.

In the large square room, its original ceiling covered with rococo motifs, the bed naturally occupies the dominant position. Of classic Adam design, lacquered in light celadon green and gilt, the bed is surmounted by an oval tester from which hangings flow to the pillars rising from the footpiece. The same colors, with some few others added, are used for the wainscoting, doors and the remaining furniture, including wardrobe and commode, both of which are shaped in the classic style but carry *chinoiserie* scenes on their panels. The upholstered chairs, arms formed of lacquered latticework, are rather inconspicuous, but the dressing table, patterned in the rococo style illustrated in the third edition of the Directory (1760), stands out like a gem. Its motif is repeated in the frame of the enormous mirror on top of the commode: fretwork scrolls, a pagoda, and low-flying birds set the tone of an exuberant fantasy in the rococo style. For all this there is a floral background of Oriental wall hangings set with vases on consoles. In this period of transition there are disparities galore, and yet there is also a harmony of colors and a balance of the various elements composing this room that create an extraordinary ensemble. Such an installation surely is a rarity.

Among the fashionable ladies staying at Tunbridge Wells in 1749 was a Mrs. Montagu who wrote a friend that she must seek out the barbarous gaudy *goût* of the Chinese – and indeed she did order some exquisite pieces of japanned furniture.[17] But there cannot have been a very wide circle of fashionable ladies able to afford this expensive new trend. This suspicion is confirmed by Dossie's handbook, published in 1758, in which we learn that the art of japanning "is not practiced so frequently on chairs, tables, and other furniture of houses except tea waiters as formerly, but the introduction of it for ornamenting coaches, snuffboxes, and screens in which there is a rivalship betwixt ourselves and the French renders the propagation of the art of great importance to commerce."[18] The type of japanning in which England took the lead was represented by the merchandise produced at Birmingham and in the Midlands as well as by the commercial use of lacquer for carriages and sedan chairs. England's chief rival was France where the introduction of *vernis Martin* and its innumerable copies had created dangerous competition. Viewed in this light, the splendid lacquer furniture used to refurnish David Garrick's villa at Hampton in 1771 must be considered an outstanding exception.[19] The actor's bedroom was hung with Chinese wallpaper. The wardrobe and other pieces of furniture were japanned green on yellow (pl. 72). Of these pieces, the wardrobe can now be seen at the Victoria and Albert Museum. It is decorated with sketchy landscapes imitative of Far Eastern scenes, painted rather lightly and varnished, though not provided with a raised underground as would have been done in earlier days. The neglect of this old technique suggests how much the art of japanning had declined.

Around the middle of the eighteenth century, the japanned commode, brought across the channel from France, became an accepted piece of bedroom furniture. Preferred was the commode with bulk set low on short legs, not the bulging *bombé* shape so popular in French (somewhat later Adam developed the serpentine front). Quite late in the century and representative of Regency style was the introduction of japanned commodes with shelves added at the sides, a somewhat lighter design based on a Louis Quinze prototype, adapted to English taste. On the other hand, japanned bookcases seemingly never found much favor; possibly the light character of decoration did not seem fitting for this kind of furniture. Illustrated is a breakfront bookcase with a straight cornice (pl. 73).

Clocks were among the favored pieces of furniture for lacquering, although they did not follow the trends in taste as closely as other objects. Over the years a sizable number of clocks were redecorated to conform to changing styles. The long-case clock, developed during the William and Mary period, stayed in great favor until well into the second half of the eighteenth century. These clocks were lacquered black, red, blue, green, and even yellow (pl. 74). In spite of the vast number that were made for sale and export, the supply does not meet the demands of present-day collectors, and so a good number of clocks made of oak, walnut, and mahogany have been "transformed" with lacquer. According to R. W. Symonds, genuine lacquer cases represent only a very small proportion of those clocks available today. Lacquered bracket and wall clocks (pl. 75) went out of fashion after 1750 and never regained popularity; nor are they sought after by collectors today.

Lacquered boxes and chests in a great variety of forms and made for any number of purposes were popular throughout the eighteenth century. The two examples chosen for inclusion here differ widely in period. Purpose and execution illustrate the divergence that was possible. The only thing these pieces have in common is the rare fact that in both instances something is known of the artists who decorated them. The large square box now in the Victoria and Albert Museum is made of metal and is signed by Marmaduke Craddock (1660–1717; pl. 78). The elegant toilet box, now in the Philadelphia Museum of Art, is lacquered in blue and is initialed JW or ML, London; as the silver marks show, it is dated 1753 (pl. 79).

Probably the oldest English japanned chairs about which we have detailed information are those made for Elizabeth Dysart, duchess of Lauderdale, and still to be seen at her former country seat, Ham House in Surrey (pl. 80). They are described in an inventory of 1683 as "12 black stoles with cane bottoms, japanned."[20] Their design is a bold yet not completely successful attempt to match oriental shapes with European forms; on the other hand, the polychromed japanned decoration is well done. More conventional types are shown by somewhat later chairs, one bearing scroll legs with carved scrolls framing the narrow caned back (pls. 81, 82). Here japanning, scarcely in evidence, does not determine the character of the chair. Another well-built chair, also dating from about 1695, has turned legs and backrails with the back and seat caned and shows only a minimum of japanning on the black lacquer ground. Both chairs indicate that before 1700 less attention was paid to japanning chairs than cabinets or bureaus, and there was little desire to create an ensemble in the Chinese style. After 1700 both the shape of chairs and the manner of decoration changed considerably. First it was the cabriole leg that came into fashion (pls. 83, 84). With this style it was possible to eliminate the stretchers connecting the legs. Caning of the back of the chair gave way to splats which were more comfortable because they somewhat followed the contour of the body (pl. 85), and upholstered seats replaced cane.

The cabriole leg dates an armchair and side chairs as made after 1700, although here cane is used (pls. 84, 87). These chairs were made for export, and certain changes were made in the specifications. Beechwood is used to replace conventional walnut because it is less expensive, lighter, smoother, and lends itself well to japanning. But beechwood is not very sturdy, so the cabriole legs required stretchers. Since the climate was hot in the Mediterranean countries where these chairs were to be used, caning was preferred to upholstery. If the chairs were for a country villa, this may explain why such lively colors as scarlet and yellow were favored. The armchair and its companions are lacquered in brilliant red and gilt. The side chairs – lacquered on a cream ground that may once have been white – is decorated with red flowers and green scrolls in a very lively pattern that suggests Moresque rather than Far Eastern inspiration. The headpieces are carved in an elaborate fashion unusual for the English market. While the side chairs can only be assumed to have been for export, the armchair is part of a set, including a number of bureaus mentioned earlier, at the Palazzo Pallavicini in Rome.

Some of the chairs exported by Giles Grendey carry his label. This is the case with a set of chairs and a daybed retrieved in 1935 from the castle of the duke of Lazcano in Spain (pl. 86). It is clear that these pieces had been given the best of care. Lacquered in a brilliant sealing-wax red, the wide expanse of wood of the splat and the broad frames offered ample background for the gilt decoration of a pattern in which European and Far Eastern motifs are combined with great elegance.

Another even more elaborately carved and decorated set in green and gold lacquer, now on display in Colonial Williamsburg, is also attributed to Grendey (pls. 88, 89). Sets of this kind mark the climax of English lacquer in the Chinese style, for shortly after they were produced the desire for lacquered furniture declined. When the Chinese fashion made a brief reappearance in the days of Chippendale, the nature of chairs had changed, leaving little room for decoration of the lacquered surface. Upholstered chairs had arms of latticework, such as those in the Chinese bedroom at Nostell Priory (pl. VII). As chairs became lighter, open paling and fretwork left little space where lacquer, beyond its color, could be effective. Color and brilliance, the basic qualities of lacquer, were still in favor, but lacquer was no longer applied when satinwood came into use. Chinese ornaments were replaced by classical figural motifs and floral design painted in oil, following the trends inspired by Robert Adam. This indeed was a departure from the *chinoiserie* lacquer painting that had dominated the scene for so long.

Insofar as English furniture is concerned, these changes marked the end of the lacquer craft in England. True, Chippendale's Directory still carried designs in the Chinese style which might have persuaded a cabinetmaker to execute them in lacquer instead of mahogany, but neither Hepplewhite nor Sheraton presented many models which would lend themselves to lacquering. If color was desired, the painted chair with little or no ornamentation was favored, especially if the chair was to be much used.

Independent of this evolution in furniture had been a steady growth in the production of lacquer articles made of tin or papier-mâché. Merchandise of this kind was developed with the intention of industrializing the production of lacquer. Although such production began in the eighteenth century, discussion will be postponed until the final chapter.

The art of japanning came to the American colonies not much later than the year 1700.[21] That most of the evidence we have of its existence in the new world is found in pieces originating in Boston may seem strange at first glance: one would not expect the Puritans to favor such fashionable exoticism. Presumably the wealthy citizens of Boston, in order to uphold its role as leader of the colonies in matters of convention and style, were persuaded to accept the English taste for *chinoiserie*.

A high chest of drawers dated around 1700 is considered one of the oldest American-made lacquer pieces in existence (pl. 90). In general appearance it follows the William and Mary style and resembles one of those English chests on a stand which now are so rare. The rather crude design of the lacquered decoration indicates that the japanner did not have a coherent pattern to follow. There is a considerable disparity between his work and the good craftsmanship of the cabinetmaker.

The manner in which japanning was done in the colonies differed in a number of ways from the practice customary in England. In the colonies, maple was preferred for the front of a piece of furniture and pine was used for the less showy parts and for carved ornaments. Maple and pine were much smoother woods than the oak or deal used in England, and for this reason it was not thought necessary to prepare the ground carefully as was done in England. As a rule, no gesso ground was applied; instead, the ground was painted and decorated and a clear varnish applied. Raised lacquer was built up with white sizing which was polished; then colors were applied and metal dust or other refinement was sometimes added before the final touch of a few coats of varnish. These simplified techniques presented no difficulties; the real problem was to find suitable patterns to copy. In some instances designs were copied from Dutch or oriental pottery or from patterned textiles, but there was never the vast amount from which to choose as there was in Europe.

Certain painted panelings, although unlacquered, bear a *chinoiserie* design and must be regarded as intended to introduce japanning (pl. 101). Two chairs in the William and Mary style, now in the Los Angeles County Museum, were probably made around 1700 in New England, possibly in Boston, at the same time as the chest of drawers mentioned above (pls. 97, 98). They are distinguished by the red lacquer with which they are covered, the gilt decoration of Far Eastern motifs, and turned legs ending in carved feet in Spanish style. That even in the early days of the colonies lacquering was not an uncommon way of decoration is indicated by the existence of such lacquered chairs as well as chests of drawers, always a prominent piece of furniture in such an ensemble. In fact, the *Boston News Letter* in 1712 advised its readers that Nehemiah Partridge on Tremont Street not only had "an Engin which grinds chocholate very well, If any Person would have Cochoa ground," but also had "all sorts of Japanware" for sale.[22] By 1739, when Boston had a population of considerably more than 12,000 inhabitants, one John Waghorne through the columns of the *Boston News Letter* made it known that he was not only an instructor of vocal psalmody but that he would be glad to teach "ladies to japan in the newest method."[23] A year later he told his customers that he had "lately received a fresh parcel of materials for the new method of japanning which was invented in France, for the amusement and benefit of the ladies, and is now practiced by most of the Quality gentry in Great Britain with the greatest satisfaction." The reference is probably to *découpure* or *lacca povera* techniques. Obviously by 1730 japanning had become a genteel pastime and remained so during the following decades if the number of teachers who offered their services is any indication. With japanning so very much in vogue, it is possible to assume that professional japanners were very much in demand.

Two highboys probably made in Boston[24] about 1725–30 have the same shape as the earlier piece, although cabriole legs have been substituted (pls. 92, 93). In both pieces it is evident how much the design has improved over earlier examples.

Fortunately we are fairly well-informed about a later group of lacquer furniture and the method of its production.[25] A high chest of drawers, now in the Winterthur Museum, carries on the backs of its drawers the inscription of one "Pimm" (pl. 94). John Pimm is known to have been a cabinetmaker active in Boston on Fleet Street in 1736 (he died in 1773). We are fairly certain that the japanning of this piece was done in raised work by one Thomas Johnson, who had his workshop "at the Golden Lyon on Ann Street," according to the business card he engraved for himself (fig. 15).[26] The card also reveals why we venture this attribution since it is decorated with two cherub heads which are also found in the gilded ornamentation of the chest of drawers as well as in that of a highboy and lowboy or low chest (evidently a dressing table) which form an ensemble now at the Metropolitan Museum (pls. 95, 96). Pimm placed his name on the highboy to make certain that it was not mistaken for the work of some other cabinetmaker while in the shop of the japanner. Under these circumstances it is fair to assume that not every piece japanned by Johnson was made by Pimm.

The Pimm-Johnson pieces as well as others are made of pine with maple fronts and are in typical Queen Anne style with broken scroll pediment and cabriole legs. They are richly decorated, with carved scrolls gilded like the rest of the decoration. Unquestionably Johnson was a most competent japanner; his raised decoration compares favorably with similar pieces executed in England. Johnson carried japanned furniture in stock or took orders to have it made. He advertised looking glasses of various types as well as chests of drawers, tables, bookcases, clock cases, and other items. (Other lacquered chests of drawers attributed to Pimm are to be seen at the Harrison Grey Otis House in Boston and in Colonial Williamsburg.)

In any well-to-do household, in America as in England, the clock played an important role. Although cases for bracket clocks were seldom made in the colonies, the tall long-case clock was extremely popular. A well-known English clockmaker, Thomas Wagstaffe (1724–1802), a Quaker who had close contact with merchants sending goods to the colonies, exported clocks with japanned cases to Boston.[27] Wagstaffe's customers in Philadelphia, however, preferred to have their cases made locally. A clock now in the Henry Ford Museum at Dearborn, Michigan, and signed by Gavin Brown, Boston, 1766, is placed in a case of perfect Queen Ann style with a domed top (pl. 99). The japanning, probably done in a Boston shop by an experienced lacquermaster, is raised work on a tortoiseshell ground.

Lacquered furniture is also known to have been produced at Newport, Rhode Island, and Hartford, Connecticut. A representative piece from Connecticut, made around 1720–30 and now in the Winterthur Museum, is of rather unique shape with widely curved legs and unusually flattened feet (pl. 91).[28] As Joseph Downs suggested, the japanning design may have been inspired by crewel work for lack of Far Eastern patterns. Matching this piece is a low chest of drawers now in the Metropolitan Museum.

In Philadelphia japanning was not greatly appreciated, although late eighteenth-century advertisements refer to the shop of Sebastiano Martini (late of Paris and London) who offered for sale japanned trays as well as his services in painting, varnishing, and gilding.[29] Philadelphia's reputation as a source of fine furniture does not rest on the production of whimsical *chinoiserie* but on the great masterpieces of mahogany furniture of the Chippendale period.

A rather large and handsome mirror made in New York City has been handed down for generations in the John Blekker family (pl. 100). It was japanned in the period 1730–40 by a very skilful member of the trade. New York newspapers carried the advertisements of Gerardus Duykinck and his son who were prominent as japanners in the period 1735–50.[30] They also stocked materials for japanning, including "prints of sundry sorts, readily colored." The reference again is to the fashion for *lacca povera* techniques among amateur japanners. Although we know the fashion was practiced in the American colonies, no pieces are known to have survived. Advertisements of japanners continued to appear in New York papers as late as the mid-seventies, but by that time, in England as well as in the colonies, interest in lacquer as an embellishment of fine furniture had diminished greatly. Panels and furniture of lesser value (pl. 101) and of a more common character, Windsor chairs, for example, may have continued to be lacquered.[31] Gradually chairs of this kind were mass-produced and, in the nineteenth century, were painted or stenciled to give the impression of lacquer.

1. H. Clifford Smith, "A Jacobean Painted Cabinet," in *Burlington Magazine*, 31 (1917), 234–40; John Irwin, "A Jacobean Vogue for Oriental Lacquer," in *Burlington Magazine*, 95 (1953), 193.
2. R. W. Symonds, "English Furniture in the Chinese Taste," in *Connoisseur*, 97 (1936), 89–94.
3. John Masefield (ed.), *William Dampierre's Voyages*, 2 vols. (1906), 1:609.
4. R. W. Symonds, "Furniture from the Indies," in *Connoisseur*, 93 (1934), 283–89; 94 (1934), 38–44; Margaret Jourdain and R. Soames Jennyns, *Chinese Export Art* (London, 1950). A bureau cabinet made in the Far East and combining conventional and exotic forms is illustrated in Francis Lenygon's *Furniture in England from 1660–1760* (London, 1914), fig. 417.

5. W. A. Thorpe, "A Group of Chinese Secretaries," in *Apollo*, 23 (1936), 323–29; R. W. Symonds, "The English Japanners' Trade," in *Connoisseur*, 100 (1937), 234–45; E. T. Joy, "A Japanned Bureau-Cabinet," in *Connoisseur*, 171 (1969), 103.
6. R. W. Symonds, "Giles Grendey," in *Apollo*, 22 (1935), 337–42; R. W. Symonds, "English Eighteenth-Century Furniture Exports to Spain and Portugal," in *Burlington Magazine*, 78 (1941), 57–61; R. W. Symonds, "A Royal Scrutoire, English Furniture in Portugal," in *Connoisseur*, 105 (1940), 233–36, 267; Ralph Edwards and Margaret Jourdain, *Georgian Cabinetworkers* (2d ed.; London, 1946), fig. 47; Sir Ambrose Heal, *The London Furniture Makers* (London, 1953), pp. 110, 118, 219, 236, 237.
7. Theodor Lunsingh Scheuerleer, "The Decorative Arts," in *Catalogue of the Exhibition "The Orange and the Rose,"* Victoria and Albert Museum (London, 1964), p. 28.
8. John Stalker and George Parker, *A Treatise on Japanning* (London, 1688; reprint, 1960), p. xv.
9. R. W. Symonds, *English Furniture from Charles II to George II* (New York, 1929), p. 21.
10. Heal, *The London Furniture Makers*, p. 269.
11. R. Edwards, *The Shorter Dictionary of English Furniture* (London, 1964), p. 203.
12. R. Edwards, *The Shorter Dictionary*, p. 664; R. W. Symonds, "Giles Grendey," p. 341.
13. Nicholas Edwards, "A Bantam Work Coffer," in *Connoisseur*, 148 (1961), 289–91.
14. Hans Huth, "English Chinoiserie Gilt Leather," in *Burlington Magazine*, 71 (1937), 25–35; E. A. Entwisle, *The Book of Wallpaper* (London, 1954); R. Edwards, *The Shorter Dictionary*, p. 435.
15. Carl Grommelt and Christine von Mertens, *Das Dohna'sche Schloss Schlobitten in Ostpreussen* (Stuttgart, 1962). Before the destruction of Schlobitten, there was a large amount – more than seventy pieces – of lacquer furniture at the manor, most of it listed in an inventory of 1728. Although listed in the inventory as a writing table and described in Grommelt and von Mertens' book as of Berlin make (p. 484, illustration no. 115), the piece illustrated here (pl. 61) the author believes to be a dressing table made in England. The counts of Dohna purchased much of their inventory abroad. It is also known that in 1717 a "meuble" was brought from an English dealer in Berlin, although this is believed to have been the state bed – definitely of English origin – in existence before 1945 (p. 172, illustration no. 104).
16. "Nostell Priory," in *Connaissance des Arts*, no. 55 (1965), 52–63.
17. Arthur Oswald, "Mrs. Montagu and the China Taste," in *Country Life* (1962), pp. 1328–29; Hugh Honour, *Chinoiserie* (London, 1961), pp. 137 ff.
18. R. Dossie, *The Handmaiden to the Arts* (London, 1758), pp. 406 ff.
19. Ralph Fastnedge, *English Furniture Styles* (London, 1955), p. 159.
20. Ralph Edwards, *A History of the English Chair* (London, 1951), no. 44.
21. R. W. Symonds, "English Export Trade in Furniture to the Colonies," in *Antiques* (June–October, 1935).
22. Irving Lyon, *Colonial Furniture of New England* (1892), p. 95.
23. G. Dow, *The Arts and Crafts in New England, 1704–1775* (Topsfield, Mass., 1927).
24. Joseph Downs, *American Furniture in the Queen Anne and Chippendale Period in the H. F. duPont Winterthur Museum* (New York, 1952), no. 187; Lydia Powell, "The Influence of English Decoration on American Furniture," in *Apollo*, 68 (1958), 104.
25. Joseph Downs, "American Japanned Furniture," in *Bulletin of the Metropolitan Museum of Art* (March, 1933), p. 44; Downs, *American Furniture*, no. 188; Joseph Downs, "American Japanned Furniture of the Eighteenth Century," in *Connoisseur*, 108 (1941), 210–15.
26. The only copy of the business card known to exist was mentioned by Downs in his essay on American japanned furniture in the *Bulletin of the Metropolitan Museum of Art*, p. 44. It was attached to a long-case clock owned in 1933 by Mr. Philip Spaulding of Boston, since deceased; the present whereabouts of the clock is unknown.
27. Martha Gandy-Fales, "Thomas Wagstaffe Clocks," in *Connoisseur*, 151 (1962), 193–201.
28. Downs, *American Furniture*, no. 186.
29. A. C. Prime, *The Arts and Crafts in Philadelphia, Maryland, and South Carolina, New York 1721–1785* (New York, 1929).
30. G. Dow, *The Arts and Crafts in New York 1726–1776* (New York, 1938).
31. Marion D. Ivesen, *The American Chair* (New York, 1957); Shirley Spaulding, "The Decline of Japanning," in *Antiques*, 66 (1954), 483.

CHAPTER IV ITALIAN LACQUER

... bisogna amarsi di una buona
pazienza e non avere fretta
ANGELO MARIA ALBERTI GUIDOTTI, 1764

Any discussion of eighteenth-century Italian art is certain to conjure up a vision of Venice. Why does Venice seem to represent so exclusively the Italian *Settecento?* During the Renaissance, European travelers and patrons of the arts found many centers in Italy of absorbing interest, but during the seventeenth century the situation changed gradually. Some of the smaller courts had been dissolved, and many works of art, including entire collections, had been sold to collectors north of the Alps. There were many changes in Rome itself after the death of the Barberini pope, Urban VIII (1644). In these times of straitened finance, there were far fewer patrons of the arts. The building of churches required several generations of donors before they could be completed. As a consequence of these many factors a number of Italian artists looked elsewhere for employment and received invitations from foreign countries, where they were welcomed. Venetian artists were especially in favor, for they were quick to adapt their art to suit the special requirements of the church or palace they were commissioned to build or decorate. Called to work in Madrid, in Vienna, in London, in Würzburg, these great ambassadors enhanced the renown of Venice throughout Europe. At the same time, attracted by its fame, splendor, and cosmopolitan reputation, all manner of men, princes and adventurers, artists and scholars, flocked to Venice. Even later, when tragic circumstances put an end to the political life of the city, the memory of its great past never faded. That is why the evocation of the Italian *Settecento* brings to mind the image of the *città nobilissima*, the city of which there was – and is – no equal.

During the eighteenth century, Venice was in desperate straits because of the shattering financial and territorial losses it had sustained. Nevertheless, it was the only city-state in Italy which had retained its ancient social structure and still seemed to be powerful. Although its conservatism in matters of government remained adamant, it was eager and open-minded enough to further artistic innovations. Venetian taste was distinguished by its love of brilliant coloration and so it could not fail to seize upon the opportunities offered by the practice of decorating furniture with lacquer.[1] As lacquer grew in popularity in the fashionable world, Venetian artisans exported their wares all over Europe.[2] According to the traveler Misson, the presence of strangers "causes a prodigious trade in things otherwise of no great moment as equipages, coaches, gondolas, liveries, habits of ceremony, as also in furniture, paintings ..." At the time of carnival, princes, kings, and aristocrats from every corner of Europe descended upon the city. There is an episode in Voltaire's *Candide* in which a cavalier meets six masked men who are addressed as "majesties." This he accepts as a carnival joke, but to his amazement he learns that the men in truth are six lately deposed kings who have come to forget their troubles in the carnival spirit of Venice. As if this were not enough, when the cavalier returns to his lodgings he learns that three more royal personages have arrived, but by now he is no longer impressed. As a result of these royal sojourns, there are a number of northern chateaus in which one finds a lacquer mirror or a commode of Venetian origin, souvenirs of a forgotten tour or possibly brought back to serve as patterns for the court cabinetmaker to copy.

Today the majority of Italian lacquer on the art market or found in collections is supposed to be of Venetian origin, probably because this attribution fulfils the wishes of collectors. The exceptions are pieces with some French traits, called Piedmontese, and others with an especially exuberant style, supposed to be Sicilian. Some of the simpler pieces, particularly those in the style of the late eighteenth century, suggest Genoa or Milan. Painted furniture thought to look like lacquer, perhaps with some simple carved motif added, is claimed for Brescia or the *terra ferma*, the hinterland of Venice. Most of these attributions are vague and rest on uneasy ground.

In the 1630s there seems to have been a hiatus in the activities of Venice as a lacquer center, and lacquer decoration inspired by the Near East came to a halt. The earliest positive record of Venetian lacquer unquestionably in the Far East style is furnished by the French traveler Misson who visited Venice in 1688 and noted that there was a lively business in lacquerware at all prices.[3] Misson, a Huguenot who lived in England and must have been acquainted with Far Eastern lacquer as well as with English copies made after the Restoration, found the Venetian lacquer trade extremely active, a sign that it had been going on for some time. Probably one may date the beginnings of trade in Venetian examples of Far Eastern lacquer at approximately 1660. As far as the needed varnish was concerned, Venice had its traditional recipes, but there was also the special varnish invented by Father Coronelli (1650–1702), the official cosmographer of the *Serenissima*, who made globes protected by varnish.[4] Coronelli stated that its main ingredient was sandarac, known for its durability and hardness, and this remained one of the chief ingredients of Venetian lacquer. In 1691, as we have noted, the picture painters seceded from the guild of the *depentores*; as a result, the remaining craftsmen were better able to look after their specific interests, and the authorities were more inclined to take their side when difficulties arose.

What do we have today of Venetian lacquer production of the seventeenth century? It seems strange indeed that after the glorious beginnings discussed in the first chapter there is so little known about what might have been fashioned in Venice in the latter part of the seventeenth century. Even Lorenzetti and Morazzoni, who did so much to clarify what we know of eighteenth-century Italian lacquer, have little to say in this regard. Was the production of nearly half a century wiped out? This would be hard to believe had not something similar happened in Turin. When the *Mostra del Barocco Piemontese* was in preparation in 1963, determined efforts were made to present authentic pieces of seventeenth-century furniture. There were very few to be found, and yet contemporary inventories of the residences of the dukes of Savoy abound in listings of sumptuous furniture made for the court. "Where all this furniture went is a mystery indeed," writes Vittorio Viala in the catalogue of the exhibition, "imagination alone will never conjure up a true impression of these once rich palaces of Piedmont."[5] This complete loss in Piedmont makes it less astonishing to find a similar situation in Venice, even though there once must have existed a large quantity of early lacquer considering the great output of lacquer around 1700 and later.

In order to discover what kind of lacquer was made in Venice, one must start with two lacquer pieces, an armchair and a table, illustrated in Molmenti's great book on Venice.[6] These are known to be of Venetian origin and once formed part of the furnishings of a villa at Lonigo, the property of the Venetian family Giovanelli. The present whereabouts of the chair is unknown, but the table is owned by a collector in Milan. The armchair is carved in a heavy, sprawling style somewhat in the manner of Andrea Brustolone (1662–1732) and its shape is no surprise, but the table has a most unexpected appearance. It is an extraordinarily pure rendition of a design in the "lobar" style as it was practiced, for example, by the silversmith Paulus van Vianen in the Netherlands at the beginning of the seventeenth century, to be copied until well into the 1660s by followers on the continent and in England. The design is full of vigor and restrained energy.

There is another table at the Cà Rezzonico Museum which is so like the one from Lonigo that it too must be of Venetian origin (pl. 102). It was made to serve as a stand for a type of cabinet usually considered to have originated in Augsburg. Similar cabinets made throughout the seventeenth century were exported all over Europe. In this case it is most likely that the cabinet as well as the table received their *chinoiserie* ornaments after the two had been combined at Venice. The table is lacquered in green and shows the same *chinoiserie* motifs and mother-of-pearl inlay as the Lonigo chair and table. It is quite possible that both tables once served as stands for cabinets; they may have formed a pair.

If we accept three other pieces of furniture published by Morazzoni as genuine, we learn more about early Venetian lacquer.[7] These pieces certainly date from the seventeenth century. Their Venetian origin could have been established by Morazzoni by a pedigree or perhaps by the type of wood used – *cirmolo*, a species of Alpine fir customarily used in Venice. One, a cabinet of a type usually called Dutch, decorated in the Far Eastern style and on a stand with high tapering legs connected by diagonal, curved stretchers, was formerly owned by the Principe Giovanelli, as were the pieces mentioned earlier. The second piece is a pulpit desk on a stand of turned bulbous legs, connected by stretchers, on bun feet and decorated in the Far Eastern manner – a type which might well be considered of English origin. The third piece is a bureau with a desk with two small drawers on top and two large ones underneath, all lacquered with *chinoiserie* of a style often seen in northern countries.

If we may judge from these few pieces of furniture, we may conclude that Venice used as models furniture originating in England and in Holland and at the same time began to use Far Eastern patterns of decoration becoming fashionable in the north. Indeed, it seems logical that lacquering in the Far Eastern manner should have caught on in this manner, since lacquer from the Far East was arriving at northern harbors. The incorporation of mother-of-pearl inlay seems to have been a truly Venetian trend and one carried over from older times. It was used in combination with floral and ornamental motifs of European character, predating the influx of oriental motifs. An especially fine example is the stem of a crucifix crowning an alms box at the church of San Zaccaria (pl. 105).

Here the symbol of a bunch of grapes made of mother-of-pearl appears within European decoration. The same is true of certain rare frames made of mother-of-pearl and now used for pictures; originally they may have been mirror frames like those exhibited at the National Gallery in Prague (pls. 103, 104). The technical execution of this kind of lacquerwork would have offered no great problem since its use was an age-old tradition of the members of the guild of *depentores*.

In the eighteenth century it seems that English influence in the making of furniture made itself felt even more strongly. This must have been the case in the following examples, both made in Venice. One was an upright bureau in the form of the early *credenzino* with drawers below, a cupboard at the top with small drawers and compartments, and a shelf in the middle which could be pulled out for writing purposes, the other a *cassetone con alzata*, a desk or bureau in two stages with a writing compartment covered by a sloping lid. There was no precedent for such designs in the history of Italian furniture since there had never been much demand for tall pieces of furniture in Italy. Even the Renaissance cupboard had been taken over from northern countries.

Hereafter we find writing cabinets crowned by a double bonnet head of the familiar English type, though often adapted to Venetian taste. There is, for example, a cabinet with pointed arches at the top, lacquered in black and covered with large *chinoiserie* motifs (pl. 106). For some of these secretaries it is hazardous to attempt to determine English or Venetian origin from a photograph.[8] Unmistakably Venetian in origin are a pair of upright secretaries now in the museum of the Castello Sforcesco at Milan (pl. 107). They are narrow, with slightly curved bottom parts and doors accentuated by rounded, heavy moldings carried above the curved and broken pediments on either side. Most remarkable are the feet shaped as heads, reminiscent of one of the best-known products of Venice, the *mori* or blackamoors, i. e., representations of young Moors in elaborate dress standing or crouching and holding platters which serve as stands.[9] These figures never lost their popularity and continued to be made and copied up through the nineteenth century in Venice and elsewhere (pl. 114).

Another secretary, extremely slender, appears especially elegant because of its curved outline and its flower decoration on a yellow lacquer ground (pl. 108). In the arrangement of pediments, finials, and other details surmounting the cornice there is a great variety in all Venetian secretaries. Typical are those with glass doors, often with etched ornaments, produced in Murano. Even shapes of secretaries or bureaus vary considerably. The front of the lower drawers may be curved or the outline broken in other ways, corners leveled, and pilasters set against the narrow, canted planes. A bureau might have narrow sides slanting back in a curve, with the middle protruding. Such variety lends extraordinary liveliness to these desks and makes them differ markedly from their English prototypes.

The decoration of bookcases and secretaries varies as much as does their shape. Frequently they are decorated with ornaments and flowers, indicating that as early as 1720 Venetian lacquerworkers not infrequently, if it was called for, emancipated themselves from the *chinoiserie* style. An example is the upright secretary decorated in the *lacca povera* manner with added gesso ornaments, undoubtedly the work of a skilled artisan and not of an amateur (pl. 109).

VII. Bedroom, by Thomas Chippendale, about 1770

VIII. Door, once in Cà Rezzonico, Venice, about 1750
IX. Bureau-cabinet, decorated with oil paintings, Rome, about 1715

X. Harpsichord, Gérard Dagley, Berlin, about 1710

The commode as the favorite piece of furniture in the eighteenth century was developed with special zest in all of the countries which contributed to eighteenth-century style. The extravagance with which these commodes were shaped is shown by the one illustrated here, now owned by Stanford University (pl. 112). It is lacquered in light blue and decorated with flowers in natural colors.

The tops of Venetian commodes and consoles were usually made of marbelized wood. If marble was used, it was set into a wooden frame which never protrudes beyond the body. This way of using marble dispels any effect of heaviness. In creating these commodes, console tables, stands, and a variety of accessories, the Venetian *depentori alla chinese*, as they were sometimes called, achieved their greatest success. Unlike Renaissance chests which do not depend so much on their surroundings to be fully appreciated, Venetian furniture should be seen in the ensemble for which it was created. To paraphrase Talleyrand's statement that France could never be enjoyed again as it had been before the Revolution, one might say that those who have never seen a Venetian room completely furnished in lacquer, as originally intended, cannot imagine the brilliance, the elegance, the sheer vibrancy of such an ensemble. In 1934 the Palazzo Donà delle Rose was the last to be divested of its treasures, especially its extraordinary amount of lacquerware. Picture low-ceilinged mezzanine rooms filled with charming, small-scale pieces of furniture provided for the sole purpose of making life comfortable and pleasant. Here were sofas and armchairs and small tables with trays on which to set cups of chocolate during the *conversazioni*. The ensemble for one salon numbered over fifteen items, among them a mirror for a mantlepiece, large commode (*cassetone*), two smaller ones (*commodini*), as well as a number of sofas and chairs, all carved, lacquered, and decorated in pink and blue with flowers in natural colors. The crowning piece of the Donà lacquer was a cradle in the shape of a shell swinging from the branch of a tree. One branch extended upward to hold a tiny baldachin from which floated the curtains. All was decorated with vines, flowers, and birds lacquered in their natural colors.[10]

In mid-eighteenth century, Venetian lacquermasters were at the height of their skill. No longer exclusively concerned with *chinoiserie*, the lacquermasters used their imagination to contrive the kinds of decoration that would enhance the spirited scrollwork surrounding a mirror or to shape the curved bottom and lid of an otherwise indifferent box belonging to a toilet set. In 1754 some twenty-five lacquermasters with more than double that number of workmen in their shops were active in Venice; by 1773 their number had risen to forty-nine.[11]

One of the most elegant of interiors must have been the grand salon of the palazzo called Cà Rezzonico, which unfortunately was denuded not only of its furniture but its doors not long after the beginning of this century. When the palace was made over into a museum, it was at least possible to recapture something of the original elegance by installing the contents of a salon from the palazzo Calbo-Crotta, still well-intact even to its old silk wall hangings.[12] This set of furniture is lacquered in green and gilt. The carvings of the mirror frame and the console table under it are extraordinarily rich and done in a most spirited manner (pl. 110). The chair seats still have ornamented silk covers which match the wall hangings, and there are curtains flowing from the lacquered cornices (*bonne-*

grazie) over doors and windows. The commode from this ensemble must be considered typical of the Venetian style of lacquering in shape as well as in design (pl. 111). Although the decorations leave little of the surface untouched, the design is so well balanced that the effect is not one of overdecoration. The grotesque figures do not disturb the blissful atmosphere of the eternal Chinese landscape. Instead of the lively fresco in color which once covered the entire ceiling of the Calbo-Crotta salon, the ceiling is decorated now with a small painting by Francesco Guardi in the center, flanked by enormous Murano chandeliers from which hundreds of candles sparkle down upon the whole colorful ensemble.

One of the Rezzonico doors was returned by the Accademia gallery, the other was split and the two sides are now in two separate collections in the United States (pl. VIII).[13] The decoration of the door that remains in Venice indicates the color scheme that governed the salon. It is lacquered in yellow, with two panels one above the other showing raised figural groups lightly tinted and gilded and surrounded by rich garlands of flowers joined by ribbons tied in bows. These floral pieces painted in warm colors surrounding figural centers represent one of the loveliest Venetian creations. The figures represent the "serious" fashion of *chinoiserie* of the 1740s. Their quality and the fact that Giovanni Battista Tiepolo is known to have decorated some of the ceilings of the palace have given rise to the suggestion that he may have painted the doors. But there is no valid reason for such a belief: the style of these decorations, partly on raised gesso, is nothing like Tiepolo's or even like that of members of his workshop. Nevertheless, stories persist that Tiepolo, Pittoni, and other painters decorated furniture. There may have been exceptions: there is a bureau, probably of Roman origin, decorated with oil paintings (pl. IX). In general, it would have been highly unlikely that painters, members of the *Collegio dei pittori*, as the gathering of "art" painters established in 1691 was called, would have cooperated with the lacquer *depentores*.

In considering settings for lacquer furniture, attention should be directed to a certain kind of suite found in and around the Piazza San Marco. These were the innumerable small *casini* maintained by members of noble families where, after large official affairs, during carnival or on other festive occasions they gathered with their friends for a *conversazione* before they scattered to their often-distant palaces. Invariably chocolate was served, and there were any number of small chairs, stands, and consoles adapted to the needs of the always small but richly appointed rooms (pl. 113). Lacquer, finely decorated on a softly colored ground of celadon, light blue, or yellow, was preferred, and it is this sort of furniture that collectors today most prize. Mention has been made of one of the most popular products of Venice, the figures of blackamoors serving as stands for trays or candelabras. A most delightful set, its glittering colors intact, has been preserved in the imperial suite at the Abbey of St. Florian in Austria. The set was made in 1729, by the Venetian Giovanni Giuliani and the Austrian Leonhard Sattler, both vying with each other to express their skill (pl. 114). Once used in suites like those of the *casini* is a pair of frames made to fit embossed wax portraits with the arms of the Rezzonico family placed within a graceful array of curves, the branches and flowers polychromed and gilded on a yellow ground (pl. 115).

Few of these suites outlasted the Republic, and only one remains today, though without its furnishings (pl. 116). It is located west of the Piazza San Marco, close to the Ponte dei Baratteri (no. 4939), and once belonged to Donna Elena Priuli, wife of the procurator Federico Venier, one of the Republic's highest dignitaries in the late eighteenth century. This casino was rejuvenated for the exhibition of the *Settecento Italiano* in 1929.[14] The apartment itself is intact, including the delightful stucco ornamentation on ceilings and walls. There is still a spyhole (*diago*) in the wall and a secret exit through one of the built-in cupboards. For the exhibition the room was furnished with all the appointments it once might have contained, and of course lacquer furniture predominated. Many of these *casini*, often mentioned by Casanova, were short-lived because they were kept under surveillance by those who feared that the opportunity for privacy might nurture political conspiracies or be dangerous in other ways. The only rooms with lacquer furniture still *in situ* are some in the Palazzo Querini-Stampaglia, now a museum.

Of Venetian-made chairs, a certain type often seen in paintings by Longhi is distinguished by the very wide, rather flatly molded frame which surrounds the upholstered back (pl. 117). The chair illustrated is lacquered in red and decorated with small flower motifs. Some Venetian chairs follow English patterns of the Queen Anne period; French models are not often used, and the *bergère* is completely unknown. Toward the middle of the eighteenth century and after, English patterns and derivatives are frequent. A typical Venetian pattern is a chair in which moldings in the back are twisted into a figure eight, while two moldings pleated into each other accompany or frame the apron (pl. 118).

One piece of furniture which differs considerably from anything so far mentioned resembles a heavy commode but is in fact a sales desk (*banco di negozio*) with an opening at the back for the vendor (pl. 124). It may have been used in a fashionable coffeehouse, a gambling place, or a shop. A similar piece is seen at the Ca' Rezzonico which had been used as a desk for a pharmacist. Its cumbersome appearance is somewhat lightened by the skill with which the rocaille curves are applied in the graceful ornaments that frame the flower arrangements.

Among Venetian specialties were lacquered pincushion containers, boxes and trays in a variety of sizes, candlesticks, and toilet sets, usually comprised of eight pieces (pls. XII b, 119). Another popular piece was the game table or game board (pl. 120, 121). Two stringed instruments may also be mentioned. They are charmingly decorated, but there is some question whether they may be claimed for Venice. The one without a case belongs to the inventory of the Palazzo Doria-Pamphilij in Rome and may date from the 1730s (pl. 123). The other, formerly in the Collection Adolf Loewi, Los Angeles, with a scene of jugglers on the lacquered case, may date from the early eighteenth century; the instrument itself may have been redecorated later (pl. 122).

With the last quarter of the eighteenth century came a change in style: rigid Louis XVI forms replaced the fancies of the Louis XV period, surely to the dismay of the artisans in Venice. Variety in shape and color had nourished the brilliant fantasies of the Venetian lacquermaster, and they may have been reluctant to accept the change. The year 1780 marked the period of transition, as suggested by the green lacquer commode once owned by the Falier family (pl. 125). The end came soon. Not only did lacquer go out of fashion, but first the French Revolution and then Napoleon began to change the face of Europe. Venice ceased to be the rendezvous of international society. In 1797 the treaty of Campoformio ended the existence of the *Serenissima Repubblica di San Marco;* Venice was now part of the Austrian empire.

The art of lacquering remained dormant until the late nineteenth century, when this craft and other accomplishments of earlier days once again found favor. Undoubtedly the Venetians' skill and feeling for shape and color still existed, but they were used only to recreate what had been admired during the great epoch of the eighteenth century.

Second only to Venice in importance as a producer of lacquer was Turin, the residence of the king of Savoy, Vittorio Amadeo II (1666–1732). In an effort to emulate the palace at Versailles, Vittorio had commissioned Filippo Juvara (1678–1736) to remodel the old Palazzo Madama. In spite of the grandeur achieved after this and other changes had been made, Montesquieu sarcastically referred to Turin as the biggest village in the world. Nevertheless, in spite or because of this derogatory comment, Lord Chesterfield recommended that his son visit and become acquainted with "the most polite society" in Turin. From these remarks one can well imagine that with all its elegance the spirit of Turin could not compare with the cosmopolitan atmosphere of Venice.

The example set by the king was followed by the aristocracy of Savoy. Palaces in and around Turin were built and furnished on a lavish scale. Rich furniture inlaid with ivory was in fashion, as were lacquer pieces, although these were in vogue only among the upper circles of society, unlike Venice, permeated with the spirit of the age, where elegant furniture was not a privilege solely of the *nobili.*

Perhaps the most striking lacquer room of the period was – and remains – that constructed in the royal palace of Turin about 1735 (pl. 126, 127, 129). It was based upon a design by Filippo Juvara.[15] Far Eastern lacquer panels for the walls were supplemented most skilfully by a local lacquermaster, Pietro Massa. Lacquered in gold and red on a black background, the panels are fitted into a framework of carved and gilded wood in a design of great elegance, the whole executed on a most opulent scale. Massa's talent in adapting his work to that of the Far East is remarkable. Indeed, the difference between his excellent work and that of an anonymous master who worked ten years earlier in a more modest room in the palace is strikingly evident. The nature elements in this secondary master's work are acceptable enough, but his figures of Roman warriors seem rather naïve (pl. 128). By luck, a set of six stools made for this room are still in existence (pls. 138). Lacquered with a Chinese motif, the vigorously curved cabriole legs give them their particularly Italianate character. At Stupinigi, the king's summer residence outside Turin, the light decoration is perfectly in keeping for a hunting lodge, albeit one of enormous size (pl. 130). In the king's apartments are some elegant rooms with painted silk wall hangings in Louis XV style, and here Francesco Servorcelli decorated some furniture. A corner cupboard, utilizing arabesque ornamentation of a somewhat classical design on a background of yellow lacquer, stands out against the colorful walls (pl. 131). At the time this piece was executed, about 1750, the fashion for *chinoiserie* had waned, though soon it would return to favor.

In contrast to the splendor of the court at Turin, a country seat, the Villa Vacchetti at Gerbido, was furnished in a much more sober manner. A room from Gerbido is now in the W. R. Nelson Gallery of Art in Kansas City (pl. 132). Its architectural structure represents an earlier style than its *chinoiserie* panels, gilt on red lacquer. The panels were probably executed in the 1740s in this sparse yet graceful manner, perhaps patterned after Coromandel screens.

In demand in Venice and yet rare in Turin was the tall, upright secretary or bureau; in its place was a rather capriciously designed secretary which originally must have had a mirror or door instead of a glass window (pl. 133). Lacquered in blue with rich gilding and with its ingeniously curved and rounded top, this piece has the quality of a sculpture. Indeed, although no opportunity is missed to curve a line or bend a plane, there is sufficient restraint in the design of the desk to prevent its form seeming to be an exaggeration. Its shape is rather powerful, and the piece as a whole is important enough to stand in a palace suite. The same may be said of a commode, sold at Christie's in 1955, which is lacquered in green with gilt decoration (pl. 134). Its well-balanced *bombé* shape indicates French influence. Turin also produced, as did Venice, a variety of accessory pieces of furniture. Some followed the French trend in the use of hoof feet (*pieds de biche*) with heavily carved stretchers, but they lack the lightness of Venetian furniture (pls. 135–139).

During the eighteenth century, the once-powerful Republic of Genoa was obliged to defend its interests with very uncertain means; it was involved incessantly in struggles with revolutionaries and other would-be usurpers, to the point where it offered no encouragement to a pleasure-loving society.[16] Nevertheless, some lacquer was produced in Genoa, although neither in the quantity nor with the charm of the lacquer from Venice. The strong accent on color and the sheer grace of Venetian furniture would not have seemed appropriate in the massive structures the Genoese aristocracy built on hill slopes. The lacquer of Genoa is not as well executed as that of Venice; sometimes the lacquer was applied to the wood without much, if any, sizing underneath, and monochrome color schemes all-too-often prevailed in the decoration. When the French traveler Lalande visited Genoa in 1765, he noted that several well-known lacquermasters were at work and that the technique called *vernice della Madalena*, developed years before by a master living near the church S. Madalena, was still in use, indeed its name had become a generic term like *vernis Martin* in France.[17]

Not much lacquer of importance can be traced to the princely residences in Modena, Ferrara, and elsewhere. Like the princelings of small states in the Holy Roman Empire, these rulers modeled their style of living on that of their more powerful counterparts. In so doing, they copied the styles in Turin and in Venice. In 1748, when Parma became the residence of Duke Philippe de Bourbon Parma and his wife, the Duchess Louise-Elisabeth, daughter of Louis XV, French influence was very strong in the court. The ducal palace was rich with superb French furniture, including a lacquered commode, now in the Palazzo del Quirinale in Rome, created by the cabinetmaker Bernard van Risenburgh.[18]

During the early eighteenth century, the throne of Saint Peter was occupied for the most part by members of such ancient families as the Albani, Conti, Corsini, and Orsini who were bent on preserving old customs and traditions. It is significant that when Clement XIII (1758–1769) became pope, this scion of the Rezzonico family could not be reconciled to departure from his home in Venice. The baroque age had turned the city into a *Roma moderna*, and such it was to remain.

In Rome, the fashion for lacquer was never fully accepted, and indeed delicate work of this kind would have been dwarfed in the serene halls of Renaissance and Baroque palazzi. All the same, there were some early beginnings; we have already mentioned the English lacquermaster William Smith who worked in Rome. A hundred years later, around 1720, Bonanni mentions a lacquermaster in the Via dei Coronari near the Piazza Navona. He is said to have produced lacquer caskets, writing desks, and tables decorated with gilt arabesques and foliage, but apparently not in the Chinese style.[19] Around the middle of the seventeenth century, the well-known painter of flowers, Mario Nuzzi (1622–1673), called Mario dei Fiori, is supposed to have decorated some furniture.[20] While this claim has not been substantiated, we do know of a bureau (pl. IX), most probably of Roman origin, painted in oil and decorated with mythological scenes attributed to the painter Sebastano Conca (1680–1764) and his shop. It carries the motif of Annibale Caracci's "Galathea" in the Galleria of the Palazzo Farnese. It is the tradition to claim that in 1714 this bureau was in the dowry of Principessa Elisabeta Farnese when she married Prince Philip of Anjou-Bourbon, later king of Spain as Philip V. Although the technique of its decoration is an exception to the rule, this bureau suggests the general shape of lacquered bureaus as they were fashioned in Rome. Among its characteristic features are the carved and sweeping curves decorating all four corners and a more monumental shape than is customary in Venetian bureaus.[21] Fortunately there still exist a few distinguished pieces of lacquer in the possession of other great families that can give us some idea of unquestionably Roman trends.

A small commode, dated about 1750 or earlier, is owned by Principe Urbano Barberini (pls. 141, 142). Two other commodes of similar shape are in the Palazzo Pallavicini (pl. 144). All three are representative of a certain type of Roman commode on high cabriole legs. The uprights where sides and front meet are accentuated by columnar members from which the sides swing back and curve outward. The front is also curved. This shape gives the commode a sturdy appearance, well-suited to carry a thick marble top, very different from the thin marble tops only used rarely in Venice. The Barberini commode is decorated with *chinoiserie* in raised gesso in gold on blue lacquer. The pair of Pallavicini commodes are lacquered in light gray, perhaps somewhat faded from a light blue, with a gilt floral decoration. A larger commode of the same type, decorated in a more lively fashion with an arrangement of flowers on a cream – once probably white – ground, is owned by the Los Angeles County Museum (pl. 143). An unusual article of the same period belonging to Principe Barberini is a microscope with Chinese decoration in gold on black lacquer, signed by its learned maker, a Jesuit father, Paulus Maria Petrini (1704–1773; pl. 140).

Under the rule of the Bourbon kings, Naples and Sicily remained the last Spanish stronghold in Italy. If the atmosphere of the court had not been so inert, the spirited artisans of Naples might well have rivaled the artisans of Venice. It seems that repression of the spirit endangered the artistic impulse and the creative force that might have contributed to the rococo style which developed so richly elsewhere in Italy.

The palace of Caserta, with its fabulous waterworks begun by Vanvitelli in 1762 and completed around 1770, was to be the great achievement of the eighteenth century, rivaling both the Escorial and Versailles. Unfortunately, the result, executed in what Carl Justi once called a style of "august tedium," must be considered a failure. Certainly the idea of lacquer could not have thrived in this rigid atmosphere, nor could the elements of rococo take root within the dry classicism of a building devoid of inspiration.

Palermo, on the other hand, was a place of colorful character, and the palaces of the nobility reflected the livelier trends of the eighteenth century. A lacquer cabinet from one of the country seats shows every indication of having been inspired by Juvara and his craftsmen in Turin. Fragments of this room have been installed in the Villa Viscaya in Miami, Florida (pl. 145). While the design of the lacquer panels and their framing is closely related to the more impressive Chinese cabinet in the royal palace at Turin, the flower patterns follow a purely European style of exuberant design. Even today when the room no longer has the unity of its former appearance (original wainscoting and wall hangings have been replaced), the remaining doors, the decorated mantlepiece, and the mirror panels opposite combine to make this room a most impressive ensemble.

Fragments of another Sicilian room of most regal splendor are installed at the Musée des Arts Décoratifs in Paris (pl. 146). And yet its presentation in a museum makes it difficult to appreciate how splendid it once was when ceiling, draperies, and furniture formed a complete ensemble. One may gain a similar impression from still another Sicilian hall now installed as a private theater in the Italian embassy in Paris. A characteristic example of Sicilian furniture is a commode with a low apron set on short, stubby legs and decorated with flowers on a blue ground (pl. 147). The "gilding," as is frequently the case in Sicilian furniture, is in fact "mecca gold," that is, silver leaf coated with varnish to give the effect of gold.

Under the rule of the Bourbons, the shipping trade of the Kingdom of the Two Sicilies gravitated toward England, and English lacquer furniture was shipped to Naples, just as, later, chairs of the Chippendale and Hepplewhite period were exported to Italy and frequently copied in bastard form.

1. Eduard Baccesci, *Mobili laccati Veneziani del Settecento* (Venice, 1962); S. Levy, *Lacche Veneziane Settecentesche* (Milan, 1967); Giulio Lorenzetti, *Le lacche Veneziane del Settecento* (Venice, 1938); Giuseppe Morazzoni, *Mobili Veneziani Laccati*, 2 vols. (Milan, 1954).
2. Malachy Postlewayt (ed.), *The Universal Dictionary of Trade and Commerce* (4th ed.; London, 1774), the article "Venice." This is a later edition of Jacques Savary des Brulons (ed.), *Dictionnaire Universel de Commerce*, 4 vols. (Copenhagen, 1762), 4:118, "Venise."
3. Maxime Misson, *Nouveau voyage de l'Italie*, 2 vols. (La Haye, 1698), 3:217.
4. Vincenzo Coronelli, *Epitome cosmographica* (Venice, 1693), as quoted in Morazzoni, *Mobili Veneziani Laccati*, 1:16.
5. *Mostra del Barocco Piemontese, Catalogo a cura di Vittorio Viale*, 3 vols. (Turin, 1963), 3:1–5.
6. Pompeo Molmenti, *La storie di Venezia nella vita privata*, 3 vols. (Bergamo, 1910), 3:323, 324.
7. Morazzoni, *Mobili Veneziani Laccati*, 1: pl. XIII, Stipo (cabinet), pl. LXII, Scrivania (secretary), pl. CLXXVIII, Cassetone a ribalta (secretary).
8. Morazzoni, *Mobili Veneziani Laccati*, 1: pls. XVI–XIX. Compare R. Edwards, *The Shorter Dictionary of English Furniture* (London, 1964), p. 97, fig. 19.

9. Molmenti, *La storia di Venezia*, 3:327, n. 2.
10. Arno Schönberger and Halldor Söhner, *The Rococo Age* (New York, 1960), pl. XV.
11. Morazzoni, *Mobili Veneziani Laccati*, 1:53.
12. Molmenti, *La storia di Venezia*, 3:328 (illustration of former setting of the room).
13. One side of the door is owned by The Art Institute of Chicago, the other side is in a private collection. See *Cathay Invoked* (exhibition catalogue, California Palace of the Legion of Honor, San Francisco, 1966), no. 132.
14. *Il Settecento Italiano. Catalogo della Mostra delle Lacche Veneziane del Settecento* (Venice, 1929). See also Aldo Rava, "Il ridotto Venier," in *Dedalo* (1920), p. 452.
15. *Mostra del Barocco Piemontese*, 1: pl. 1.
16. Giuseppe Morazzoni, *Il Mobile Genovese* (Milan, 1949); Luigi Cannonero, *Barocchetto Genovese* (Milan, 1962).
17. J. J. Lalande, *Voyage d'un Français en Italie, 1765–66*, 9 vols. (Paris, 1786), 9:376.
18. Chiara Briganti, "Comment Madame Infante a meuble sa résidence à Parme," in *Connaissance des Arts*, no. 161 (July, 1965), pp. 48–57.
19. Filippo Bonanni, *Trattato sopra le Vernice* (Rome, 1720), here quoted from the French edition (Paris, 1720), p. 108.
20. Giovanni Mariacher, "Lacquer," in *Encyclopedia of World Art* (New York, 1963). On Nuzzi, see Lione Pascoli, *Vite de' Pittori*, 2 vols. (Rome, 1736), 2:57.
21. *Catalogue Lempertz-Auktion 500, Köln. Alte Kunst*, no. 1621 (November/December, 1968). A most unusual Dutch linen closet, decorated all over with conversation pieces painted in oil in the eighteenth century and completely destroying the structural aspect of the cupboard, is illustrated in *Connoisseur*, 171 (1969), 73.

CHAPTER V GERMAN LACQUER

> ... die zu grosser Potentaten
> Belustigung erfundene Laquierkunst
> GÉRARD DAGLY, 1696

Because none of the member states of the Holy Roman Empire engaged in seafaring enterprises in the Orient, the fashion for lacquer did not spread as quickly or as vigorously among the German states as it did in England and Holland. When we do find early traces of the Chinese fashion, they lead to the seaports of Hamburg and Bremen. Thus the 1689 inventory of the Electress Dorothea, wife of Frederic William of Brandenburg, mentions "Hamburg lacquer trays on stands with turned columns," which indicates that Hamburg did have some trade in lacquer articles.[1] This is not the first mention of the lacquer trade. In the city archives we learn of an *Indianischer lackwerker*, Evert Sachsenhausen, in 1622, and of another, Marcus Albrecht, in the period 1641–57. Other than these brief notes, nothing is known of the work of these men.

A number of lacquermasters are known to have worked in Hamburg toward the close of the seventeenth century, perhaps encouraged by Hamburg's growing fame as a city of music – and of musical instruments decorated in lacquer. Georg Philip Telemann and Philip Emmanuel Bach were important to the musical life of the city, Arp Schnitger was building his famous organs, and there were some fifteen known makers of stringed instruments, some of whose families had worked in the trade for several generations. The best-known of these were the Fleischer, Zell, and Hass workshops.[2] Most of the clavichords they made were decorated in lacquer, the outside of the case in lively red, green, and gilt, the inside in lighter colors. On the inside of the lid there was usually a painting in oil of a European scene, often depicting a musical gathering. In instruments from the Hass workshop we recognize various styles in *chinoiserie*, indicating that a number of different hands were at work. One instrument, made about 1723, is decorated with a scene of more or less European figures clothed in a kind of Chinese garb against a background of naïvely drawn buildings and plants (pl. 148). In strong contrast to this design is that by another artist, around 1732–55, who was more skilful and had a knowledge of Far Eastern patterns (pls. 151, 152, 153). He makes a sincere attempt to depict rocks, plants, houses, and a few scattered figures in a truly Chinese pattern, though the result is a *chinoiserie* of so individual a style that his work is easily recognizable. Stringed instruments with this kind of decoration are in the Belle Skinner Collection at Yale University and in the museums at Oslo (pl. 150) and Copenhagen (pl. 154). A cabinet in the museum at Oslo, patterned after the English type with a double bonnet top, is decorated by the same hand, further indicating that the lacquermasters of Hamburg also decorated furniture which followed English patterns (pls. 152, 153).

A clavichord made in 1728 by Christian Zell, a master related to the Fleischer family, was decorated by yet another artist whose work is superior to that of the Hass masters (pl. 149). There is an unusual competence and elegance in his decoration, and he gives his work a rather special character by including among his "Chinese" figures a number of pet apes. A decade later when it was the fashion to ridicule the Chinese, the apes are depicted in human costumes.

Although to date no later pieces of Hamburg lacquer have been found, it can be assumed that with the constant influx of goods from England the lacquer trade prospered in a modest way as long as it was the fashion. An old photograph of a fragment of a lacquered window frame, once part of a red lacquer room, seems both of very good quality and unique (pl. 155). Nothing is known about the room or the house from which it came except that it was located in the oldest quarter of Hamburg and dated from about 1700. Years ago the Hamburg museum tried to purchase the house, then during World War II the house was completely destroyed in an air raid.

In Bremen there is evidence of only one lacquerworker. In 1688, Nicolaus Woltmann applied for permission to practice his art "of pruning flowers as well as lacquer work," having learned both trades during a stay of ten years in England.[3] Woltmann was granted permission with the restriction that he was not to engage in cabinetwork unless lacquer was to be added to a cabinet, table, or other article. Woltmann's point that he had learned his trade in England is significant because it indicates, as does the Hamburg cabinet now in Oslo, how much the lacquer trade in northern Europe depended upon English antecedents. Unlike Hamburg, however, where musical instruments were made and lacquermasters were in demand, Bremen had little incentive to engage in the lacquer trade.

Brunswick was another center influenced by English lacquer, probably because George I of the house of Brunswick-Lüneburg ascended the British throne in 1714. The first known lacquermaster in Brunswick was Johann Christoph Lesieur, born in Hanover, who became a citizen of Brunswick in 1717.[4] His name would indicate that he was descended from one of the Huguenot families who sought asylum on German soil. Lesieur seems not to have prospered in his business. Two lacquered chests of drawers have survived in the possession of the ducal house of Brunswick (pl. 156). Since they are undoubtedly of Brunswick make, they probably could not have been made by anyone other than Lesieur. Considering Lesieur's dates, these chests must have originated about 1720, although their shape would date them a generation earlier. The same is true of their decoration, composed of elements taken from Stalker and Parker – once again showing the strength of English influence. In spite of the backwardness of his style, Lesieur must have been fairly competent in his work if we can trust the descriptions of the lacquerwork he had in stock when he applied for a permit to hold a lottery because his business was so poor. There was good reason for this lack of business. Because of the close connections with England, the court and the nobility gave much of their patronage to English cabinetmakers, a preference one can readily understand in view of Lesieur's rather clumsy furniture. These purchases caused the local cabinetmakers so much concern that in 1749 they complained about the importation of English chairs and cabinets. After Lesieur's death in 1739, the making of lacquerwork in Brunswick continued on a small scale well into the second half of the eighteenth century when the craft became an industry through the efforts of the Stobwasser family, following English trends – not those of the fashionable cabinetmakers in

London but those initiated by the thriving workshops of Birmingham and Pontypool which were engaged in lacquering tin and papier-mâché (see chap. VIII).

In southern Germany the most important trade centers were Augsburg and Nürnberg. In these cities the arts and crafts had flourished for centuries, and here the art of the Italian Renaissance had been introduced north of the Alps. In spite of the open-mindedness of these cities to new trends and ideas, neither of them harbored lacquer shops of importance which might have established trade as was the case with Augsburg silver or Nürnberg ceramics. The curious thing about this neglect of lacquer was the fact that publishers and printers in both cities took a strong interest in *chinoiserie* and lacquer fashions. Most of the many tracts on the art of lacquering were published in Nürnberg, and printers in both cities published many series of prints either of *chinoiserie* or cut-outs intended to be used in the *lacca povera* technique. According to one Nürnberg historian, the goldsmith Johann Heel (1637–1709) introduced *Indianische Lackarbeit* when he moved from Augsburg to Nürnberg in 1668.[5] But none of his work, or the work of any other lacquermaster in the city, is known today.

Concerning Augsburg, Paul von Stetten, the eminent chronicler of its crafts, writing shortly before 1780, had this to say: "There have been artists who initiated the Chinese and Japanese way of lacquering but they never attained the finesse nowadays given to this kind of work by French and English artists. Thirty or forty years ago [1740–50] we had a special fashion much indulged in by amateurs and ladies. They painted household articles, tables, trays, screens, toilette cases, in red, blue, and yellow. On this undercoating specially engraved, colored and cut-out designs were pasted and then varnished. This was common practice in Germany as well as in Spain and other countries. Today people no longer think of lacquering, nor is there much they can read about it in order to learn this kind of art."[6]

While lacquer production in Hamburg prospered as auxiliary to the manufacture of musical instruments, the elements essential to a thriving business were missing in large cities when there was no residing prince, no court, no "nobility and gentry." After all, according to the outstanding lacquermaster of Berlin, Gérard Dagly, lacquer had been "invented to delight potentates." Even where there was a court – Brunswick, for example – the lacquer craft could not succeed if it had to compete with English imports of far better style. As well as the "potentates" there were the high dignitaries of various courts who furnished their palaces and country estates in the current fashion wherever possible. A typical example was the manor of Schlobitten in East Prussia, built around 1700, which was wantonly destroyed in the aftermath of World War II. Schlobitten belonged to the counts, later the princes, of Dohna who for generations had served at the court of Berlin. While the Dohnas apparently never employed a lacquermaster of their own, they acquired lacquer furniture in Berlin, Holland, and very probably England (pls. 61, 171).

A somewhat farcical counterpart to the grandeur of the lacquered furnishings of Schlobitten is presented by a cupboard made for a nobleman of Danzig or some other Baltic city (pl. 157). Although in general shape it follows the style of the region, it has a rather whimsical appearance, decorated in red lacquer with stiff chinoiserie scenes. A glass cabinet decorated in similar fashion may also have originated in the same region (pl. 158).

To get an idea of the kind of lacquer produced in the old German empire it is not necessary to follow developments in each of the many states within its confines. Instead we need only study some of the leading workshops conducted under the auspices of various rulers who were interested not only in artistic output but also in how these workshops contributed to the development of commerce.

The most important lacquer shop in Germany was that of Gérard Dagly, established in Berlin in 1686 at the court of Brandenburg. Dagly was born not long before 1665 in Spa, in the bishopric of Liège, a well-known and fashionable watering place and a city that had a tradition of lacquermaking. Many members of Dagly's family had been active in this craft since the early seventeenth century and also had held high positions in the government of the city. Usually most of the circumstances surrounding the life and work of early lacquermasters remain shrouded in obscurity, in part because their constant search for better lacquer recipes caused them to be regarded as alchemists who guarded their secrets. In Dagly's case, however, the Berlin archives offer as much information about his life and work as one could hope for.[7] When the architect Andreas Schlüter came to Berlin in 1694 to build a palace for the Elector Frederick III (after 1701, King Frederick I), Dagly was one of the few highly qualified craftsmen already doing work for the court who could participate in the creation of the new building. Yet in spite of his great activity, Dagly remained a completely forgotten man until 1935. No information about his work in Berlin had been collected for over two hundred years, nor was any of his furniture known. Only the Belgian historian Albin Body, writing about the craft of lacquer in Spa in 1898, mentioned details about Dagly's ancestors originally published in Berlin in 1761.

After learning the trade from his father, Dagly joined the French colors for a time, then went to Berlin to take up his profession. There are two possible reasons why Dagly may have left Spa for Berlin. He may have been a member of the Reformed Church and as such followed in the wake of the French Huguenots who sought asylum with the Elector of Brandenburg after the Edict of Nantes in 1686. Or again he may have been recommended to the Elector Frederick William II by the Prince of Orange who had known the Dagly family when one member served as mayor of Spa. The elector's interest in Far Eastern work began while he was at school in Leyden. At that time, in 1634, he bought some lacquered Japanese riding sticks as a gift for his father.[8] During his reign he corresponded for over twenty years with the Batavian representatives of the Dutch East India Company, urging them to send him products of all kinds for his curio collection. Thus it seems plausible that the elector would have invited a lacquermaster such as Dagly to serve at his court.

In any case, on 12 June 1687 Dagly received a diploma as a *Cammerkünstler* (chamber artist) in recognition of his "special knowledge in gilding and doing lacquer work." His duties were to varnish and lacquer tables, trays, candlestands, cabinets, and the like. After the death of the elector in 1689, his successor, Frederick III, confirmed the agreement but stipulated that Dagly was to receive "lodging, one pot of wine, four pots of beer, two loaves of bread daily, fodder for two horses, wood and coal," all the raw material he needed, and 1,000 *ecus* a year as well as the title of *Kunstkammer Meister* (Master of the

Curio Cabinet). This placed Dagly in charge of the upkeep of objects in the curio collection in addition to his regular work as lacquermaster. Frederick III was as interested in the Far East as his father had been and continued to acquire Chinese and Japanese objects, including Coromandel cabinets, porcelain, and soapstone carvings.

His familiarity with the contents of the curio collection must have been most stimulating for Dagly in creating his own lacquer. Four of his lacquer cupboards were made especially as receptacles for curios (pls. 166, 167, 168). In 1696 Dagly again received a new title and new duties as *Intendant des Ornaments* (Superintendent of Interior Decoration). In this capacity, in addition to his other duties, he was to "design ornaments for the decoration of the palaces" and keep them in good repair. This meant that he had to produce, paint, and varnish stucco and other decorations. The creative side of this work was probably limited by the arrival of Andreas Schlüter in 1694, who began construction of the palace and soon after took charge of design in all the other residential buildings. But supervision of the technical execution of the decorative work must have remained in Dagly's care. We know that he maintained a large workshop under the direction of his brother Jacques (born 1665 in Spa, died in Paris in 1728) whom he had called to join him. In this shop workers were organized in groups to make stucco figures, gild and paint ornaments, and produce lacquerwork. Apparently it was not easy to maintain discipline among workmen of many different nationalities. There was also difficulty in keeping secret lacquer recipes and guarding such valuable materials as gold leaf, varnish, and paints. Thus it came about that Dagly and his men kept the courts busy with various controversies and complaints: Were the men overworked? Were they betraying their master by stealing and selling goods or by running away to join a competitive shop? One lawsuit took nine years and ended with no clear-cut decision. Such trials plagued Dagly, and in 1696 he petitioned the elector to allow him the privilege of being the only one to make and sell lacquerwork in Berlin. This plea was cunningly argued. By reasoning that lacquer had been invented for the enjoyment of great potentates but the craft was now being prostituted by "quacks and idiots" who were seeking to lure away from him the very men he had taught his secrets, Dagly argued that private citizens were now being given a chance to buy lacquerwork that had not even been offered first to the court. It was high time, Dagly claimed, to put an end to these "bunglers who are nothing but pretenders in the art of lacquering and still have the effrontery to offer their own trash as products from his shop." Some of these complaints echo those made by Stalker and Parker about "ignorant knaves" who provided bad lacquerwork. The elector immediately granted Dagly the privilege he sought "in view of the extraordinary knowledge he had acquired in the field of lacquering." In 1702 the privilege was renewed and more precisely defined in Dagly's interest.

Dagly now felt it possible to undertake other activities, leaving his shop in the care of his brother. He endeared himself to the elector's librarian by explaining how he might save money by using varnished silver in place of gold leaf for the titles stamped on the bindings of books. In fear that Dagly's death might deprive them of the secret, the librarian begged him for the recipe of the varnish. It was recorded as follows:

4 quarts *Spiritus Vini*
4 quarts *Gummi Lacca*
2 quarts *Gummi Sandarac*
4 lots *Sanguis Draconis*.

Among the problems Dagly set himself to study were how to preserve human or animal flesh and birds with their feathers intact, what colors and plasters would protect houses in all weather, and how to prevent wood from rotting. The same questions were of interest to scholars of the time, and soon such men as the philosopher Gottfried Wilhelm Leibniz and a number of the courts began to consult Dagly.

Apart from his scholarly interests, Dagly looked for new ways to make money. Since lacquer could be used in decorating buttons, the knobs of canes, sword guards, and hats, Dagly first sought to manufacture steel buttons which were to be gilded or lacquered. Again, he sought a monopoly, claiming the privilege he had been granted in selling lacquer in Berlin should be extended to cover lacquered buttons as well and demanding that the authorities confiscate buttons made by others. In 1697 the elector decreed that he had no intention of halting the progress of arts and crafts in Berlin and could only suggest that Dagly mark his products so that it might be considered a crime to copy them. It is remarkable how considerate the elector was, and from this one can conclude how valuable he deemed Dagly's services. In 1740 a chronicler remarks on the button industry in Berlin some forty years before, "producing engraved, damascened and lacquered buttons, sword guards and snuffboxes. Such work had been introduced by a Frenchman [undoubtedly Dagly] and Swiss and Palatine craftsmen."

In addition to his other duties, in 1705 Dagly was commissioned to restore the paintings in the royal palaces, for which he was to receive a special honorarium. Dagly claimed to have invented a varnish that would "revive" any faded varnish obscuring the paintings. The master started the job with great zeal, and in no time at all the pictures he had treated "looked like new, as if they had been painted only a few days ago." Unfortunately, this beauty lasted only a short time, and soon the pictures, once shining like mirrors under many layers of copal varnish, appeared duller than ever; many were permanently spoiled. Dagly was violently attacked for this failure by no less a personage than Joseph Werner, the director of the Royal Academy of Arts.[9] In his own defense, Dagly printed in 1706 an augmented tract on restoring paintings which he had first published in 1702. Included was a favorable report on the restoration of paintings contributed by the Royal Commission in an effort to justify the master.[10]

Busy as he was working for the court, Dagly still found time to accept commission from private customers. One of these was the margrave of Schwedt who ordered "a red lacquered desk with silver bands around its 13 drawers." Other pieces went to the landgrave of Hessia.[11] It is also known that Dagly lacquered harpsichord cases for the Berlin firm of Rost and Michael Miethke.[12] Miethke's instruments were not made after 1719 but continued in favor throughout the eighteenth century. So far, no piece by Dagly has been found which carries his signature or any mark that might be recognized as his, although in 1702 he received permission to place a mark and a number on every piece made in his shop once it had been examined by a commission. Of course it was not Dagly's custom to mark pieces delivered to the court. At the same time, his workmen were forbidden to establish themselves anywhere in Prussia, nor were they allowed to make, import, or sell lacquerwork. In recognition of this agreement, Dagly promised to furnish to the court each year a piece of lacquer valued at 100 ducats.

From 1700 Dagly began to enjoy a certain degree of fame in German countries. A traveler from Frankfurt, Zacharias Conrad Uffenbach, came to Berlin in 1702 and looked up Dagly, "who was incomparable in matters of lacquer."[13] He had special praise for Dagly's four lacquer cabinets in the curio collection (pls. 166, 167, 168). Two years later, Dagly was a topic of discussion in letters written by the Duchess Elisabeth Charlotte of Orléans ("Liselotte") to her aunt, the Electress Sophia of Hanover: "Apparently there are good craftsmen in Berlin who know how to make fine things, maybe it is an Indian." In reply the electress wrote the duchess that this "Indian knows many secrets, e. g., how to prevent wood from rotting."[14] Thereupon Liselotte sarcastically advised that "ladies who frequently visit the outdoors should spread Dagly's varnish over their faces to preserve them." In 1705, the Electress Sophia sent her royal son-in-law in Berlin a novel item received from London, a lacquered case in which to place one's pocket watch. It could either be hung up or placed on a table. She meant the gift as a pattern, because the electress was certain that Dagly could make a much better one.[15]

During his last years in Berlin, Dagly came in close contact with Leibniz, with whom he had earlier discussed some of the problems he was trying to solve.[16] He had discovered a formula to *rendre la chair incorruptible* (to make flesh incorruptible) and was willing to sell the secret to a university if Leibniz could help him to do so. Dagly assured Leibniz that he could preserve the flesh of man or beast in perfect condition and that indeed he had proved this to the king. We do not have Leibniz' reply, but he seems to have continued to hold Dagly in great esteem, recommending him to the duke of Brunswick and pointing out how successful Dagly had been in serving the landgrave of Hessia who had asked advice about a durable cement for his waterworks at Kassel. Besides, Dagly had "an excellent knowledge of everything concerning lacquer." From the tone of the letters they exchanged, Dagly and Leibniz must have been on friendly terms, for Dagly writes of personal matters, illness, and his embarrassment when unable to attend a court reception because he felt so *incommode dans mes jumpes* (meaning *jambes* – legs) and begs Leibniz to make his apologies to the Electress Sophia. In 1710 Leibniz was informed that Dagly was about to prove to the British ambassador that he had found a means "that would be useful to the British fleet" to impregnate wood against damage caused by insects or other pests in American waters. Somewhat earlier, in 1705, Dagly offered to explain some of his secrets to a suitable person chosen by the king of Prussia. These secrets pertained either to the problem of protecting plaster, cut stone, or wood against weather damage or to his lacquer and varnish for rejuvenating paintings and copying Far Eastern lacquer work. In return, Dagly received several thousand talers, including arrear payments for earlier services. In addition he continued to receive his salary, but he seems to have had time to travel to Holland to other courts when asked for advice.

Although Dagly was only about fifty years of age when he tried the cure at

Schlangenbad, he was badly crippled by arthritis. Along with his failing health, his family life was unhappy. He had married a young Huguenot in 1688 but was later divorced. He then abducted his two daughters with the intention of having them educated in the Catholic faith but succeeded only in angering his former wife and even his sovereign who for once was so irate at the folly of his trusted subject that he commanded Dagly to return the girls immediately.

The death of the king in 1713 brought to a close the great artistic era he had encouraged. As his successor, the soldier-king Frederick William I, wanted to save money and had little interest in art, he dismissed most of the artists who had worked for the court, including the two Dagly brothers. Jacques went to Paris and entered the service of Louis XIV, where we will meet him again; Gérard continued as consultant to various courts. In 1715 Dagly was in service of the Elector Palatine Jan Wilhelm at Bensberg (Rhineland) who was building a huge *retraite de chasse* patterned after Versailles. Dagly died in Bensberg in 1715.[17]

That it is possible to ascribe a group of lacquer furniture to Dagly and his shop is due to a singular chance. In September, 1694, Christoph Pitzler, an architect traveling to continue his studies, visited Berlin and as was his custom made notes (fig. 9 a) of what he saw, often illustrating them with clever drawings. When he came to Schloss Oranienburg, he remarked "... it is beautifully furnished and is equipped with cabinets and chairs made in Japan, also there are here some made in Berlin by Dagly, one in the manner of porcelain in blue on white" (pls. 160, 161, 163, 165).[18] Evidently the colors were chosen to match the porcelain room at the palace. A year later, an Italian traveler from Siena, Fra. Alessandro Bicchi-Ruspoli, arrived in Berlin on a political mission.[19] Interested in matters of art, he jotted down what he saw and noted that a court painter whom he met was making beakers, cups, and plates of wood to replace those of silver which served as decoration. These wooden pieces were given the color of porcelain and executed with great subtlety. Fra. Alessandro added that there was a secret about the varnish used; it was said to be made with mercury and arsenic, which of course was not the case. In both instances the reference is undoubtedly to Dagly.

The cabinet enameled in blue on white was an unusual item (pl. 160), and since in 1935 the one listed in the inventory of the royal household was known to have been at Oranienburg, it is certainly safe to venture that this was the cabinet decorated by Dagly. With this cabinet as a clue, much of Dagly's *œuvre* can be identified. Some of the work seen by Fra Alessandro probably supplemented the Dutch pottery and Far Eastern porcelain vases decorating the so-called porcelain room of the palace of Charlottenburg, much of it destroyed during World War II. According to an inventory of 1704, these wooden items were gilt outside, lacquered green and red inside, and decorated with white, red, and green or gold and silver flowers. Other entries are marked as being by Dagly: lacquered tin sugar containers, one decorated in color and with the figure of a lynx painted in red, as well as a matching bottle. These entries provide an importance piece of information, for they confirm that Dagly knew how to lacquer tin. Since these items were made before 1704, the date of the inventory, they predate anything of the kind known to have been made in France or England.

XI. Harpsichord, detail, plate X

XII a

XII b

XII a. Margravine Sibylla Augusta of Baden, about 1700
XII b. Lady at her toilette table, detail, by Pietro Longhi, about 1750

Fortunately, more examples of Dagly's furniture have survived, although not the blue and white cabinet; another one, decorated with an unusual border on the side of the doors, was also destroyed during the war (pl. 161). This border, a feature of the Dagly workshop, shows a pattern of a flower, like a stylized chrysanthemum, alternating with vines with angular and pointed contours not unlike thistles. The panels themselves with their *chinoiserie* are fashioned to look as much as possible like Far Eastern patterns (pls. 164–168). Various motifs – buildings, trees, birds, and rocks – are copied closely and are well-spaced, leaving wide areas free, although perhaps not always free enough. These motifs are repeated on a number of cabinets, tables, and harpsichord cases, all from the Dagly workshop. One interesting motif is that of a fence rising diagonally across the panel with smaller panels inserted between the rails and showing charmingly sketched scenes. The human figures are never caricatures, and a serious attempt has been made with oriental garb to suggest their Eastern counterparts, although the hairdos often resemble European *toupets* (pl. 165). Among the groups of figures most often repeated are two dancers with flying sleeves and two or three musicians, all copied from Kang Chi vases in the Charlottenburg Chinese room (pls. X, XI). Another group, a seated dignitary with two servants standing behind him with fans, is borrowed from a Dutch print by Peter Schenk the Elder (fig. 6d). On the door of the blue and white cabinet this group was depicted seated at the top of a palace stairway (pl. 160). The sides of the cabinet are not oriental in spirit and may have been executed by a lesser artist of the shop. The stand with its scroll-shaped legs is typical of Dagly's work and was often repeated. It is decorated with European vines resembling ivy spread loosely over the whole structure and across the edges.

Another cabinet decorated in white bears all the usual Dagly shopmarks on the inside (pl. 159). The outside is decorated with raised lacquer of an extraordinarily fine quality. Except for some birds in the sky that lack the delicacy of an oriental original, the cabinet gives the impression of being an authentic product of the Far East. It repeats a motif copied from a Japanese chest owned by the court. The stand itself reveals its domestic origin. Unquestionably this raised lacquer represents the finest work the shop could produce and must have been executed by Dagly himself, who claimed that he could copy any Far Eastern product. Another cabinet, made of camphor wood of Japanese origin, with a Dagly stand has authentic oriental raised lacquer on the front (pl. 162). The sides are decorated with versions of the oriental pattern which originated in the Dagly shop (pl. 163). A cabinet on a stand, now at the palace in Stockholm (pl. 164) and very probably a gift of Frederick the Great to his sister Queen Ulrike of Sweden, is decorated in the same manner. Dagly's hand may also be recognized in one of the surviving cabinets he made for the curio cabinet (= room) in the palace in Berlin (pls. 166, 167, 168). Both doors executed in raised work are dominated by Chinese phoenixes in an otherwise sparse decoration leaving the sky empty. The curved top and the turned legs show the familiar vines. This outstanding piece shows Dagly's skill in design and execution. The black lacquer is of so fine a quality that it can scarcely be distinguished from Far Eastern lacquer. A print published in 1696 shows a view of the curio cabinet in which the elector's art collection was kept (pl. 167). Dagly's cabinets are here seen *in situ;* whether they were crowned by sculptural groups remains questionable. Among other products of the Dagly workshop are two harpsichords, one decorated in black and the other in white. Astonishingly enough, the white harpsichord has not turned yellow (see chap. II, note 11; VI, note 21), as is so often the case with French lacquer of the period (pls. X, XI).

A number of tables, including some once in the manor of Schlobitten in East Prussia and undoubtedly furnished by Berlin lacquermasters, show decorative elements unlike those attributed to Dagly (pls. 169–171).[20] This point raises the question often asked in tracing work done in the shop of a prominent master: how well are we able to distinguish the work of various hands in the shop? The quantity of lacquerwork produced in Berlin in the early eighteenth century was certainly enormous, and we must assume that most of it came from Dagly's shop because of the privileges granted to him. Besides tables, there were candlestands, mirrors, frames, and other items, many of which survived the 1943 bombing.[21] When we consider Dagly's many duties, it seems unlikely that he could have done much of this work himself, although certainly his was the hand responsible for the finest raised lacquer produced in the shop. What his brother Jacques was capable of producing we are not apt to discover, but he too must have been a master since he was later called to Paris. Martin Schnell, who probably worked for Dagly and later worked in Dresden, must also have distinguished himself. Whatever individual handmarks these men may have used it is no longer possible to identify. While the very best pieces stand out because of their quality, the shop undoubtedly produced run-of-the-mill objects as well, and these are more difficult to attribute.

After 1713, when Dagly's shop closed, others in Berlin took up the craft of lacquer; if anything, the trade flourished once it was no longer necessary to respect Dagly's privileges. Among those who may have troubled Dagly as a competitor was Andreas Völkert (active ca. 1708–33). We know that he made some furniture for Queen Sophia Dorothea, the wife of Frederick William I.[22] One piece is described as a cabinet made to contain a watch collection, "blue inside and decorated in black and gold on the outside." In appearance like an English cabinet on a stand, it was decorated with a headpiece showing a carved coat of arms made by the English sculptor William King (active ca. 1705–56) who worked at the court. His work is somewhat in the manner of Grinling Gibbons. A lacquered fire screen in Charlottenburg carries the initials of the queen lacquered in red with decorations in gold (pl. 176). The style of this piece so much resembles some large cupboards with drawers at the base and stands for vases on top that it is very possible that this type of furniture may have been made by Völkert around 1725 (pls. 174, 175). Lacquered in red within and blue without, the cupboards were decorated with caricatured Chinese scenes bordered in the Bérain style. The queen, as has been noted, was most interested in lacquer and was one of the amateurs who amused herself by learning *lacca povera* techniques.

Among the early lacquermasters in Berlin whose work can be identified is David Pennewitz.[23] He was known as the manager of a stoneware shop at Plaue near Berlin, established in 1714. Here he not only lacquered stoneware vases but also executed a lacquer room for the manor of Plaue, later owned by the counts von Königsmarck. Fortunately, this richly decorated room was preserved during the last war and is now in the

Märkische Museum in East Berlin (pl. 177). The decoration includes European motifs, the figures of musicians and mythological scenes surrounded by Bérain motifs, as well as some *chinoiserie* scenes taken from Stalker and Parker. These designs bear some relationship to designs found on leather screens made in Dresden, to be mentioned later. We know that Pennewitz once worked in Meissen and there had access to the prints used as patterns by the Dresden leatherworkers.

After the great flourish of lacquer in Berlin up to 1720, little more is heard until well into the period of Frederick II (1740–1786) when the king asked the Martin family of Paris to send a representative to Berlin. Jean Alexandre Martin arrived in Berlin in 1747. In 1753 he lacquered the "flower" room in the Palace of Sans Souci in natural colors on a yellow ground.[24] Before 1765, he also did the king's study in the New Palace, decorating it with polychromed garlands of flowers contrasted with carved and silvered ornaments on a yellow background. Both decorations, still in existence, were probably based on designs by Johann Christian Hoppenhaupt the Younger in the late rococo Potsdam style. To replace Martin, who returned to Paris in or before 1767, another French lacquermaster, Sebastian Chevalier, arrived in Potsdam in 1766.[25] Chevalier lacquered the "oval" room at the New Palace in yellow and green and added polychromed flowers as if the walls were trellised (pl. 181). Another room was lacquered with panels in "flesh colors" alternating with white pilasters. Both rooms have kept their original appearance and are in good condition. Later Chevalier established a workshop in Berlin and engaged in the making of lacquered furniture. A number of his delicate little tables, called *quatre-pieds*, lacquered in black, red, or green and decorated with lively painted polychromed flowers and finely wrought mountings in bronze, either gilt or silvered, still survive in the New Palace (pls. 178, 179, 180).

Undoubtedly Chevalier maintained connections in Paris, for in 1773 the king allowed Chevalier's son to return there to further his knowledge of his father's profession and thus prepare him to follow in his father's steps. In 1780 Chevalier was living in a house owned by the government, with permission to remain there for his lifetime. Here he managed a large establishment and produced furniture as well as lacquered iron and tin products. A government report in 1781 asserted that Chevalier's work was as good as any made elsewhere and granted him the exclusive right to produce tin merchandise, at the same time forbidding the importation of similar products. In the year 1782 he made goods valued at 6,000 talers, about as much as the value of the lacquerware produced by Jean Guérin and Bellin, two masters of French extraction who also had shops in Berlin. Around 1790, Chevalier was commissioned to do two lacquered rooms at the newly built *Marmor Palais* at Potsdam for Frederick William II. Upon the death of the king in 1797, Chevalier's pension was cancelled and he fell on evil days. The last we know of his career is that he applied to the Russian government for permission to transfer his workshop, including twelve assistants, to Russia. Permission was denied.

Closely following Berlin in importance as a lacquer center was the city of Dresden. In 1692, Elector Frederick III of Brandenburg paid Dagly 200 talers for a cabinet done in white and gold to be presented to Elector Johann Georg of Saxony on the occasion of his wedding. Frederick III was so delighted by the cabinet that he awarded Dagly a gold medal as *douceur* for his effort. Two years later the elector of Saxony died and was succeeded by Augustus the Strong (1694–1733). Perhaps this fine cabinet gave the new ruler some idea of the exquisite lacquerwork being done in Berlin and made him wish to establish a similar shop in Dresden. Unfortunately, the war in which he was engaged, together with his desire to become the king of Poland, left him little opportunity to do anything about his plans to embellish his palaces. In 1703, Martin Schnell, who worked for Dagly in Berlin, was presented to Augustus at Marienburg in East Prussia during one of the king's journeys to the Polish theater of war.[26] Here Schnell was able to display some of his lacquerwork. Although Augustus is known to have been impressed, it was not until Charles XII of Sweden withdrew from Dresden in 1707 that Augustus could resume his earlier plans. In 1710 Schnell was hired at a salary of 3,000 talers as "court lacquermaster" with the task of establishing a workshop equipped to execute large orders for lacquer.

Before Schnell's arrival, the principal lacquermaster in Dresden was Heinrich Teschau. Teschau both built and decorated furniture (Schnell did not do any cabinetwork) and is known to have furnished "a coffee table decorated with Japanese figures" for Queen Eberhardine whose cabinetmaker he was. In spite of this title, apparently Teschau was not considered sufficiently gifted to fulfil the needs of Augustus and thus lost out to Schnell.

Schnell, born around 1685 in Stade near Bremen, is known to have worked in Dagly's shop about 1703. Where he learned japanning is not known. A few years after Schnell's arrival in Dresden, Augustus built or remodeled three palaces renowned for their decor: a Japanese palace (1716–17), an Indian palace at Pillnitz (1722–23), and a Turkish palace (completed in 1719). In the latter, the king received his guests dressed in Turkish costume. The Dresden archives supply a good deal of information about the lacquer furnishings Schnell supplied for all of these buildings. In 1717 he produced "Cabinets, Clavicembaloes and screens" worth 1,145 talers, and in 1724 he fitted the treasure cases in Augustus' treasure house, the so-called Green Vault, with fine gilt moldings on a green and red lacquer ground. Schnell worked not only for the king but for a number of the king's favorites, including Count Brühl and Count Wackerbart, and his name appears in records in both Dresden and Warsaw until 1740, when he probably died. Like Dagly, Schnell never signed any of his pieces, and we assume he employed a large number of workmen, all of whom remain anonymous.

Between 1712 and 1716 Schnell received a salary from the porcelain workshop at Meissen for lacquering and decorating stoneware pieces with *chinoiserie* and ornaments in the Bérain style on a red and blue ground (pl. 182). He also decorated vases turned in wood in the same style.[27] These were used simply for ornamental purposes – placed on top of a cabinet or some high shelf – and no one cared what material they were made of as long as they filled the space. They were a kind of make-believe, typical of the baroque age. Bérain ornamentation was also used on some tables with very fine raised lacquerwork, very probably produced by Schnell. Böttger and his associates at Meissen were glad to avail themselves of the opportunity of decorating with lacquer because as yet they did not have a sufficient scale of colors to decorate their wares, and, too, the use of lacquer enabled them to dispense with a second firing which always offered certain dangers. With use, however, lacquer colors wore off, and today such pieces with colors intact are extremely rare. Some pieces of Böttger stoneware decorated in the style of Japanese Guri lacquer are preserved at Schloss Favorite near Baden-Baden, and a fine stoneware coffeepot, probably decorated by Schnell, was sold at auction at Sotheby's in 1952 (pl. 183). Two other remarkable pieces, almost certainly by Schnell, are in the Metropolitan collection in New York. One is a so-called Pilgrim bottle of about 1715 in the standard shape of a silver wine container lacquered with a delightful polychromed *chinoiserie* landscape (pl. 182). The other piece represents Pantaloon, of the *Commedia dell'Arte*, with his bearded mask and characteristic red garb. As soon as a sufficient variety of colors was available which could be safely fired and so made to last, Meissen discontinued the practice of decorating ceramics with lacquer.

A few words might be said about the use of lacquer to decorate certain groups of faïence vases, though this has nothing to do with Dresden and very little to do with the use of lacquer as it has been considered here. In the faïence workshop established in Frankfurt in 1660, lacquer was used to cover the unpainted surfaces of vessels decorated with a blue underglaze in order to lend contrast to the decoration. A vase now at the Bayrisches National Museum in Munich is decorated with a brownish red lacquer (pl. 184). In Ansbach, some vases decorated with a blue underglaze are lacquered with black, red, and gold to enhance the pattern (pl. 187). Other workshops occasionally used the same technique since it simplified work, although it never added the brilliance that is the special quality of lacquer.

Another group of vases, often seen on the art market and represented in a number of collections, has caused considerable discussion concerning date and origin even though the artistic value is rather low. These pieces are of porcelain as well as faïence, and a number of them may even be of Far Eastern provenance. They are vases or covered jars, some lacquered in bluish green, others in scarlet, usually with borders of segments of white marguerites with yellow centers (pls. 185, 186). It now seems likely that these vases, of various origin, were decorated in a rather obscure shop in Berlin around 1790.[28]

Returning once again to Martin Schnell and Dresden lacquer, it must be stated that while one cannot distinguish between Schnell's raised lacquerwork and that produced by his employer Dagly, a number of details in the shape of the furniture lacquered in Dresden distinguishes it from that produced in Berlin. The Berlin cabinet and table stands were usually fashioned of scrolls connected by flat, inwardly curved stretchers. In Dresden they are often more complicated and some have legs in the shape of pilasters (pls. 188, 189). A cabinet on a stand, which may be attributed to the Schnell workshop, is owned by the Rijksmuseum in Amsterdam (pls. 192, 193). The decoration on drawers and doors is framed by lines and certain motifs showing replicas of huge oriental vases. The same decoration is found on a number of Dresden cabinets.[29] The pediment composed of half-round segments is a feature typical of Dresden but not of Berlin.

Fortunately, before the holocaust in 1945, Rudolf von Arps-Aubert thoroughly studied all of the Dresden furniture, and many of the pieces lost in the destruction of the city can be examined in his published work. It is clear that English, or possibly Dutch, examples of lacquer furniture were available for study in Dresden so that artisans could copy certain bureau cabinets and long-case clocks of the English type. English lacquer chairs made for export must have been familiar to the maker of chairs for Schloss Moritzburg, now a museum, near Dresden. They closely resemble the English chairs in the Palazzo Pallavicini in Rome (pl. 84).[30] Another chair with exquisitely fine lacquer decoration on a white ground that has kept its color is dated 1719 and shows the coat of arms of Saxony (pls. 200, 201).[31] It is almost certain to have been executed in Dresden.

Among bureaus in Dresden, now badly mutilated, is one that Arps-Aubert, Holzhausen, and the recent catalogue of the Dresden museum consider to be English.[32] It is quite possible that this is the case. Certainly the bureau resembles one illustrated in Edwards' *Shorter Dictionary*, although the fact that it is made of alder wood and the drawers of oak would be unusual in English furniture.[33] And yet this attribution is of special interest because it suggests that Dresden workers did have an English model to copy.

Most Dresden cabinets as well as a number of very fine tables show workmanship of the highest quality (pls. 190, 191, 194, 195). A japanned table mirror in the Rijksmuseum shows some very fine painting on the metal sheet covering the back (pl. 199). It carries the royal Saxon coat of arms, testifying to its origin in Dresden. The very delicate *chinoiserie* shows some relationship to decorated porcelain.

Schnell's versatility enabled him to apply lacquer not only to furniture and stoneware but also to leather and linen. Even with lacquer decoration the leather remained sufficiently pliable so that it could be used for covering chairs as well as for wall hangings and screens. At the hunting lodge Schloss Moritzburg, for example, were some sixty rooms with leather hangings and twenty-four *dozen* decorated leather-covered chairs. Six rooms were hung with "red and gold Venetian leather," four with "blue and gold Hamburg leather."[34] In this instance "Hamburg leather" almost certainly means leather imported, perhaps from Spain, by way of Hamburg. Schnell is known to have lacquered six leather screens in the period 1731–35 as well as linen hangings decorated with Chinese figures for the king's "Japanese palace." Unfortunately, none of these still exist. To gain some idea of how this kind of japanned leather may have looked we can study the panels of a leather screen painted in oil by Johann George Näcke (pl. 198). The panels are decorated with figures from Italian *Commedia dell'Arte*. There are also some leather chairs decorated in a similar way.

Schnell of course was not the only lacquermaster in Dresden. Probably more important than his predecessor, Heinrich Teschau, was Christian Reinow, listed as employed by the court in 1717. In 1731 his salary was 100 talers – more than received by Schnell – so he must have enjoyed a good reputation. Reinow, an architect by training, is known to have done some lacquerwork in the Green Vault of the treasure house of Augustus the Strong. He also specialized in marbelizing and the restoration of paintings and, late in his career, he furnished lacquered cupboards and trays. Maria Josepha, wife of Frederick August II and archduchess of Austria, had a special fondness for lacquer. Between 1720 and 1733 she employed four lacquermasters as well as engaging the services of Schnell and Reinow.[35]

To conclude these observations on Dresden lacquer, one must consider two most elegant bureau cabinets, one now at Schloss Moritzburg, the other made for Heinrich, Count Brühl, the powerful minister of the court of Frederick August II (pls. 196, 197). Judged by their style, these pieces originated in the 1740s. They are magnificently lacquered, gold and red on the outside, blue and gold on the inside, in striking contrast, enhanced by a brilliant display of ormolu fittings somewhat in the style of those used by Cressent and surely of French origin. The base of the Frankfurt cabinet is modeled like a piece of sculpture, its feet ending in great upward curves. The impression is much like certain pieces of Italian furniture made in Turin. These exquisite pieces are the last known to have been produced in Saxony. With the advent of the Seven Years' War with Frederick the Great in 1756 there came an end to the expensive refurbishing of the royal palaces. Dresden lacquer, unfortunately, sometimes is in a poor state of preservation today; it is fragile and often peels from its surface. Much Dresden lacquer has been repaired and not infrequently spoiled in the process.

So far we have reviewed German lacquer as it was developed in certain cities under especially favorable conditions. Although this resumé reflects lacquerwork only in a somewhat small segment of Germany and not always in the centers where artistic interests flourished, it does illustrate much of the best produced in Germany. Why this is so and why the remainder of Germany as well as Austria show only a very spotty production of lacquer may require some explanation.

That part of Germany not yet discussed comprises more than fifty sizable territories and nearly one hundred and fifty smaller regions ruled by princes. Each prince, of course, owned at least one residence in his "capital" as well as a country manor. The great houses of Bavaria, Baden, Hesse, Württemberg, and a number of others, including those of the princes of the church, each owned a number of often sumptuous palaces, manors, and hunting lodges, to which must be added all the garden pavilions and similar buildings in which lacquer furniture was much in evidence scattered throughout the parks and grounds. During the first half of the eighteenth century, most of these rulers were involved in building and would never have considered omitting lacquer in their plans for decoration. Unquestionably the possibilities for the use of lacquer were staggering, and yet when we examine what is left today we realize that its quantity is no more impressive than its quality or originality. Many lacquer rooms have been dismantled, of course, and much of the especially vulnerable lacquer furniture has disintegrated or has been painted over. Lacquer of miscellaneous origin only here and there resembles examples of the English or Dutch style or, more rarely, is remindful of Italy. Usually a local style is followed (pls. 157, 158). The artisan has simply lacquered a piece of furniture that otherwise might have been veneered or left with a plain wood finish. No German style materialized in the Rhenish manner of Aix-la-Chapelle and Liège, none in the Bavarian manner of Cuvilliés. The reasons are obvious: there was no commercial center for lacquer in Germany where workshops could be developed over several generations to supply the needs of the country. Augsburg and Nürnberg might have become such centers, but their major contribution to the lacquer trade was the publication of prints and tracts. In other cities and in princely residences the need for lacquer was so limited that an itinerant lacquermaster or even a local painter could fulfil all commissions. Thus even princes had little chance to hire a lacquermaster and usually had to be content with those who offered their services.

One of the most richly appointed residences was that of the Bavarian court at Munich. During his years of exile as a result of the Austrian occupation, Max II Emanuel, elector of Bavaria (1662–1726), lived in Brussels and at his Château de Bearn near St.-Cloud and knew the splendors of Versailles. On his return in 1715, he began to redecorate his palaces in Nymphenburg and Munich. During the last decade of his life, when the fashion for *chinoiserie* was at its height, he personally provided the idea for the design of a pavilion at Nymphenburg (1717–19). The plans for his *maison des Indes*, called the Pagodenburg, were carried out by his architect, Joseph Effner.[36] The lower story was decorated with blue and white tiles, the upper story was provided with two lacquer rooms – one in red, the other in blue – both decorated with "Indian flowers and birds" (pl. 202). Set into the wall were Chinese-silk panels, later replaced with hangings of painted rice straw. Probably the artist was an otherwise completely unknown Father Edmund who worked for the court in 1717 and could execute designs "in the Chinese fashion." His colors seem to have faded rather quickly, for fifty years later, in 1769, the painter Ambrosius Hörmansdorfer had to restore his work. Hörmansdorfer also worked for Max Emanuel's son, Clemens August, elector of Cologne, at his summer palace, Schloss Brühl, near Cologne, of which we will hear more later. He also worked as a decorator in the porcelain shop at Nymphenburg as Schnell had done at Meissen. This suggests that lacquermasters and porcelain painters had certain mutual interests.

The pavilion at Nymphenburg still has its original furnishings, including two Japanese chests inclosed in precious Parisian lacquerwork and shaped as commodes (pl. 222). As late as 1763, Max Emanuel's grandson, Max III Joseph (1745–1777), had a corner room at Schloss Nymphenburg refurbished with Coromandel screens (pl. 203). Since there were not enough screens to cover the walls, they were supplemented by lacquer panels executed by Johannes Georg Höringer who previously had worked in stucco (pl. 206). These paintings, executed with remarkable bravura, even improve on the Augsburg prints from which their pattern was taken (pl. 207). Although these prints were published by Martin Engelbrecht in Augsburg as early as 1720, no harm was seen in copying them forty years later in spite of changing fashions in *chinoiserie*.

In the following decades, the court followed French trends. A number of French lacquer pieces were imported, including a desk attributed to van Risenburgh (pl. 225) and a number of other pieces. Although it is hardly likely that a lacquermaster of importance worked in Munich for any length of time, there are some pieces made in Bavaria which must have been produced in Munich or in nearby Augsburg. There is a clock, and a stand dating from about 1725, probably made for one of the South German courts in early eighteenth-century style and decorated with colorful lacquer showing quite animated *chinoiserie* (pl. 204). The bracket clock, probably made in Munich with a movement by a Munich clockmaker, is lacquered in gay colors on a yellow ground and is representative of the Bavarian rococo style (pl. 205). Finally, to mention an example, there is a sedan chair lacquered in silver on blue, made for the court around the middle of the eighteenth century (pl. 208). A number of other sedan chairs and carriages, now in the Carriage Museum at Nymphenburg, indicate that toward the end of the eighteenth century the lacquer trade in Munich was rather active, although there is almost no documentary material in evidence.

An admirer of the Pagodenburg was the widowed margravine, Sibylla Augusta of Baden-Baden, who saw this *maison de plaisance* in 1722 and was so enchanted by it that the elector sent her elevations of the building. Although greatly interested in *chinoiserie*, she never succeeded in building a similar pavilion. This passion she shared with her husband, the margrave Ludwig Wilhelm, called *Türken-Louis* because of his distinguished service as a general in the long struggle with the Turks. His Near Eastern contacts as well as the Turkish weapons, costumes, lacquerware, and silver he brought home from the wars as booty must have instilled in him a strong interest in everything Eastern.[37] In an inventory made after his death we find listed a set of his nightgowns repeating the pattern of the lacquer toilette case in his bedroom.[38] The lacquer room at his palace at Rastatt, begun in 1704 and completed in 1707 after the death of Louis, is mentioned by a well-known traveler, Johann Friedrich von Uffenbach, who saw the panels lacquered in brilliant color in the storage room of the palace.[39] Apparently the room had been dismantled after the death of the husband because Sibylla Augusta wanted to instal it in another place. Ludwig Wilhelm also owned a manor in Bohemia called Schlackenwert for which he planned a lacquer room. The panels were to be decorated in gold on black and red with chinoiserie framed by tiles.

Upon the death of her husband, Sibylla Augusta, a lady of strong character and decided ideas, ruled for twenty years during the minority of her son. During this period she built a charming summer palace (1710–12), called *Favorite*, near Baden-Baden.[40] Over the centuries the palace has undergone a number of changes, and yet its eighteenth-century character has been preserved together with a good many of its furnishings in their original settings (pls. 210a, 210b). The table shown here may be of Dutch or English origin; it is made of oak and sycamore wood. In the drawing room are a number of mirrors with "Indian flowers," and there are seventy-two paintings in lacquered and decorated frames showing members of the court in Turkish costume in commemoration of some special *fête* (pls. 209a, 209b, XIIa). A number of the other rooms, later changed, were furnished with wallpaper, hangings, and ceilings decorated with *chinoiserie* and filled with porcelain, many of the pieces displayed on lacquered stands or tables. The palace is a rare place which still impresses us with the spirit of a day when *chinoiserie* reigned supreme.

A day's journey by coach from the summer palace was another summer residence, Ludwigsburg, where in the days of the margravine Duke Eberhard Ludwig of Württemberg resided. It was built in an extravagant and sumptuous manner to please the duke's *maîtresse en titre*, Countess Grävenitz. Of course a lacquer room was to be included, and in 1714 a plan was invited from a painter in Prague, Jan Adalbert Ignaz Kratochwill (b. 1667, d. before 1741).[41] This master must have been of some repute, since in 1712 he had been granted an imperial privilege whereby he was made exempt from guild duties for his skill at executing "Indian work." His price for a plan was 9,000 guilders, so shocking a demand that it was dismissed as "excessive pretension." To gain an impression of what his work would have been like, we can consider a lacquer room he had executed about 1709 for Count Wenzel Adalbert von Sternberg for his palace (now the National Gallery) within the area of the castle at Prague (pls. 213, 214). It is still in excellent condition with all its decoration intact. (The master's wife, Marie Anna, herself an artist and named court painter, is known to have painted Chinese figures on mirror grounds in the 1730s, and was still alive in 1741.) The Sternberg room, painted around 1709, is of major importance on its own merit and because it provides us with an idea of the type of lacquer rooms in vogue in Austria and its crown dominions. Apparently the room was designed as a background for porcelain displayed on brackets and console tables. Medallions lacquered in blue and white decorate walls colored in black and showing scattered figural *chinoiserie* delicately polychromed. All of these decorations are organized in an architectural setting leaning to the seventeenth century. The height and the unusual dimensions of this room give it great style.

When Kratochwill's bid for the lacquer room at Ludwigsburg proved unacceptable, a lacquermaster from Nürnberg, Johann Jacob Sänger, was asked to submit his conditions. He guaranteed that his lacquer would be of a permanent character and fireproof, and further claimed that he had just completed a room at Rastatt. The final statement is difficult to accept, for in the early twenties Sibylla Augusta was no longer interested in Rastatt and certainly did not continue to build there. All the same, Sänger's room turned out to be one of the most remarkably elegant and certainly one of the finest ever executed in Germany (pl. 211). The panels were decorated with dashingly conceived landscapes, in part using raised lacquer, with birds and dragons painted in greenish blue and yellow on a black background. The panels are framed in dark red and brown, with some of the surface glowing in luster colors, the carvings all gilded. The lambrequin motifs appeared in blue, and the carved vases and Chinese figures set on consoles were done in red and yellow. The duke was so enchanted by Sänger's work that in addition to his honorarium of 6,000 guilders he was presented with two medals and 400 guilders.

Sänger left Stuttgart in 1722 and traveled to nearby Ansbach, the court of the margrave of Brandenburg-Ansbach, who was married to Sophie Friederike, a sister of Frederick the Great. When he arrived the old palace was being remodeled and was not ready for decoration, and he moved on elsewhere. At this juncture we lose track of this most accomplished master who was also an architect and had published a number of architectural designs.

Lacquer was not in great favor at Ansbach. We have record only of a room with stucco decorations completed in 1763 by Johann Christoph Eberlein, a lacquermaster of renown.[42] Eberlein and his brother Andreas specialized in lacquer items used by the military, including swagger sticks, bullet cases, boxes, and beakers. The brothers had a widespread clientele throughout Germany and were known for the excellent quality of their very hard lacquer. They established a shop in 1745, and in 1757 they were given a license to protect their wares from imitation although this proved no protection. Somewhat later, Johann Heinrich Stobwasser passed through Ansbach and managed to learn the secret of their lacquer. How Stobwasser made use of this information when he established himself in Brunswick will be discussed in Chapter VIII.

Some fifteen miles north of Ansbach is Bayreuth, the capital of Brandenburg-Bayreuth, ruled by Margrave Carl Wilhelm Friedrich (1729–1757). Wilhelmine, his wife, was the favorite sister of Frederick the Great, and her liveliness, her gift for observation, and her taste and knowledge of art made her very different from her more retiring sister at Ansbach. Painting and lacquerwork were among the ways Wilhelmine found to express herself, and in recognition Frederick presented his sister with four Coromandel panels. Wilhelmine, proudly but with some exaggeration, noted in her memoirs that they were of quite "enormous price and probably unique in Europe."[43] Since Wilhelmine was to order the decoration of the palace (1736–40), she resolved to instal the panels in a Japanese room in the "Eremitage" close to Bayreuth (pl. 212). Because there were not enough panels to cover the walls, the princess herself arranged to have stucco applied and incised the decoration which was then lacquered. Modestly, she does not mention her handiwork in the memoirs, written before 1744, except to say that all furnishings *s'accordent avec cette boiserie* (unite in effect with the woodwork). The only reference to her own activities is in mention of the margrave's room, later redecorated, which was done *d'une espèce de vernis j'ai trouvé l'invention* (in a kind of varnish I had invented). Also installed around 1750 were three other rooms of "Chinese" character, with figures in raised lacquer executed by Johann Christian Jugd, a lacquermaster who went to Berlin in 1763 to work for the court.

In making the rounds of the diminutive courts of Germany, it is worthwhile to stop at that of the Prince of Schwarzburg-Arnstadt in Thuringia, even though there is very little lacquer to be found there.[44] We do meet an interesting personality and find an unusual pastime. The Princess Augusta Dorothea (1666–1751) with her father, Duke Anton Ulrich of Brunswick, and her sister, Elisabeth Christine, wife of the Emperor Charles VI, had been converted to the Catholic faith. Living in entirely Protestant surroundings, having no children and being estranged from her husband, she led her own life at Augustenburg, the manor she had built for herself. In her household were two Franciscan fathers who shared her strong artistic inclinations. To while away the time, the idea was conceived of producing a set of miniature rooms or scenes showing the happenings of everyday life in town and country, at the court, and in the cottage. The princess with her ladies, with girls from Arnstadt to sew, the two Franciscans modeling the heads and hands of figurines in wax, a cabinetmaker, a silversmith, tinkers, and anyone who was needed went to work. The result after many years of toil were twenty-six most delightful miniature houses with eighty-four rooms and four hundred and eleven figurines. There was a squire receiving his tenants, ladies at a card game, a visitor at court, a group of men smoking, a nurse with a baby, maids making up a big state bed, a chamber quartet, a lady buying silk in a shop, a barber, a baker, a country fair – in fact almost every kind of scene one can imagine. In a number of these rooms are tiny tables, chairs, and other pieces of lacquer furniture made in Arnstadt. In a replica of the palace China room are small lacquer drums resembling those brought back from Turkey by the margrave of Baden-Baden. The shelves of this room contain tiny faïence pieces made to order in the manufactory of Dorotheental, established by the princess in 1715. Although sizes and dimensions of the miniatures are not always quite accurate, the rooms depict admirably actual scenes and events of the day and undoubtedly belong among the minor marvels of the century for the insight and understanding they offer of the period.

In neighboring Rudolstadt, the capital of the principality of Schwarzburg-Rudolstadt, the ancestral castle of Heideggsburg was partially restored in the eighteenth century. A lacquer room was installed with German lacquer panels set in a sumptuous architectural decor. Nothing is known of the origin of this setting.

Accounts kept at the court of Count Carl Ludwig of Hohenlohe (1674–1756), who resided in the still-well-preserved manor of Weikersheim, owned by the princes of Hohenlohe and now in the territory of Swabia, give us information about some of the sources of the inventory acquired around 1700. The court had its own staff of cabinetmakers, some descended from the Sommer family, a clan of artisans working at Künzelsau. A quarter of a century earlier H. D. Sommer had worked in the style of Boulle, though in a way entirely his own.[45] Now, in 1711, a descendant, Johann Eberhard Sommer, fashioned a number of tables and other items lacquered in black and gilt or silvered. Two large cabinets, still placed in the bedroom for which they were made, are probably his work (pls. 215, 216). They may have been lacquered by a local painter, Johann Konrad Hoffmann, who had been sent to Amsterdam to be trained in the art of japanning by one Balthasar Schayd. This detail reveals that the courts of both North and South Germany depended upon the fashions of the Netherlands as long as there was easy access to western waterways. The two cabinets are so typically Dutch in appearance that if offered on the art market with origin unknown undoubtedly they would be proclaimed as Dutch.

Unlike the lacquered work at Weikersheim, a room in the *Neue Residenz* at Bamberg of the Prince Bishop Lothar Franz von Schönborn, one of the greatest builders of the eighteenth century, has been called traditionally the "Dutch room." Completed about 1719, its walls are divided into small panels, the centers decorated in gold and blue with borders in blue on white (pl. 218). All of this very delicate painting reveals great understanding of Far Eastern patterns, probably stimulated by oriental porcelain. Nevertheless, there is no reason to believe that the decoration was executed by a Dutch painter. A desk (pl. 217) dating from about 1730 and acquired by the Bayrische National Museum in 1968 may once have been part of the inventory of the *Neue Residenz*. Its shape is clearly related to work done by the well-known court cabinetmaker Ferdinand Plitzner. Since no other lacquer connected with the court at Bamberg has been recognized, this desk of gilt on black lacquer is of considerable interest. Many of the somewhat awkward *chinoiseries* were copied from prints published by J. Christian Weigel.

There would be little point in cataloging all of the lacquer rooms that still exist in the manors of the great families listed in the *Almanac de Gotha*, but it may be of some interest to speak of one of the princes of the church and the part he played in the fashion for lacquer. It is Clemens August, elector of Cologne (1700–1761), the fourth son of Max Emanuel of Bavaria and one of the great art connoisseurs of the eighteenth century, a prototype of his time. Among the many palaces he caused to be built or restored, Augustusburg, later called Schloss Brühl, near Cologne is the most extraordinary. Its staircase is probably the most grandiose of the baroque period. The Indian room (pl. 219) in this palace undoubtedly was given the prince's personal attention, as an eminent student of the period, Kurt Roeder, has attempted to prove.[46] When the palace was bombed during World War II, the room was severely damaged and only some ruined panels have been salvaged. It was lacquered in white, with a perfect satinlike finish, the walls divided into oblong panels and decorated with *lacca povera* work. It is very possible that around 1730 Clemens August and members of his court cut these prints from a great number of contemporary volumes on botany and geography and then mounted the color prints in new ensembles of European flowerpieces. This anticipates a type of porcelain decoration which became fashionable after 1740 when European motifs were used as well as Chinese. As usual the prints were lacquered and in time turned yellow, thus making the entire decoration homogeneous. At a later date, probably around 1750 according to Kurt Roeder, the dado and doors were decorated by porcelain painters who chose oriental motifs to create a most delightful *chinoiserie* in exquisite colors. Clemens August's interest in lacquer was shown anew by some Far Eastern panels at Falkenlust, a hunting lodge near Brühl, a most exquisite little place, in part decorated by the French master Gilles Marie Oppenord, with some needed additions by a domestic worker.[47]

With Clemens August, the story of German lacquer of the eighteenth century comes to a glorious climax. During its development it did not always exhibit such fine results as those produced under the aegis of this Wittelsbach prince, but no one can deny the great variety existing in German lacquer or the care given in creating it even at small courts remote from such centers as London and Venice.

1. Walter Stengel, *Alte Wohnkultur in Berlin* (Berlin, 1958), p. 73.
2. Armin Conradt, "Hamburger Musikinstrumente des 18. Jahrhunderts mit Lackmalerei," in *Jahrbuch der Hamburger Kunstsammlungen*, 9 (1964): 29–48.
3. J. Focke, *Bremische Werkmeister aus alter Zeit* (Bremen, 1890), pp. 238 f.
4. F. Fuhse, *Vom Braunschweiger Tischlerhandwerk* (Braunschweig, 1925), pp. 51–80; Ludwig Baron Döry, "Englische Chinoiserien auf Braunschweigischen Lackmöbeln," in *Braunschweigisches Jahrbuch*, 40 (1959): 144–48.
5. J. G. Doppelmayr, *Historische Nachrichten von den Nürnbergischen ... Künstlern* (Nürnberg, 1730), p. 262.
6. Paul von Stetten, *Kunst-Gewerbe und Handwerksgeschichte der Reichs-Stadt Augsburg*, 2 vols. (Augsburg, 1779), 1: 261.
7. (Karl Heinrich von Heinecken), *Nachrichten von Künstlern und Kunstsachen* (Leipzig, 1768), pp. 32–34 (written by Abraham Humbert in 1761); Albin Body, *Essais historiques sur les ouvrages peints, dites "Boîtes de Spa"* (Liège, 1898), contains information about the ancestor of Dagly in Spa and repeats details of the biography by Humbert; Hans Huth, "Lacquerwork by Gérard Dagly," in *Connoisseur*, 95 (1935): 14–18; Hans Huth, *Europäische Lackarbeiten* (Darmstadt, 1955), p. 30, no. 19, contains references to the pertinent Berlin archives, partially destroyed during World War II; remaining documents are kept in the archives at Merseburg (East Germany).
8. Leopold Reidemeister, "Der Grosse Kurfürst und Friedrich III. als Sammler ostasiatischer Kunst," in *Ostasiatische Zeitschrift*, Neue Folge 8 (1932), pp. 175–88.
9. Hans Müller, *Die Königliche Akademie der Künste* (Berlin, 1896), pp. 51, 54, 77.
10. Gérard Dagly, *Recueil des Mémoires des diverses experiences faites au sujet de la conservation des tableaux* (2d ed.; Berlin, 1706). A copy is in the university library at Cologne.
11. Stengel, *Alte Wohnkultur*, pp. 75, 76; A. Holtmeyer, *Die Bau- und Kunstdenkmäler im Reg.-Bez. Kassel*, 6, I (1932): 334.
12. Stengel, *Alte Wohnkultur*, pp. 75, 76.
13. Zacharias Conrad Uffenbach, *Merkwürdige Reisen*, 4 vols. (Memmingen, 1753), 1: lxviii, lxiii.
14. Before 1945: Hohenzollern Haus-Archiv, Berlin

(see n. 7). Copies of letters X, 27, 1704; XI, 23, 1704, in *Rep. 56 Liberalia*, pp. 137, 176.

15. *Briefwechsel König Friedrich I. mit seiner Familie*, edited by E. Berner (Berlin, 1901), p. 79, no. 136, XI, 25, 1705.
16. "Berichte des Sekretärs der Brandenburgischen Societät der Wissenschaften Jablonski an Leibniz 1700–1715," edited by Adolf Harnack, in *Abhandlungen der Preussischen Akademie der Wissenschaften* (Berlin, 1890).
17. Body, *Essais historiques*, p. 41.
18. Christoph Pitzler, "Reysebeschreibung durch Teutschland" etc. (1694), unpublished manuscript, Codex Th. Ch. No. 9436, p. 434, Technische Hochschule, Berlin-Charlottenburg. Although the manuscript was lost during World War II, the passage concerning the blue cabinet had been photographed and is illustrated (fig. 9a). It reads: "[Schloss Oranienburg] ist fein meubliret und hat viel schräncke und Kästen von Japanischer arbeit auch etl[iche] so in Berlin von Tagli gemacht worden, sonderl[ich] auf porzellan art weiss und blau." Tagli stands for Dagly.
19. Fra Alessandro Bicchi, "Berlino e sua corte," in *Rassegna Nazionale* (1888), 39: 584 ff.
20. G. Grommelt and C. von Mertens, *Das Dohna'sche Schloss Schlobitten in Ostpreussen* (Stuttgart, 1962), illustrations nos. 121, 126, 191.
21. A number of sidechairs and armchairs (pls. 172, 173) belonging to the seventeenth-century inventory of Charlottenburg carry pairs of impressed capital letters, such as PL, on the outside of the back rails below the seats. According to Wilhelm Slomann, in *Actes du Congrès de l'histoire de l'art* (Stockholm, 1933), reprinted in *Burlington Magazine*, 65 (1934), pp. 156–70, pl. III B, the initials are those of supercargoes who went to the Far East and returned with some furniture which they were allowed to mark and offer for sale. Although the chairs may have been in the East, they certainly were not lacquered there; the lacquer is of very mediocre quality and the decoration *chinoiserie*. Sir Ambrose Heal, in *London Furniture Makers from the Restoration to the Victorian Era* (London, 1953), p. 260, maintains that the initials seen on chairs of English origin were brandmarks applied by the chairmakers. It is hardly possible that the marks on the Berlin chairs could be interpreted in this way; they show many different letter pairs, whereas a commission for chairs almost certainly would have gone to a single artisan.
22. Stengel, *Alte Wohnkultur*, pp. 78–79, 81.
23. Stengel, *Alte Wohnkultur*, pp. 84–85, illustrations nos. 15, 16, 17, 18.
24. F. Nicolai, *Nachrichten von den Baumeistern* (Berlin, 1786), p. 149; F. Nicolai, *Beschreibung von Berlin und Potsdam*, 3 vols. (Berlin, 1786), 3: 1216, 1237, no. 9. The "flower cabinet" is illustrated in Georg Piltz, *Sanssouci* (Berlin, 1954), pls. 26, 27.
25. Nicolai, *Beschreibung*, 2: 546; 3: 1239, no. 18; Stengel, *Alte Wohnkultur*, pp. 89, 90–91; the former Hohenzollern Haus-Archiv, Berlin, Rep. 9, Kc 1780, Minute 1738; I. N. Ouchanova, *Lacques Russes au L'Ermitage* (Leningrad, 1964), p. 12.
26. Rudolf von Arps-Aubert, "Sächsische Lackmöbel des 18. Jahrhunderts," in *Zeitschrift des deutschen Vereins für Kunstwissenschaft*, 3 (1936): 342–68; Arps-Aubert, *Sächsische Barockmöbel 1700–1770* (Berlin, 1939).
27. W. B. Honey, *Dresden China* (London, 1934), p. 53; Walter Holzhausen, *Lackkunst in Europa* (Braunschweig, 1958), p. 259; Arps-Aubert, "Sächsische Lackmöbel," illustrations nos. 4, 5.
28. These vases are illustrated in Holzhausen, *Lackkunst*, nos. 198–202. Stengel, *Alte Wohnkultur*, p. 90, overriding earlier attributions by Sauerland and Falke, suggests that the Kayser establishment in Berlin decorated this group of vases around 1790.
29. Arps-Aubert, "Sächsische Lackmöbel," illustrations nos. 14, 18; Holzhausen, *Lackkunst*, illustrations nos. 128, 129, 130. Illustration no. 128 is a product of Dresden, not of Berlin as indicated.
30. Arps-Aubert, "Sächsische Lackmöbel," illustration no. 23.
31. A correct interpretation of the data concerning this chair may be found in the catalogue of an exhibtion held in Berlin; see E. Berckenhagen, *Katalog der Ausstellung Barock in Deutschlands Residenzen* (Berlin, 1966), no. 267.
32. Arps-Aubert, "Sächsische Lackmöbel," illustration no. 24; Holzhausen, *Lackkunst*, illustration no. 59.
33. R. Edwards, *The Shorter Dictionary of English Furniture* (London, 1964), p. 76, illustration no. 14.
34. Arps-Aubert, "Sächsische Lackmöbel," pp. 347–348; Arps-Aubert, "Sächsische Handwerker," in *Freiheitskampf* (Dresden, 7 October 1934), p. 5.
35. Arps-Aubert, "Sächsische Lackmöbel," pp. 347–348.
36. Louisa Hager, *Nymphenburg* (Munich, 1955).
37. *Katalog der Ausstellung "Der Türkenlouis"* (Karlsruhe, 1955).
38. A. M. Renner, *Die Kunstinventare der Markgrafen von Baden* (Bühl, 1941), p. 86.
39. Gerhard Peters, *Das Rastatter Schloss* (Karlsruhe, 1925) p. 66.
40. Rudolf Sillib, *Schloss Favorite* (Heidelberg, 1929).
41. Werner Fleischhauer, "Das Indianische Lack-Kabinet in Ludwigsburg," in *Festschrift Julius Baum* (Stuttgart, 1952), pp. 187–95; K. V. Ha-

rain, *Ceske maliratvi od doby rudolfinke do smrti Reinerovy* (Prague, 1915), p. 128, contains information on Bohemian painters and includes data on Kratochwill; Albert Ilg, *Die Fischer von Erlach*, 2 vols. (Vienna, 1895), 1:444.

42. Heinrich Kreisel, *Residenz Ansbach* (Munich, 1939), p. 71.

43. Albert Savine, *Une residence Allemande, Souvenirs de la Margravine de Bayreuth* (Paris, n. d.), pp. 146, 147; Heinrich Kreisel, *Eremitage* (Munich, 1934), p. 21. Here quoted is the inventory of 1758 which states that there were only four Far Eastern panels and that the remainder were decorated by the princess. Also notes from pre-1945 State Archives in Berlin (Dahlem, Rep. 96, 19. A); for present whereabout see n. 7.

44. Karl Gröber, *Das Puppenhaus der Fürstin Auguste Dorothea von Schwarzburg-Arnstadt* (Kronstein, n. d.); Christof Roselt, *Kunstsammlungen im Schloss zu Arnstadt* (Eisenach, 1956).

45. Hans Huth, "Zwei Möbelwerkstätten des 16. Jahrhunderts" (H. D. Sommer), in Pantheon, 5 (1929): 23–29; Graf Adelmann, "Barocke Möbel im Schloss Weikersheim," in *Württembergisch Franken*, N. F. 28/29 (1954): 242–68.

46. Kurt Röder and Walter Holzhausen, *Das indianische Lackkabinet des Kurfürsten Clemens August in Schloss Brühl* (Tübingen, 1950).

47. The lacquer at Falkenlust is illustrated in Holzhausen, *Lackkunst*, illustrations nos 95, 96, pl. xiv. The entire building is treated by Trude Cornelius in *Katalog der Ausstellung Kurfürst Clemens August* (Cologne, 1961), p. 127, pl. 99. See also E. Renard, *Clemens August Kurfürst von Köln* (Bielefeld, 1927).

CHAPTER VI FRENCH LACQUER

Quelle découverte plus utile que
le vernis!
JEAN-FELIX WATIN, 1773

Le gôut Chinois en France, Madame Belevitch-Stankevitch's extremely interesting study of French taste during the period of Louis XIV, was written to advance the thesis (put forth by Henry Havard and Emile Molinier) that French rococo style, unlike Italian rococo of the same period, was influenced by a vogue for the Chinese. Although this theory is no longer accepted, this book is still most valuable because it offers such a complete account of the subject. Louis XIV, Cardinal Richelieu, and Cardinal Mazarin as well as other dignitaries were all avid collectors and acquired as many items imported from the Far East as they could lay their hands on. Even ordinary citizens could acquire Far Eastern objects from a number of dealers in Paris and especially at the annual fair held at St.-Germain. A poem by Paul Scarron written around 1640 gives an idea of what was for sale at the fair.[1]

Lead me to the Portuguese
  Where we see at little cost
The merchandise of China;
  Here we find gray amber,
Beautiful work of lacquer,
  Fine porcelain
  From the celestial country
  Or from paradise.

In France the fashion of copying Far Eastern goods seems to have begun at Nevers when glazed pottery was used as a substitute for oriental porcelain in the 1640s. When the same practice began in lacquer we cannot say, since not a single piece of French lacquer in the Far Eastern style and dating from the middle of the seventeenth century has been recognized as yet. Nevertheless, it seems that one Louis Le Hongre decorated two cabinets at Versailles with lacquer panels in 1655 (there were also some well-known sculptors in the same family).[2] We know also that in 1666 a lacquermaster named Perigon provided for Versailles black lacquered cabinets in the Chinese fashion, decorated with silver, as well as two candlestands in similar style.[3] During the same period a number of other pieces "in the Chinese style" were added to the inventory of the royal household. It is not always possible to determine whether these additions were imported or of domestic make, nor is there any way of determining how "Chinese" in style they were. We gather from some of the entries that they must have been of French origin, and we gain the impression that there cannot have been much of the "Chinese" about their appearance except the fact that they were lacquered. Here is a description of one "lacquer cabinet." On its upper part

XIII. Bureau, formerly at Hôtel de Châtelet, Paris, about 1770

XIV. Commode, French, about 1740

it "was decorated with a large ornament engraved in silver showing putti, grotesques, and festoons, in the middle of which was a bust of a female surrounded by garlands of flowers." In front it opened up into arcades resting on terms wrought of silver connected by festoons; the base was formed of six female terms, probably carved in wood and connected by festoons. The description recalls those sumptuous cabinets decorated with tortoiseshell, stone inlay, and ebony often pictured in Flemish paintings of the seventeenth century. Fine examples of such pieces may be seen at the Rijksmuseum in Amsterdam and at the museum in Strasbourg.[4] The cabinet described here was probably square, its façade divided by terms, with perhaps a recess in the center, the whole crowned with a pediment wrought of silver showing putti and a female bust; the base was a stand formed by terms probably carved in wood and connected by richly flowing garlands. No Chinese motif is mentioned, and indeed it would have been out of place in such an ensemble. What distinguishes this piece from older cabinets of the same general type is the fact that it was covered with lacquer against which the silver decoration was probably extremely effective.

Before the royal workshops in Paris became celebrated for their excellent products, Antwerp was one of the centers specializing in the making of sumptuous cabinets. Florence, too, was famous for its cabinets, noteworthy for the excellence of stone inlay. As soon as it became known that the court at Versailles demanded superlative craftsmanship, some of the finest artisans in Flanders and Italy offered their services. Thus, Pierre Golle, maker of fine cabinets, from the Netherlands, and the Italian, Domenico Cucci, an extraordinary cabinetmaker well-versed in many arts, came to Paris. Cucci's work is known from a cabinet with fine stone inlay as well as carving, gilding, and bronzework of a most unusual quality.[5] Of Golle we know less, but an entry in the *Journal du Garde Meuble* of 3 May 1677 tells us that on that date he furnished a table "varnished in the manner of stone," suggesting that he had mastered the lacquer technique.[6] Cucci and Golle, like the better known Philippe Caffieri and André-Charles Boulle, carried on their craft at the *Manufacture Royale des Meubles de la Couronne*, established in 1667 at Les Gobelins under the direction of Charles LeBrun. Within this establishment a workshop, *Ouvrages de la Chine*, was set up in 1672, although no mention is made of it in any known documents until around 1713 when a new master was engaged. It was in this shop that Golle must have worked, if indeed he was not its master. It may well be that the shop was given such a name because lacquer in the Chinese manner was produced there, although originally perhaps without any idea of decorating it in an exotic manner or giving pieces so decorated an unusual shape. In the early years of this establishment the lacquer produced there was probably considered a useful replacement for ebony veneer or stained pearwood. Lazare Duvaux, an art dealer in the period of Louis XV, points to the custom when he speaks of furnishing a number of pieces "with polished varnish to imitate veneer."[7] We may conclude that hardly any furniture with *chinoiserie* decoration existed in France in the 1660s and 1670s; certainly it could not have been in great favor at the court of Versailles.

Of considerably later date was a lacquer workshop established by a member of the royal court, Louis Henry Duc de Bourbon Condé (1692–1740), who had been exiled to his estates at Chantilly. According to a contemporary biographer, Louis de Sanrobert, writing around 1760, this shop produced some excellent lacquer; even the great connoisseurs were apt to be misled as to its origin.[8] The duke also maintained a porcelain factory and employed a number of artists, among them the engraver Jean Antoine Fraisse, who in 1735 produced a *Livre de dessins Chinois* inspired primarily by the collection of works of art from the Far East owned by his patron. These designs were used in the porcelain workshop as well as by the lacquermaster. Unfortunately we have yet to identify a single piece of lacquer produced at Chantilly.

Some of the lacquermasters at work in the last decade of the seventeenth century are mentioned in the *Livre Commode*, an invaluable directory of artisans published by Abraham Pradel in 1692. There were, for example, Langlois, father and son, who could imitate entire pieces of Chinese furniture as well as Chinese screens; Sieur Desessarts, who copied carved as well as raised lacquer; and Sieur Paty, who did minor lacquerwork. Since we know of no piece of French lacquer which might date from this period, we must rely on a print dated 1688 to give us some idea of what lacquer of the time may have been like (fig. 9b). We see a stringed instrument in the late baroque style. Only the sides are lacquered and decorated *à la Chine*, and as usual the oil painting inside the lid is done in European style. Another piece is a desk which once belonged to Madame de Sevigné (pl. 220). It is very likely that it was made to order in the Far East, following specifications to assure that it would be appropriate in a French setting. Like the stringed instrument mentioned above, it is restrained in taste and uses only a minimum of oriental ornamentation. It seems possible to state that both pieces represent more sober tastes than those current in the court at Versailles. Still another example of the period are Daniel Marot's suggestions for a Chinese room, published around 1700. He called for lacquer panels showing distinctly Chinese subjects. Marot also proposed to make full use of a rich setting of blue and white porcelain or pottery of oriental make or style. In spite of these foreign elements, the dominant element of the ensemble is French. How rarely an Eastern object was allowed to produce an effect of its own may be judged from a French commode seen in the Pagodenburg near Nymphenburg (pl. 222). This piece, dated about 1715, was composed of an Eastern cabinet set on a French stand which diminished considerably the oriental impression of its lacquerwork.

In 1713, for reasons unknown, a master was needed to take charge of the *Ouvrages de la Chine* shop at Les Gobelins. The lacquermaster Jacques Dagly, who had been dismissed in Berlin the year before, was able to accept the position and was called to Paris. That a complete outsider was hired would indicate that no suitable person was available in Paris. We may also infer that the shop was run inefficiently by the fact that upon his arrival Dagly took steps to apply for a patent to protect the lacquer formula he intended to use – very probably the one he and his brother Gérard had developed in Berlin. Like Gérard, Jacques Dagly (1669–1729) was a native of Spa. We know that he did much to organize his brother's shop in Berlin. In Paris, Dagly took as partners two painters, Pierre de Neufmaison and Claude III Audran. On 28 November 1713 an edict granted the petitioners the right over a period of twenty years to produce a lacquer with which to cover all kinds of pliable materials including linen, silk, and leather and to be used to protect furniture decorated in color. Dagly's lacquer was called *vernis de Gobelins*.

Dagly's work for the court of Versailles included the lacquering of some rooms in the Cabinet d'Antiques near the royal chapel. A chronicler of the day, Louis-François Dubois de Saint Gélis, remarked that Dagly and his associates "know very well how to create designs in the Chinese manner, to such an extent that they produce items quite in the taste of the Chinese. Their lacquer, which stays pliable, is also much used, all kinds of furniture are made with it, and it compares very well with authentic pieces from China. If this lacquer becomes spotted, one takes a sponge and one may even clean it after some time has passed."[9] (It is also mentioned that the artificial pigeons which the king used during shooting matches were made of parchment covered with *vernis des Gobelins*.)

To gain an idea of the kind of decorations produced in Dagly's workshop, one may study those designs which came from the estate of Claude III Audran and are now owned by the National Museum in Stockholm (fig. 11).[10] Included are drawings for the decoration of carriages, panels, stringed instrument cases, tabourets, and tables. Since Audran was one of Dagly's partners, they may have shared their designs. When Peter the Great of Russia came to Paris in 1717, Dagly's shop was one of the showplaces he visited. Dagly remained in charge of the shop until his death in 1728 at the age of sixty-five.

Dagly was succeeded by his partner, Pierre de Neufmaison (b. about 1672), who boasted the unusual title, *Cavaliere del ordine di S. Giovanni*, perhaps indication that while in Rome he had worked in the service of a cardinal. After Dagly's death, Neufmaison produced lacquer used for carriages and woodwork and on linen *en façon de la Chine*. When Neufmaison died in 1752, a number of *Berlines* (carriage bodies), finished and unfinished, were listed as part of his estate. The legacy is mentioned here only because of an unusual chair acquired by the Carriage Museum at the Château de Compiègne, a so-called *chaise à gondole*, a seat intended for use in a sleigh or a small cabriolet (pl. 256). It is decorated with some mediocre *chinoiserie* and dates from not long before the middle of the eighteenth century. Attention is drawn to it only because it bears a rather odd inscription, something very much like a signature in simulated Chinese characters and resembling the name Dagly. The combination of letters is scarcely accidental, and yet it is impossible to consider it proof of origin. In the first place, the style of the piece is too late; it lacks Dagly's quality; finally, Dagly is not known to have signed any of his work, and certainly it seems highly improbable that any artist would sign his name in such an obtrusive way. We can only conjecture that the chair was among the unfinished pieces in Dagly's shop and was discovered after his death by Neufmaison or another who undertook to finish it and, for some mysterious reason, affixed Dagly's name.

By order of the king, Neufmaison was succeeded by his son-in-law, Charles André Tramblin, noted for his excellent varnishes and gilding.[11] The king's private theater and his opera house, neither any longer in existence, were decorated by Tramblin. In 1761 Tramblin went to Vienna to lacquer some carriages for the emperor. He did so in so splendid a manner that henceforth his work was considered equal to that of the Martins. Somewhat later Tramblin migrated to Russia, was unsuccessful in establishing himself there, and committed suicide. Upon his departure from Paris, the *Ouvrages de la Chine* was abandoned.

Perhaps even in Dagly's lifetime, and certainly after his death and during Neufmaison's regime, the shop lost its reputation in the world of fashion as far as lacquer decoration of furniture in the Far Eastern style is concerned. And yet the technique of lacquering remained in constant use, quite often combining European ornamentation and oriental motifs, sometimes in a burlesque style.

It is generally forgotten that Antoine Watteau engaged in lacquerwork. After Watteau left Gillot in 1704 he is supposed to have accepted odd jobs including the decoration of lacquerwork on carriages. From 1708 on, when he joined Claude III Audran in his workshop at the Palais du Luxembourg, Watteau undoubtedly did a considerable amount of decorative work. The Warneck Collection contains some panels, parts of decorations for stringed instruments, which have been attributed to Watteau.[12] It is also claimed that they are *vernis Martin*. These claims contradict each other, since the Martins did not begin their activities until a considerable time after Watteau's death.

A number of engravings after decorative designs by Watteau were published by Gersaint about 1734. Included is a design for the top of a harpsichord, undoubtedly to be executed in lacquer (fig. 12). Advertisements published in *Mercure* (1756–57) mention *clavecins*, including one made by Ruckers, the Antwerp master, supposedly decorated by Watteau[13]. It is more than likely that these decorations are simply based on designs by Watteau.

A surprising discovery by Carl Nordenfalk, director of the National Museum at Stockholm, is worthy of mention.[14] He found that at least three paintings by Watteau – *Leçon d'amour*, *Sérénade italienne*, both at the National Museum in Stockholm, and *L'accord parfait*, in the collection of Lord Iveagh – had been painted on segments of lacquered carriage doors. Furthermore, an X-ray of *Léçon d'amour* revealed that under the surface was a painting of a coat of arms dating from around 1708, when Watteau was working for Audran. The panels of the other two paintings had been cut from a second door also decorated with a coat of arms of about the same period. Professor Nordenfalk concluded that Watteau himself had painted the coats of arms. Certainly both are more spirited than is usual for such decorations. The ornaments are much like those by Marot, fashionable around 1708.

Another similarity is revealed by X-ray (pl. 223). The decoration of the coat of arms resembles those seen on certain lacquered boxes usually claimed to be of French origin. A particularly attractive lacquered box is owned by the Victoria and Albert Museum (pl. 224). Examples such as these would seem to indicate that decoration of French lacquer of the period was no longer confined to Chinese motifs. Unfortunately, little else is left to indicate the style of lacquer fashionable during the Regency period, from the second decade of the eighteenth century. It would appear that at this time lacquer was not nearly as popular in France as it was in England and Italy. But fashions change, and during the Louis XV period lacquer became immensely popular.

A commode dating from about 1725 is typical of the indecisive manner of the period of transition (pl. 221). Although heavy in appearance, it is shaped along Regency lines. In its decoration it seems to follow the style of Persian miniatures but with the addition of flowers in European style. Our knowledge of French lacquer remains sporadic until well after the ascension of Louis XV in 1726. During his reign not only did the style of decoration change completely but also some of the basic working conditions for artists and artisans. Trends in fashion were no longer initiated solely by members of the court; other members of the nobility as well as persons highly placed in society began to introduce ideas of their own. In this respect it is interesting to note that Louis XV hated the color black and never ordered black lacquer furniture, and yet black lacquer became extremely fashionable.[15] Away from the court, as we have noted, Louis Henry Duc de Bourbon Condé established his own lacquer and porcelain shops, both of which won much prestige. Interest in the new and the unusual was encouraged by the *marchands-merciers* whose activities have been elucidated properly only in recent years by Pierre Verlet and Francis Watson.[16] These decorators and furniture dealers were the interior decorators of their day, referred to rather sarcastically by Diderot as *marchands de tout et faiseurs de rien*. One such dealer, Lazare Duvaux, kept records of his dealings with his clients, and these have become one of our prime sources of knowledge about French cabinetmaking of the finest quality.[17] Madame de Pompadour was one of his customers, and we have learned much about both her purchases and her taste, which was extremely influential. These dealers or agents, no longer restrained by the commands of the court, responded to the ideas or perhaps the not-all-too-clear wishes of their clients and suggested what might be provided to please them. Much later, in the days of Marie Antoinette, when Dominique Daguerre had become the Duvaux of the day, small clay models (*maquettes*) were made up to help customers visualize the finished products they were commissioning.

As fashions changed, there was dwindling interest in furniture considered too ostentatiously oriental. In the 1730s it became the fashion to integrate *lacque*, the oriental product, and *vernis*, the French imitation, within the ornamental scheme of the piece of furniture to be enhanced. The same kind of integration was the rule in organizing the decor of an entire room. Often the furniture was designed and placed by the architect in charge of the design of the paneling. Instead of making a piece of lacquer the center of attention, lacquer was used in a more subdued way. In the decoration of a great commode, lacquer was applied like an inlay of veneer and surrounded by spirited curves of glittering bronzework, in contrast to the somber tones of the lacquer. A commode decorated in this fashion no longer appeared to be simply an oriental object and was more likely to harmonize with its surroundings. This suggests how completely alien to French taste was the trend to oriental decoration, if not the lacquer technique itself. The technique became no more than an auxiliary, to be used or rejected at the whim of the purchaser. Although it was most usual to employ a tripartite design for the front of a commode, there was infinite variety in the way the design was enhanced with bronzework. Bronze was available in an endless number of shapes which the cabinetmaker could combine to his taste to lend accent to the lacquer. A comparison of the commodes signed by Desforges and van Risenburgh will make this evident (pls. 237, 238). Large commodes (pls. XIV, XV) meant to be placed prominently in a room were decorated with an unusual array of bronzework. A small commode, perhaps used in the private apartments of a lady, was decorated very simply with bronze lines accentuating the silhouette of the piece and ornamental stress given only to the shoulders and the center of the apron (pl. 236).

In the grand salon of a suite, a commode might dominate the long wall opposite the windows, accompanied by corner pieces (*encoignures*) (pls. 234, 236) designed to match the commode. While such corner pieces might have one or two doors, the bronze decoration framed the lacquerwork as if it were a single unit, taking no account of the division; in some instances the bronze elements reach across the dividing split between the two doors. In the corner cupboard by van Risenburgh, Paris lacquer was employed (pl. 235). Because of its high quality and the prominence given the piece, the lacquer is likely to have been a product of one of the Martin shops.

How much of our knowledge of lacquer furnishings commissioned for a single setting depends on chance was revealed quite recently in the findings of Madame Denise Ledoux-Lebard, who was able to reconstruct an entire room (pl. XIII) designed in 1770–71 for the Hôtel de Châtelet in the Rue de Grenelle (Paris).[18] All the furnishings have been identified – nine lacquer wall panels, four *armoires*, and one bureau with its *cartonnier* – but have yet to be brought together. They are displayed at the Musée des Arts Décoratifs and at the Château de Compiègne. Equally elegant ensembles of a related type are lost to us or await detection.

Since it is impossible to show examples of all the types of lacquer furniture produced so capably in this century, it is at least rewarding to consider a single kind, the writing desk, in its variety. Most often seen is the pulpit desk on cabriole legs, a design developed from a seventeenth-century chest set on a stand. The desk has graceful curves and gently modeled lacquer surfaces flowing into each other, decorated with flat or raised gilt *chinoiserie* motifs. The desk pictured here, from the Château de Bellevue owned by Madame de Pompadour, is not one of great elegance (pl. 230). What gives it its special character is its blue lacquer decoration, a color not frequently used. The raised lacquer decoration is inclosed by aventurine frames. This technique, mentioned by Watin, imitates aventurine stone, brownish-red in color, which glitters as if gold particles were scattered on the surface.[19] Aventurine is imitated by using powdered bronze on a dark ground. This technique was in great favor in mid-century when the desk for Madame de Pompadour was made but subsequently went out of fashion. Watin mentions it because he believed it would become fashionable again, as indeed it did toward the end of the Louis XVI period (pl. 236).

One of the most important pulpit desks was sold at Sotheby's on 7 July 1961 (pl. 229). It has all the elegance and fine craftsmanship associated with a French piece of great distinction. Similar in appearance is a desk formerly at the manor of Sagan in Silesia, the seat of the Duchess of Dino and Sagan, one of the great ladies of the nineteenth century, who inherited it from her uncle, Charles Maurice de Talleyrand (pl. 228).[20] Very different from these desks is one at the *Residenz* in Munich which is of much heavier construction, somewhat reminiscent of earlier pieces (pl. 225). Most likely it was ordered in Paris by the Elector Carl Albrecht of Bavaria in the period 1730–37 and probably made by van Risenburgh. The material used is Japanese lacquer, not European, a matter of little importance in this instance since it is not the quality of the lacquer that stamps the piece but the way in which the lacquer is molded to decorate bizarre shapes. The somewhat ponderous form, with antiquated stretchers carrying a huge piece of rocaille ornament, is obscured by the skilful manner in which the lacquer is used, allowing its planes to sparkle in all decorations. In striking contrast is a drop-front desk in the Wrightsman

Collection (pl. 227). In spite of its fiddleback shape, it is somewhat statuesque, the movement of its outline is measured, and there is a minimum of plasticity in its appearance. One gains the impression that the bronzework serves only to frame the lacquer as though it were a painting. This desk, one of a pair, is signed by Dubut and invites a study of the differences between the lacquer on the drawer, which is Parisian, and the two large panels imported from Japan. It is amazing to see how perfectly the European master was able to adopt Far Eastern style. Secretaries of this period are now rare, but the type was much in favor in various revivals in the nineteenth century for a number of rather well-made copies are in existence.

Price determined whether lacquer was used, either cut from gilt and black lacquered Japanese screen panels or from colored and incised Coromandel screens, or whether Parisian substitutes were provided. Since *vernis* made in Paris is often of excellent quality, a close scrutiny is necessary to distinguish between imports and domestic work. Strong cracks in the lacquer are indicative of imported lacquer, especially when the lacquer is bent and attached to curved planes, a technique cleverly mastered by Parisian artisans.

Certain cabinetmakers specialized in preparing "carcasses" – the underlying framework which lacquermasters were commissioned to decorate. The piece was then returned to the *ébéniste*, who finished it, applied the bronzework, and signed it. He also stamped his name or initials and his mark, which was registered with the guild at the *Jurande des maîtres ébénistes* (JME), whose mark was also applied. Unfortunately, these marks tell us nothing about the artists who did the lacquerwork. The lacquermaster remains forever anonymous, since the piece of furniture is registered under the name of the *ébéniste* – Roger Vendercruse, called Lacroix, signing RULC; Jacques Dubois, Jean Desforges, signing D. F.; Bernard van Risenburgh, signing BVRB, and all the others.

The creative design, superb workmanship, and well-balanced use of bronze and lacquer for commodes, flat-topped desks (*bureaux plats*), and other pieces executed by these craftsmen demand high praise, but there are a few instances when they surpassed even this perfection. One example is a certain small table of which there are a number differing only slightly. Some of these have tops or shelves made of decorated Sèvres trays, allowing us to date them rather exactly. One of these tables is in the J. Paul Getty Collection at Malibu (pl. 231); another is in the Musée du Louvre (pl. 232); both were made by van Risenburgh. A closely related table, made by Lacroix, belongs to the Camondo Collection of the Louvre, and two other tables by van Risenburgh are in the Kress Collection of the Metropolitan Museum (pl. 233). What distinguishes these tables, apart from their extraordinary elegance, is the novel way in which the lacquer is used. No longer does the lacquermaster borrow a Chinese design; color and pattern are original, developed to complement the slender silhouette of the underlying woodwork and the decoration of the Sèvres tablet. In these tables European lacquer comes into its own with a unique design and a new use of material in the very spirit of French taste. The lacquer as well as the design for these tables probably originated in one of the Martin shops. Their contemporary, Watin, remarks that the Martins were famous for their white lacquer.[21] The Sèvres tablet made a part of the Getty table is dated 1761, the table in the Louvre is dated 1766; if these tables were lacquered in the Martin shops, the lacquermaster must have been either Robert Martin, who died in 1765, or Etienne-Simon, who died in 1770. Some of these tables, unfortunately, are now somewhat marred; the lacquer, originally so perfectly in harmony, with the Sèvres tablet providing the key color, has yellowed considerably.

During the Louis XVI period, interest waned in *chinoiserie* and lacquer was used far less. Commodes of the transition period, like those shown here (pls. 239, 240), suggest that this kind of background and this shape were no longer suitable for the heavy and rather rigid bronzework then coming into style. The *meubles d'apparat* made by Riesener, Carlin, Weisweiler, Levasseur, and others for Marie Antoinette and members of the court were to have an entirely different appearance. Now Japanese lacquer panels, or close imitations, delicately decorated in gold on black and framed like pictures, often connected by richly shaped bronze festoons, appear in classic symmetry, quite alien to oriental aesthetics. Martin Carlin, a favorite cabinetmaker of the court, excelled in this kind of furniture. He provided the corner cupboards for *Mesdames de France*, the sisters of Louis XVI who lived at the Château de Bellevue (pl. 236). The contrast, or marriage, however one wishes to call it, of exotic and classical elements must have seemed a most attractive experience in its day. Only a decade or two later, about the turn of the century, the lacquer panels would be replaced by mahogany, offering a more serene background for the bronzework.

Toward the third quarter of the eighteenth century, much of the color was disappearing from the walls of salons and mansions in Paris, but was still considered fashionable in less formal country villas and summer residences. Suites were decorated in light tints of green, blue, or yellow, forming a pleasant background for lacquered furniture decorated in *chinoiserie* and set off by gold or even silver. A corner cupboard lacquered in blue and finished with silvered bronze appliques, ordered in 1743 by Louis XV for Madame de Mailly and her Château de Choisy, typifies the new trend (pl. 241).[22] Colorful furniture was produced by the great cabinetmakers as well as by others of lesser renown. Because imagination was more important than skill in planning the decoration for such furniture, an extraordinary variety resulted. A commode lacquered in blue and white and rather sparsely decorated with bronzework represents the type thought suitable for country residences (pl. 243). Another example, a small *bureau plat* with raised and gilt ornaments on a yellow ground and fitted with a minimum of bronze, may date from around 1760 (pl. 242). François Rubestuck is the maker of a commode created around 1775 and covered with an all-over pattern of lacquer which in no way respects the convex shape of the middle section (pl. 244). This lack of sensitivity suggests a loss of understanding between lacquermaster and cabinetmaker. The same is true of the choice of bronzes, which do not seem suitable. A bed table (*table d'accoucheuse*) is mentioned here not because it was designed specifically for a country residence but because it is not Parisian and does have some colorful decoration (pls. 250, 251). At first glance, this piece of rosewood veneer, resembling a toilette table, does not seem particularly striking, but the table has been made so that the upper part may be lifted off to serve as a breakfast tray. The top of the support thus revealed is lacquered in luxuriant colors – a still life of fruit in a style reminiscent of the south of France. The table was once the property of Wilhelm von Bode, who acquired it in Marseilles.

Stepping back in time to the middle of the eighteenth century, there is to be discussed a most extraordinary family of artists and craftsmen whose work is often characterized as *Martin* or *vernis Martin*.[23] The family worked through two generations; we know the names and dates of at least four members in each generation. Although we have knowledge of numerous objects produced by the Martins and their imitators, there is not one piece signed and precious few that can be authenticated. Under these circumstances, the only and admittedly inadequate criterion for attributing individual pieces to the Martin workshop is the excellence of craftsmanship (pl. XVI a).

In the first generation there were four Martin brothers, Guillaume (d. 1749), Etienne-Simon (d. 1770), Julien (d. 1752), and Robert (1706–1765). In 1730 the two oldest and most active brothers, Guillaume and Etienne-Simon, acquired a royal patent to protect the lacquer they had invented. In addition, in 1744 they received a patent for the protection of their lacquerwork *en relief dans le goût du Japon et de la Chine*. At length, in 1753, they received a patent for a lacquer consisting mostly of copal which probably was the one to become world famous as *vernis Martin*. By 1748 their establishment had been appointed *Manufacture Royale*. It consisted of three shops, one in the Faubourg St.-Martin, one in the Rue St.-Denis, and one in the Rue St.-Magloire. As the years passed production was extended from the decoration of small objects and furniture to the lacquering of carriages, sedan chairs, and the decoration of entire rooms. Certain modern techniques are evident in the use of molds of specific sizes for the production of small boxes to be lacquered.

Much of the work done by the Martins was intended for the royal court.[24] One of the brothers was asked to furnish lacquer decoration in green and gold for the *Petite Galerie* at Versailles for Queen Maria Leszczynska, wife of Louis XV. Later, between 1748 and 1755, Etienne lacquered rooms at Versailles for the dauphin and dauphine (later Louis XVI and Marie Antoinette). In 1748 the *Oratoire* and the *Cabinet à niches* at Versailles were decorated by Etienne in white, the color for which the Martins were famous, enhanced with some green. Etienne spent nearly twelve-hundred working days on this task and made some fifty trips to Versailles. Only in one room decorated for Queen Maria Leszczynska in 1756 are there still some faint traces of the original lacquer decoration of flowers and pastoral scenes. These rooms may have contained lacquered furniture purchased by the dauphin in 1748 from the dealer Lazare Duvaux.

The Martins also did a considerable amount of work for Madame de Pompadour at the Château de Bellevue for which they were paid more than 58,000 livres. The Martins also were known to have repaired precious lacquer pieces owned by Madame de Pompadour, as we learn from the *Livre Journal* of Lazard Duvaux. According to Duvaux, little was left of the original lacquer after repairs were made to two commodes in 1752. The Martins scraped off the old aventurine lacquer and replaced it with black lacquer. They also attached some of the lacquer and added raised work to conceal bad spots, completing the work by tinting the bronzes.[25] This entry confirms an assertion by Watin, the eighteenth-century authority on lacquer, that repairing lacquer was an essential part of the craft but that such repairs should never go beyond the damaged area. This restriction, rarely followed by restorers today, was not followed by the

Martins either, although Madame de Pompadour after all did receive genuine Martin replacements.

Another famous customer of the Martin workshops was the Marquise du Châtelet, hostess to Voltaire at Cirey. We know that one of the Martin's apprentices worked at Cirey, and perhaps this induced Voltaire to mention the name of Martin in several of his works and praise "those cabinets in which Martin surpassed the art of China."[26]

Members of the second generation of Martins were Guillaume-Jean (b. 1713), Etienne François (d. 1771), Jean Alexandre (1738–1823), and Antoine Nicolaus (b. 1742). Jean Alexandre, who served Frederick the Great as *vernisseur du roi* in the period 1747–66, has been mentioned in the chapter on German lacquer. He returned to Paris in 1767 and continued his work at the Faubourg St.-Martin shop, apparently the last member of the family engaged in the old trade. In the years that followed business decreased. Costly lacquer was not in great demand when customers could buy less expensive pieces offered as "in the Martin genre." Then, too, France was on the brink of the Revolution. Aristocrats were not so anxious to flaunt snuffboxes with coats of arms and other symbols of nobility. A number of snuffboxes still in existence reveal that coats of arms have been overpainted rather crudely, as if considered dangerously inciting. Whatever the case, Jean Martin gave up his business in 1787 at the age of forty-six. We last hear of him in 1794 when he was summoned to appear as a witness at a trial.

The lacquer used by the Martins for furniture was built up painstakingly. First the surface to be decorated was covered with forty-three layers of chalk white (*blanc de Meudon*) and, when required, ornaments were then carved in this ground. Next, five layers of paint were applied, followed by fifteen layers of varnish. The base of the lacquer was Brasil copal. Between coatings the surface was polished again and again until it was completely smooth. Since the Martins lacquered furniture made by a great number of cabinetmakers whose style varied greatly, style alone does not make it possible to identify their work.[27] Nor did the Martins use an easily identifiable set of designs in lacquer decoration; often they worked with designs contributed by outside painters. For instance, we know that some of their carriages were decorated by Lucas Charles, P. Dutour (d. 1785), and one of the Huets – perhaps Christophe, who died in 1759.

In spite of the large number of superb pieces of furniture lacquered by the Martins, lacquered furniture was probably not a major part of their production or even chiefly responsible for the spread of their fame throughout Europe. What made their name a generic term were certain household articles – barbers' bowls, goblets, cups, extraordinarily elegant snuffboxes, pillboxes, toilette necessities, and *carnets de bal* – charmingly decorated, generally in the European fashion, and often richly set in gold: trifling but refined *objets d'art* typical of the century. Some exquisite examples of such work now in the Wallace Collection and in the Metropolitan Museum surely must have originated in the Martin workshop (pls. 245–248). A toilette table, dating from the end of the eighteenth century, is perhaps unique – every item composing its contents is still in existence, each neatly fitted into its proper place (pl. 249). Besides items of glass and porcelain, it includes an array of lacquerware to complete the set of toilette articles. Since one is apt to attribute only the finest pieces known to the workshops of the Martins, it is important to point out that the Martins did not confine their work to such only of the greatest elegance. This table and its contents are finely executed, but the lacquer is not the most precious, but even so it might come from a Martin shop.

The household articles decorated by the Martins were fashioned of nothing more than paper. Since the sixteenth century, pap or papier-mâché was used in France for architectural ornaments. Since papier-mâché was not a very substantial material, it was Guillaume Martin's idea to glue sheets of paper together to achieve necessary thickness for the small objects they wish to produce and lacquer. This method was first described by the astronomer Jerome le Français de Lalande in a tract in a series devoted to the arts and crafts of France, *L'Art du Cartonnier*, published in 1762.[28]

The body of the pillbox or snuffbox, called *Martin*, was made up of a great number of sheets of paper *(de Caen* or *de Champey)* glued together to the required thickness. While these sheets were still wet they were pressed into a mold of the desired shape and dried in an oven until they were as firm and hard as wood. The box was then rasped and further shaped by the turner, then polished, painted, and lacquered. As an additional decoration, colored metal powders, generally brass or copper, were scattered over the wet varnish to achieve an effect of aventurine, used for borders or background.

A special item from the Martin workshops was a pillbox standardized in ten sizes, from *petit rien* and *zéro* to numbers 1 through 8. The thickness of these boxes varied, from about forty sheets for the largest one, some three inches in diameter, to fifteen or sixteen sheets for the smaller sizes. One workman could make about one hundred boxes a day, and it took from five to six days to ready them for lacquering. If it were possible to find and examine a sufficient number of these boxes, we might determine the types in the Martin shop. The Martins had an increasing number of competitors in spite of the royal patents granted to assure their exclusive license. Watin reports that in 1745, when the Martins had acquired an enormous reputation, Paris was inundated by imitations of their work, particularly "Martin snuffboxes." This brought prices down to "nothing." While imitators undoubtedly did their best to copy the outward appearance of the Martin's work, it is unlikely that they had the same expertise. Probably Dossie directs his complaints against these "charlatans" in *Handmaiden of the Arts* when he points out that French boxes were primed but did not receive a sufficient number of lacquer coatings; as a consequence, French snuffboxes had a tendency to chip and lose large chunks of lacquer.[29] The Martins, on the other hand, always maintained the quality of their wares, although they were never able to obtain the brilliance of Far Eastern products nor did their pieces age as well. In time, all European lacquer shows craquelure, and the varnish has a tendency to yellow. But in their early period the Martins produced work so like the oriental that even the most astute connoisseur accepted their products as genuine. According to Watin, writing in 1773, these masterpieces were as much in demand as was old Chinese lacquerwork.

Throughout the eighteenth century, Paris was a center for the making of musical instruments. Since lacquering was an integral part of the decoration of harpsichords and other stringed instruments, many lacquermasters must have been engaged in this line. As in furniture, there was a wide difference in quality. A little *spinettino* made around the middle of the century was given a simple but attractive decoration using a favorite *chinoiserie* design (pls. 252, 253). Another instrument, made by Johannes Goermans in 1754, was decorated more elaborately in the full style of the "jolly Chinese," with such motifs as a company of merry Chinese musicians about a harpsichord (pls. 257, 258). Majestic Parisian harps demanded the most skilful execution of carved and lacquered decoration. One such harp, dated around 1760, was acquired by the museum in Oslo from the family of the original owner, together with a portrait of the gentleman seated at his harp (pls. 259, 260). Painted at a time when *chinoiserie* was no longer fashionable, the harp is decorated with a rich display of flowers much in the style we associate with the Martin workshops. Harpsichords made by Pascal Taskin (1723–1793), born in Theux near Spa and considered one of the great instrumentmakers, are distinguished by the elegance of their lacquer decoration (pl. 261). Almost every instrument attributed to Taskin is said to have been once played by Marie Antoinette.

Even after the Revolution lacquer continued to be in demand for the decoration of carriages. The artisans of Paris had excelled in the building of carriages since the end of the seventeenth century. The excellent varnish devised by the Martins enabled the carriagemakers to give their products a perfect and stylish finish. To a certain extent, the Martins monopolized the craft; the use of their lacquer was considered a necessity both before the Revolution and for a time thereafter. For the aristocracy, a carriage decorated with *vernis Martin* was *de rigueur* – a notion for which Mirabeau castigated society shortly before the Revolution.[30] But it is quite true that it was an age when a carriage was not simply a necessity but an object of great beauty to be decorated as carefully as one's home.

Carriagemakers also made sedan chairs. A sedan chair completed in mid-century has *vernis Martin* panels on a gold ground framed by carved and gilt moldings (pl. 254). A charming little carriage (*calèche de parc*), dated somewhat earlier, is decorated with scarlet lacquer panels with gilt ornaments in the Bérain style (pl. 255).[31] Although it belongs to the old inventory of the Palazzo Pallavicini in Rome, it must be of French make. At some point it was transformed into a little rocking chair. A number of lacquered carriages, sedan-chairs, and sledges are displayed in museums at Belem, Compiègne, Hanover, Schönbrunn, and elsewhere.[32] Although lacquer decoration continued to be used extensively in the carriage trade until the end of the eighteenth century, it is true that interest in achieving unusually beautiful effects lessened with the years. To trace the decline is beyond the scope of this study.

1. Paul Scarron, *Œuvres*, 7 vols. (Paris, 1786), 7:239.
2. Henri Cordier, *La Chine en France* (Paris, 1910), p. 99; H. Belevitch-Stankevitch, *Le gôut Chinois en France* (Paris, 1910), p. 128 n. The activity of Le Hongre is here questioned.
3. Belevitch-Stankevitch, *Le gôut Chinois*, p. 129.
4. Belevitch-Stankevitch, *Le gôut Chinois*, p. 132. For illustrations of similar cabinets see *World Furniture*, edited by H. Hayward (London, 1965), illustration no. 261 and plate opposite p. 80.
5. Pierre Verlet, *French Royal Furniture* (New York, 1963), p. 101, pl. i.
6. Information most kindly given by M. Pierre Verlet.

7. Pierre Verlet, *Les meubles du XVIIIième siècle*, 2 vols. (Paris, 1956), 2 (*Les Ebénistes*): 24.
8. Gustave Macon, *Chantilly* (Paris, 1925), p. 132.
9. Dubois de Saint Gélis, *Histoire Journaillière de Paris, 1716–17*, edited by Maurice Tourneux (Paris, 1885), pp. 147–49.
10. Catalogue of an exhibition at the Bibliothèque Nationale, Paris, *Dessins du Musée National de Stockholm par Claude III Audran* (Paris, 1950), pp. 24–30.
11. Henri Vial, Adrien Marcel, and André Girodie, *Les artistes décorateurs du bois*, 2 vols. (Paris, 1922), 2:53, 172.
12. Hélène Adhémar, *Watteau* (Paris, 1950), catalogue nos. 9–12.
13. E. Dacier and A. Vuaflart, *Jean de Julienne et les graveurs de Watteau*, 3 vols. (Paris, 1922–29), 1:22, catalogue no. 206.
14. Carl Nordenfalk, *Antoine Watteau och andra franska sjutton hundratal mästare i Nationalmuseum* (Stockholm, 1953). I am most indebted to Dr. Nordenfalk for the X-ray photograph of the *Leçon d'amour* as well as for additional information he was so kind to give me. The date 1708 given to the painting is based on recognition of the combined coats of arms beneath as those of the Colbert de Seigneley and another family. A male member of the de Seigneley family married in 1708, and it is concluded that the carriage was made for the wedding. As it happened, the groom died in 1712; the door bearing his coat of arms may have been replaced by another one, thus giving Watteau a chance to acquire it as a "canvas," as Carl Nordenfalk suggests he did in another instance.
15. Verlet, *French Royal Furniture*, p. 107.
16. Not before Pierre Verlet began to study the history of French furniture had there been much understanding of the relationship between the corporations of the *menuisiers* (the craftsmen producing carved furniture – beds, chairs, and tables) and the *ébénistes* (known for making veneered pieces) with the *marchands-merciers* and *marchands-tapissiers*, the salesmen and upholsterers who served as middlemen in dealing with clients. Their dealings have been treated extensively in F. J. B. Watson's introduction to the catalogue of furniture of the Wrightsman Collection, New York. Here also is to be found an evaluation of the stamps applied to French furniture, all too often incorrectly interpreted (see note 18).
17. Paul Comte de River, *Histoire du Château de Bellevue* (Paris, 1933), p. 126; H. Corday, *Inventaires de Madame de Pompadour* (Paris, 1939), p. 63, nos. 709, 713; Louis Courajod, *Livre Journal de Lazare Duvaux* (Paris, 1873).
18. For the two pieces of furniture from the Wrightsman Collection here mentioned see F. J. B. Watson, *The Wrightsman Collection*, 2 vols. (New York, 1966), 1: no. 92, commode (here pl. XV), and no. 104, drop-front secretary (here pl. 227). The furniture from the J. Paul Getty Collection was published by Paul Wescher in *Art Quarterly* (Summer, 1955), pp. 114–35. Denise Ledoux-Lebard, "Un cabinet de travail en laque," in *Connaissance des arts*, 197–98 (1968): 62–65.
19. Jean-Felix Watin, *L'art du peintre, doreur, vernisseur* (Paris, 1st edition, 1772; 2d enlarged edition, 1773), p. 172.
20. Hans Huth "Französische Möbel in Deutschland," in *Pantheon (1930)*, 6:555–59.
21. Watin, *L'art du peintre*, pp. 238, 246 n.
22. Pierre Verlet, *Le mobilier royal français*, 2 vols. (Paris, 1945), 1:6.
23. Vial-Marcel-Girodie, *Les artistes décorateurs*, 2:15–18.
24. Pierre Verlet, *Versailles* (Paris, 1961), pp. 469–86; Henry Racinais, *Un Versailles inconnu* (Paris, 1950), p. 41.
25. Courajod, *Livre Journal*, 2:135.
26. Vial-Marcel-Girodie, *Les artistes décorateurs*, 2:15.
27. See chap, ii, n. 11.
28. Reprint of first edition, *Description des Arts et Métiers*, 19 vols. (Neufchâtel, 1776), 4:607.
29. Robert Dossie, *The Handmaiden to the Arts* (London, 1758), p. 23.
30. Courajod, *Livre Journal*, 1:cxxix.
31. Compare with *calèche* in Heinrich Kreisel, *Prunkwagen und Schlitten* (Leipzig, 1927), p. 55.
32. Rudolph H. Wackernagel, *Der französische Krönungswagen*, 1696–1825 (Berlin, 1966), offers information on many types of carriages and an exhaustive bibliography. For a review see Hans Huth in *Art Bulletin* (1967), 49:368–69.

CHAPTER VII

LACQUER IN THE NETHERLANDS, SCANDINAVIA, RUSSIA

> . . . not one in a thousand of all the stiles, chairs, gates, temples, etc. which are called Chinese, has the least resemblance to anything that China ever saw.
> William Whitehead, 1753

The beginnings of lacquer early in the seventeenth century in the northern, Protestant provinces of the Netherlands remain obscure, and only by examination of the close ties between England and Holland and by reference to English products of the period is it possible to get some idea of what Dutch lacquer may have been like. The situation did not change much before the last quarter of the seventeenth century when Dutch craftsmen were inspired to copy certain lacquer imports which had become increasingly fashionable. Possibly some indication of one popular piece of furniture may be gathered by examining certain lacquered tables of "lobar" style decorated with both mother-of-pearl inlay and floral *chinoiserie*, copied in Venice but certainly based on a Dutch original (pl. 102).

In the southern Netherlands, in what is now Flanders, Antwerp was the chief commercial center, and here a fashion of another kind was initiated. From the sixteenth century, artisans in Antwerp fashioned elaborate cabinets, many of them in a sumptuous style, decorated with inlays of stonework, paintings, embossed panels of ivory, coral, or metal, and veneered with ebony or tortoiseshell. These cabinets were exported to many countries as receptacles for curios or jewels.[1] When the Boulle technique was introduced, it was quickly adopted in Antwerp; we know that certain cabinets in this style were executed in that city.[2] One such is a seventeenth-century desk, formerly in the palace in Berlin, decorated with raised lacquer on a white ground (pls. 264, 265). In its general shape, with tapering, spiral-turned legs crowned by a rosette-like capital and connected by spandrels, it follows the Antwerp Boulle desks so closely that one should be permitted to claim this desk and others like it for Antwerp. This seems all the more possible if one assumes that the art of lacquering would have been taken up in Antwerp as soon as it became fashionable.

Another group of lacquered cabinets may also be considered of Netherlandish origin because the decorations combine arrangements of European flowers in oriental vases, a motif likely to have been copied from Dutch still life paintings of the seventeenth century. A cabinet of this kind used to be in the royal palace at Königsberg (pl. 266). Its floral decoration links it to Dutch marquetry cabinets in the style of Jan van Mekeren.[3] A rare and important cabinet, at present in Schloss Mosigkau, a state museum near Dessau in East Germany, was originally in a manor of the dukedom of Anhalt (pl. 267). The princes of this territory and their courtiers, like those of Brandenburg, had many ties with the Netherlands, and imports such as this cabinet would not have been exceptional. It should be remembered that North Germany, like other countries adjacent to the Baltic, depended on England and Holland for the import of art objects and other amenities of life. From Hamburg goods could easily be shipped down the Elbe and to the rivers beyond. The cabinet in question is lacquered on a white ground. The spiral-turned legs are of a bold shape, and the lacquered and decorated stand has three steps at the top for the display of pottery, a feature contributing to the thoroughly Dutch character of the piece.

In the next phase of the development of the Dutch cabinet it becomes virtually impossible to distinguish between cabinets of Dutch and English origin because of the striking similarities of their stands. It is made all the more difficult because a number of Dutch cabinets of this kind were placed on the English market many years ago and now are mingled and confounded with like cabinets of English origin. A cabinet of this type, dating from around 1680 and once in the inventory of the royal palace in Berlin, is probably of Dutch origin even though the seated figure on the left and some of the birds in the decoration of the doors were copied from the book of designs compiled by Stalker and Parker (pl. 268). Another cabinet on a stand, with tapering pilasters and richly designed raised lacquer, is probably of a later date, around 1690 (pl. 271). Its decoration, a conglomeration of buildings and the figures of American Indians in the style of the prints by Theodore de Bry, first published in 1590, together with the vigorous appearance of the stand, bespeak its Dutch origin.

After 1700, Dutch cabinets, not unlike their English counterparts, were designed with tapering, plain wooden legs, round, square, or polygonal in shape, connected by spandrels. The turned leg had been abandoned, and heavy gilt carving had gone out of fashion. One cabinet with a stand in this style is lacquered in gold on red, with the Dutch arrangement of steps at the top, the whole decorated with an elaborate landscape in raised lacquer, a design rather close to the oriental (pl. 270). What gives it special importance is that it is unquestionably of Dutch origin; it has remained in the same Dutch family for which it was made.[4] The shape of this piece serves to confirm the Dutch origin of a number of other cabinets, including the cabinet at Schloss Mosigkau and two others in the Kölnische Stadtmuseum (pls. 267, 269, 273).

The popularity of cabinets of this kind lasted well into the first quarter of the eighteenth century, but by then their style may have been considered quite conservative. Their general purpose was to serve as repositories for collections of curios. A lacquered cabinet for the doll's house of Christof van Brant, installed about 1700, was used for the display of a shell collection; a few shells are displayed on top (pl. 279). Later cabinets not only were of a completely different shape but were designed to serve an entirely new purpose.

Before considering how the change came about, it should be pointed out that the Dutch designed and lacquered other kinds of furniture but only rarely have examples survived. In the Rijksmuseum there is a corner cupboard with a façade somewhat like an English bureau-cabinet. It is veneered outside and lacquered rather modestly on the inside. Lacquered folding tables were apparently very popular; examples (pl. 280) of these are seen in the van Brant doll's house, and another of similar character, destroyed in the manor of Schlobitten in East Prussia, may well have been purchased in the Netherlands.[5]

A new kind of cabinet first appeared in the decade 1730–40. A showpiece, it was made to house collections of pottery, porcelain, and glassware behind glass-fronted doors usually made of mahogany. Although cabinets of this kind are not very rare even now, a large number of imitations are on the market. A genuine cabinet of the period is in the museum at Schloss Mosigkau near Dessau (pl. 277). It follows a pattern similar to that of enormous Dutch linen cabinets, although it is much smaller in size. It stands on rather high cabriole legs connected by a richly carved apron, and over the doors is a carved pediment on which a jar or vase could be displayed. The skilful *chinoiserie* of this cabinet resembles Far Eastern patterns. Lacquered showcases of this particular pattern are now rare. A little stand on cabriole legs decorated with raised lacquer is typical of the skill of Dutch lacquermasters in copying Far Eastern work (pl. 281). The use of such a stand, with a group of "Chinese" placed on it, is shown in a pastel by Cornelis van Troost (1697–1750), now in the Rijksmuseum (pl. 282).

Finally, one may point to the great number of pieces of lacquer furniture in museums or on the art market which are considered to be Dutch only by the process of elimination, since they do not seem to have been made in any of the other countries where lacquer was produced. One piece of this kind is a cabinet on a stand, the cabinet made around 1700, the stand around 1740 (pl. 274). A large and elegant writing desk, of good proportions, lacquered in green, probably made in the period 1740–50, may also be of Dutch origin (pls. 275, 276).

In the Netherlands there no longer seem to exist any completely lacquered rooms dating from the seventeenth century or the first half of the eighteenth century. At one time a paneled room at Rosenborg was considered to have been lacquered by a Dutchman named Samuel Clauszon in 1615, but this erroneous attribution was based on a misinterpretation of the data (pls. 262, 263). Probably the room was decorated in the late seventeenth century, making use of prints from the compendium of Stalker and Parker and from John Nieuhoff. The paneling with raised lacquer in another room at Rosenborg castle, first executed in the seventeenth century, was redone by Christian van Bracht, a Dutch lacquermaster working at the Danish court, in 1716. While it is difficult to distinguish between the original work and the restoration, the general design, using decorative elephants, monsters, and birds, is of a highly individual and unusual character. Also at Rosenborg is a signed lacquered vase by one of the sons of Christian van Bracht. Another traditional, so-called Dutch room at Bamberg was discussed earlier (pl. 218).

In the Gemeente Museum at The Hague is a large lacquered hall originally in the manor Buytenrust (pl. 272). *Chinoiserie* is used sparingly together with European ornamentation typical of the mid-eighteenth century, although *chinoiserie* and ornamentation may not be of the same period. Examples of the high quality of Dutch lacquer are to be seen at Huis ten Bosch, the summer palace near The Hague (pl. 278). The so-called Chinese room was decorated in the style of Daniel Marot when the architect added two wings to the manor in 1734. As a witness of this style are a marble mantlepiece and some recently discovered paneling. The black and gold decorations now surmounting the fireplace in a rich Chippendale style were added in the period 1740–50. The rest of the room was decorated about 1785, as was the neighboring Japanese room. The satinwood paneling, with insets of black and gold lacquer, is similar to the decoration of a group of commodes and other pieces from an old Dutch manor offered for sale in Amsterdam in 1961.[6] Some of the Hepplewhite chairs in the Japanese room at Huis ten Bosch are made of beechwood with small insets of lacquer, suggesting the restraint with which lacquer was used

XV. Commode, Bernard van Risenburgh (signed), Paris, after 1737

XVI a

XVI b

XVI a. Panel with monkey, *vernis Martin*, Paris, about 1730
XVI b. Russian box, Palekh, 1937

just before it went out of fashion. In fact, these chairs may well be of English origin; they are identical to one chair now in an English collection.[7]

Cultural trends in Scandinavia can be followed only if one remains aware of the entangled political ties of Denmark, Norway, and Sweden during the period under consideration. Denmark and Norway were united from 1442 until 1814. Norway became independent of Sweden in 1905.

During the seventeenth century and the early part of the eighteenth century, Scandinavian artisans were much influenced by Dutch art, and Dutch craftsmen frequently worked in Scandinavia. After the London fire of 1660, close ties were established between England and Denmark, Norway, and Sweden. Scandinavian lumber was needed to rebuild the city, and in exchange highly desired English goods were imported to Scandinavia.[8] A strong English influence lasted until the Napoleonic wars. (After this era, Scandinavia grew more closely connected to the continent, particularly through the port of Hamburg.) A great number of lacquer pieces were imported from England, providing patterns for Scandinavian craftsmen. These copies, in the main cabinets, long-case clocks, and chairs, retained certain characteristics of English furniture largely because of the conservative trend in Scandinavian society, long after these styles had ceased to be acceptable in England.

A Swedish corner cupboard, dating from the first half of the eighteenth century, is one of the earliest known pieces of Scandinavian lacquer (pl. 284). Its proportions are graceful, and the decorative landscapes are used in quite a fresh way. Although the escutcheons include royal crowns, a lacquer painting on the inside of the cupboard depicts a man counting his money – a genre picture, possibly a later addition, rather contradicting the possibility that the cupboard once had a royal owner. A small cabinet, presumably of the early eighteenth century, is decorated with *lacca povera* work using Augsburg prints dating from the mid-eighteenth century – again, possibly a later addition by an amateur (pl. 285). The tall cabinet, conservative in shape and skilfully decorated in silver on black, points to a date between 1730 and 1740 and was probably influenced by Dutch trends (pl. 283). A lacquered bracket clock, made in the Swedish province of Smaland about 1740, and a long-case clock, lacquered in gold on blue, originating in Dalarna (Sweden) around 1740, both clearly show English influence (pls. 287, 292, 293).

Among the most skilful lacquermasters active before the middle of the eighteenth century was the Norwegian, Niels Lochstoer (1714–85), who proudly signed two of the clocks illustrated here (pls. 286, 289, 290, 291).[9] Lochstoer is known to have been apprenticed in London where he worked about 1740. He returned to Norway and set up shop in the town of Braggernes. Like other artisans, Lochstoer had an inquisitive mind and since his English masters had not revealed all of their secrets to him it was necessary to conduct experiments to find suitable lacquer with which to japan wood, papier-mâché, and tin. His activities earned him a medal from his government in 1780. Lochstoer's dependence upon English style is evident, although this dependence was not peculiar to him; during this time there was a veritable craze in Norway for English-made goods.

In Denmark, a number of lacquermasters were plying their trade in Copenhagen, working much in the English tradition. There is a long-case clock in the English style, decorated in gold on black, at the Dansk Folke Museum at Copenhagen (pl. 288). The clockwork is signed by P. Mathiesen of Copenhagen. A cupboard on a stand with drawers and with a carved, arched pediment with scrolls, once probably decorated in blue on white – a rather unusual scheme – is of special interest because it carries the label of a cabinetmaker, Matjias Ortmann, active around 1750. The carvings suggest German rather than English influence.[10]

At the Danish court, lacquer furniture had been in demand since the second half of the seventeenth century. The two paneled rooms at Rosenborg castle (pls. 262, 263), executed by Dutch lacquermasters, provide ample proof of the popularity of lacquer, as do the chairs and a desk at Rosenborg imported from the Far East. During the reign of Frederick IV (1671–1730), *lacca povera* work, or *découpure* as it was called in French, was a favorite pastime at the Danish court. Frederick's first and second wife, Queen Louise (d. 1721) and Anna Sophia (d. 1741), were passionately fond of this art for amateurs, and so was the king's brother, Prince Charles. Some of the vases decorated by Louise or Anna Sophia are still to be seen at Rosenborg. A detailed list, dated 1743, describes sixty-two pieces of lacquer furniture once owned by Anna Sophia. At Clausholm castle there exists a Chinese cabinet, executed for the queen, painted though not lacquered with *chinoiserie* in a most extravagant style.[11]

All of the lacquer mentioned so far – made for burghers of the town or members of the court – is usually distinguished by some characteristics of amateur work or by a close dependence upon English or Dutch patterns, but lacquer executed for the Swedish court during the second half of the eighteenth century was quite different and owed its uniqueness to a single cabinetmaker, Niels Dahlin (master 1761, d. 1787). In the quality of his designs and the over-all character of his work, Dahlin is the equal of French artisans; we must presume he was apprenticed in Paris. He utilized Far Eastern lacquer panels cut to suit his design and framed with bronzework of a very high quality. A desk made in the period 1765–70 is a remarkable example of his craft (pl. 295). Its shape as it narrows toward the top suggests its Scandinavian origin. It is graceful and refined in appearance, betraying no sign of provincialism. Another writing desk of great elegance and rather unique detail in the way of its mechanics, lacquered in green tints and decorated with hunting scenes, was sold at Sotheby's in 1966 (pl. 294). It might well have been of Swedish origin.

Although Russia during the eighteenth century was linked with Sweden both in war and peace, the cultural trends that swept Russia at this time probably emanated from Holland. Peter the Great knew the Netherlands well, and there must have become acquainted with lacquerwork. Certainly when he was in Paris in 1717 he was shown the workshops of Dagly. The czar was impressed by fine craftsmanship and was eager to persuade artisans to come to Russia.[12] He may have been instrumental in introducing the art of lacquering from the Netherlands. In any case, when the summer residence, *Mon Plaisir*,[13] was built at Peterhof in the period 1715–25, it included a hall decorated in the Chinese manner with over ninety lacquer panels (pl. 296). The panels were executed in 1720–22 by two

Russian lacquermasters, Ivan Tikhanov and Perfil Fjodorov, two of their apprentices, and ten other workers. By 1722 the lacquer (gold on black framed in red) was complete, and the Chinese style had been imitated so well that in later years they were believed to be of Far Eastern origin. That they were the work of Russian lacquermasters was not recognized until the building was in the process of restoration following heavy bombing during World War II. Four of the panels remained intact, and from these examples artisans from Palekh, a lacquer center about which we will learn more presently, were able to restore all of the rest.

When Empress Elizabeth ordered the embellishment of the Great Palace at Tsarskoje Tselo in the 1740s, she employed a lacquermaster named Neumeier who made lacquer wall hangings for the great hall with the help of three apprentices. During the reign of Catharine II, around 1760, three lacquermasters, Vlassow, Danilov, and Gerasimov, furnished decorations for the summer palace at Oranienbaum (today Lamasonov). The traditional use of lacquer, at least at the royal court, continued well into the second half of the eighteenth century. In token of this trend are a small desk lacquered in red and black and a small cabinet lacquered in red, both with gilt decorations in the Chinese manner, now in the Hermitage Collection (pls. 297, 298). The desk must have been made after 1705, since the motifs copied are included in a book published in that year. The lacquer produced for the court may have induced some members of the nobility – Prince Scheremetjef, for example – to establish workshops utilizing serfs. We will learn more of these activities in connection with the lacquer industry in nineteenth-century Russia.

If we turn to Spain and Portugal[14] for a very brief survey, we find extant relatively few pieces of domestic lacquer. This is rather surprising when we recall the early relations of both countries with the Far East and the opportunities given their craftsmen to copy oriental imports. The historical circumstances that placed Portugal under Spanish rule from 1581 to 1640 also seem to account for close similarity in cultural and artistic trends within the two countries. Both, of course, were strongly influenced by English style in the eighteenth century – for example, in furniture, the cabriole leg and the use of caning for chairs. Also much in favor were shapes achieved by turning – legs, stretchers, and ornamental detail. Some lacquered cupboards and cabinets dating from 1700 have the traditional bulky shape upon which has been superimposed *chinoiserie* motifs with little or no attempt to adapt them to the furniture – all very much like provincial German furniture of the period (pls. 157, 158). Cabinets made after 1700 are of a lighter fashion, closely resembling the Venetian or English models they undoubtedly follow, although in eccentric outline we recognize their Portuguese origin.

There is one glorious exception – the library of the University of Coimbra in Portugal. The walls, including the shelves, are covered with lacquered panels. Between 1716 and 1723, the lacquermaster Manuel de Silva decorated three halls in green, red, and blue, to which gilt *chinoiserie* motifs were added. The decoration, enriched by all the sculptural elements of the baroque style – festoons, trophies, coats of arms, human figures – create an impression of overwhelming richness in both form and color, although the design of the *chinoiserie* is inept. In spite of its late date, the library is truly representative of the baroque century just ended. The next step in the further development of European lacquer style coincided with the decoration of the library at Coimbra. In Turin, in 1735, Filippo Juvara completed the installation of an entire room of lacquer in the royal palace, an ensemble of such dazzling splendor that it has never been surpassed.

Not every European country has been represented here, mainly because too little is known of special trends or innovation. Although Adolph Feulner[15] published in 1927 his systematic history of furniture, by now a classic, few later studies have been made of lacquer and its development in Europe. We lack a considerable amount of basic local information. The most important recent evidence was presented in *World Furniture*, a collective enterprise published in 1965 and allowing convenient comparative study. In Austria, Switzerland, Spain, Portugal, and the former "crown dominions" of Austria, Hungary and Bohemia, trends in furniture styles developed under the influence of art centers. Much originality in their production is not to be expected, certainly none to influence the evolution of European lacquer in general.

1. For example see *Apollo*, 81 (1965), plate facing p. 80; *World Furniture*, edited by Helena Hayward (London, 1965), plate facing p. 80, nos. 171, 172.
2. Hans Huth, "Zwei Möbelwerkstätten des 17. Jahrhunderts," in *Pantheon* (1929), p. 23.
3. Theodor Lunsingh Scheuerleer, "Jan van Mekeren," in *Oud Holland*, 58 (1941): 178; *Apollo*, 80 (1964): 362; Hayward (ed.), *World Furniture*, plate facing p. 81.
4. Information through the courtesy of Dr. A. Staring, Vorden, Holland.
5. Carl Grommelt and Christine von Mertens, *Das Dohna'sche Schloss Schlobitten in Ostpreussen* (Stuttgart, 1962), p. 195, illustration p. 121.
6. Vente Baron van Heeckeren, *Paul Brandt* (Amsterdam, 1961).
7. R. Edwards, *The Shorter Dictionary of English Furniture* (London, 1964), fig. 161.
8. Ada Polak, "Anglomania in 18th-century Norway," in *Apollo*, 61 (1955): 143–45; Peter Thornton, "Scandinavia," in Hayward (ed.), *World Furniture*, pp. 170, 177.
9. Anneken Pettersen, *Niels Lochstoer* (Drammen, 1934); Robert Kloster, "Et nyfunnet arbeid av Niels Lochstoer," in *Arbok Drammens Museum, 1938–43* (Drammen, 1934), pp. 55–63.
10. Tove Clemmensen, *Moebler* (Copenhagen, 1946), p. 43.
11. Clemmensen, *Moebler*, p. 178.
12. Dubois de Saint Gélis, *Histoire Journaillière de Paris, 1716–17*, edited by Maurice Tourneux (Paris, 1885), pp. 147–49.
13. I. N. Ouchanova, *Laques russes au l'Ermitage* (Leningrad, 1964), p. 6. In Russian, with French and English summaries. Profusely illustrated.
14. Artur de Sandão, *O movel pintado en Portugal* (Oporto, 1966); Grace H. Burr, *Hispanic Furniture* (New York, 1964); Rafael Domenech and L. P. Bueno, *Antique Spanish Furniture* (New York, 1965).
15. Adolf Feulner, *Kunstgeschichte des Möbels* (Berlin, 1927; 3d enlarged edition, 1932).

CHAPTER VIII THE LACQUER INDUSTRY

> We say in this country that there's no accounting for tastes, and it will be many years before mere abstract principles of choice in ornament can become familiar – I will not say to us, but to our children.
> CHARLES DICKENS, 1852

The development of the lacquer trade in the town of Spa in Belgium offers a most informative example of the transition of a craft into an industry, if only on a minor scale. One of the oldest centers of the lacquer trade, which began there before 1600 and continues today, Spa, near Liège, once contained within the Holy Roman Empire, is a French-speaking town in Walloon country, its cultural outlook influenced by the fashions of Paris. The town owes its centuries-old fame to the salutary effect of its waters, discovered early in the fourteenth century. The poet Ronsard sang the praises of Spa, and such men as Allessandro Farnese and King Henri III of France visited there in the sixteenth century. In the seventeenth century Spa became so famous for its curative water and as a popular rendezvous of European aristocracy that the name was brought into English as a synonym for watering place. The same distinguished aggregation of kings and nobles who took the waters at this so-called *Café de l'Europe* also traveled to Venice for the carnival season.

The activities of the *bourdoniers* probably were responsible for the beginnings of the lacquer trade in Spa. The term stems from the same root as the Italian word *bordoni*, the Venetian makers of staffs or staves for pilgrims and travelers bound for the Holy Land or the Orient.[1] Long sticks of this kind, generally with a big oval knob at the head, became popular among the invalids who came to Spa to take the cure, and their popularity soon spread to those who had simply come to Spa to enjoy the season. Nobles and even some of their ladies flourished sticks as a grace note to their costumes. It was a custom in Spa to present a *bourdon* to dignitaries among the guests (the earliest record in the office of the mayor mentions that two sticks were given to a foreign dignitary in 1600). Soon other objects were lacquered and sold as souvenirs of Spa – small bowls, brushes, and bellows to blow away hair powder, among others. In 1684 the Marquis Villaret de Joyeuse was presented with a casket and other objects, and in 1689 gifts presented to another worthy gentleman included a mirror frame, a powder box, and other objects valued at 114 florins. In the same year we learn something of the cost of lacquered objects made in the style of the Far East, although this does not necessarily mean that they were the first in Spa to have been lacquered in this style. Decorative motifs were taken from works by Dutch landscape painters and possibly those genre scenes in the style of Teniers. During the era of Louis XIV, "nymphs" in the manner of Coysevaux or Coustou were favorite patterns.

The earliest printed source which tells about the lacquer made in Spa is a pamphlet by the physician Edmond Nessel, published in 1689.[2] He has this to say: "It is a pleasure to see thousands of niceties [*milles jolités*] made in lacquer, done *à la façon des Indes*." He mentions both flat and raised work, gilt, many colors, the lacquer "highly polished in very solid fashion." The physician specifically mentions work done in mother-of-pearl, ivory, tortoiseshell, English pewter, copper, and silver and refers to the Boulle technique and mother-of-pearl inlay combined with lacquer decoration. Some examples of objects of this type, though dating from the eighteenth century, are exhibited in the museums of Liège and Spa (pls. 299, 300).

In 1729, the ubiquitous Baron Pöllnitz, one of the most inquisitive writers of the eighteenth century, journeyed to Spa and wrote a booklet about the *gallantries* of the watering place.[3] He gives a good deal of information about lacquer and describes some of his visits to various shops in the company of ladies. One lady "bespoke a magnificent equipage for her toilette and a Duchess another one, raised with gold foliage and with arms and cypher on every box. With another complete toilette set all the boxes were of black Japan, with China figures in gold and embossed." Baron Pöllnitz adds: "... my lady ordered one in blue like lapis lazuli with landskips in camayeu." A toilette set such as this cost fourteen Pistoles, One of the ladies could not resist buying a varnished cane decorated with "a little cupid who was spitting a heart near a fire," with the inscription "I make roast meat of 'em."

Baron Pöllnitz admired the way the lacquermasters "mimick Japan so exactly that it is difficult to find the difference." The miniatures "show their beauty and coloring through the varnish as if they were painted on vellum. We saw a table for fifteen Pistoles which had but fourteen pictures out of Ovid's Metamorphoses ... we found a hundred sorts of pretty items such as *quadrillé* boxes [chip containers], watch cases, dessert trays, canes, tobacco boxes ... of all prices according to the work and the workmen ... all are not equally good. The Xhrouets [or Chrouets] ... were excelling in fable and history ... Le Loup in landskip and perspective ... Dagly at the 'White Pigeon' made the best varnish ... and had a special taste for fruits and flowers, whether flat or embossed. As these knick-knacks are the only things manufactured at Spa everybody works at this business that does not let lodgings, we went to a dozen of these shops."

A master not mentioned by Pöllnitz was Vincent Rousseau (1676–1720), who evidently specialized in pastoral scenes on the lacquered boxes he signed (pl. 302). Pöllnitz and his friends also bought "toys" for a lottery they planned to hold to please the ladies. They selected pin boxes, scissor and tweezer cases, necklaces, work baskets; the chief prize was to be a complete set of toilette boxes (pl. 305).

In another booklet, *Amusements d'Aix-la-Chapelle*, Baron Pöllnitz relates that this not-quite-so-fashionable watering place was an outlet for the lacquerwork produced at Spa. A generation later, J. P. de Limbourg[4] published *New Amusements of the German Spa* and presented a picture of the lacquer trade very much as described by Pöllnitz. The artisans of Spa had begun to decorate small pieces of furniture (pl. 303) – tables, corner cupboards to hang on walls, and candlestands. They utilized "Japan ink on white ground, leaf gold on brass and copper, blue, yellow, black, and green, in imitation of China or shell work [perhaps meaning tortoiseshell] with close copies of nature." There were "historical subjects, the prospects about Spa ... whatever a purchaser will pitch upon or require ... the varnish ... gives a peculiar lustre ... nothing can look more genteel." The price for a "toilette box on black ground, designs in relievo or embossed work, gilt with coat of arms," was 10 louis d'or, another on green ground and "very gay" was only 6 louis d'or, and a quadrille box was priced at 1 louis. One such toilette box, decorated with biblical scenes, which the master would not part with under 100 ducats, probably did not sell, as only "ideas of a gayer nature would gratify the curiosity of the fairer sex." A speciality of Spa heretofore unmentioned was a small container called a *bergamotte* in which visitors carried anise or fennel seed as a costive agent against the savage effects of the water. A similar container for orange blossoms was called an *orangette*. These containers were decorated and lacquered with all kinds of motifs among which the *scènes galantes* were not in the minority. With the growth of the lacquer trade and the related *tabletiers* (makers of knickknacks) and *toilettiers* (makers of toilette boxes), there came a need for such craftsmen as turners and cabinetmakers. During the season, some five hundred or six hundred workers were kept busy (pls. 304–306).

The basic wood used for items of furniture was from the plane tree, the alder or linden. After it was shaped, it was soaked in water from the Pouhon spring, reputed to be rich in tannin, which gave the wood a brownish color and was said to fortify it against worms. No undercoating was applied, but the ground colors were solved in glue. After the decoration had been applied with gouache colors, the piece was lacquered with sandarac and polished a number of times.

The fame of the lacquer trade at Spa spread beyond the limits of the city, and a number of lacquermasters were called to serve at various courts. In the service of Clemens August, Elector of Cologne, was Renier Roidkin (after 1722 and before 1741, when he died at his home in Spa), who always signed as *dessinateur et peintre en vernis*.[5] Although none of his lacquer is known today, it is likely that he did such work in some of the many establishments of the prince. Clemens August visited Spa many times, and a probable souvenir of a summer's stay was a *boîte de Spa* decorated with the electors's coat of arms (pl. 301).

In 1763 the Margrave of Bayreuth called one of the Xhrouets to his residence. Another member of the family, Lambert Xhrouet, a master turner, was asked to teach his trade to the Emperor Francis I, who, like other members of the nobility, found turning to be a genteel hobby. A lacquermaster, Jean Hubert Tahan (1777–1843), deserted the trade to join the painter Jacques Louis David during his exile in Brussels. Toward the end of the eighteenth century, a Scots nobleman persuaded Vincent Brixhe (b. 1756), a lacquermaster of Spa, to establish a shop in Scotland. He was followed by one H. Henrard, who later returned to Spa. About these masters who settled at Mauchline and Cumnock in Ayrshire more will be said later.

The French Revolution and the wars that followed did much to damage Spa and its lacquer industry. After 1815, the lacquer industry revived and flourished throughout the century and to some extent helped to restore the international fame of the watering place. George Sand, while living in Paris, tried her hand at decorating boxes from Spa. She mentioned painting "flowers and birds in microscopic size."

At the London Exhibition of 1851 the industry had a chance to display its products, but there was a noticeable decline in interest, and by 1898 Albin Body, chronicler of the lacquer trade, could write that soon the once famous trade would be nothing more than *une douce reminiscence.*[6] In more recent years, encouraged locally by a growing interest in the traditions of the past, there has been a revival of the trade in Spa. Designs have been produced which challenge the more conservative style, and *bôites de Spa* are once more for sale in the town.

"Pontypool" was once a generic term for japanned tinware, a product which won customers for English goods throughout the civilized world. Although Pontypool was probably not the first place in England to produce lacquered tinware, it was certainly the first to manufacture japanware of excellent quality on a sound commercial basis. With the rising demand for these goods, the japanning industry spread to Usk, Birmingham, Wolverhampton, and Bilston.[7]

There were no secrets in the manufacture of japanned tinware as there had been in the closely guarded recipes of the old lacquermasters. To be sure, the manufacturers at Pontypool guarded their processes, but these were the result of technical expertise and accessible to anyone interested in seeking them out. Unquestionably the new technological information was based on the experience of generations of craftsmen, but added to it was knowledge of chemical reactions, the result of research and experimentation. In addition, progressive ideas in management made production more economical. The new system of production evolved through a number of experimental stages until it, too, became more efficient. The early craftsmen produced lacquerwork to suit the tastes and desires of individual customers, but toward the end of the eighteenth century lacquerware, first of tin and later of papier-mâché, was manufactured with the idea of satisfying a market, wherever that market could be developed.

Early in the eighteenth century and for decades thereafter there was little competition between the two types of producers as long as their merchandise went into the hands of two distinctly different kinds of customers. A lady of quality would always prefer her finely lacquered wooden toilette set to the sober Pontypool tins, but the average man and woman in England or a farmer in the British colonies were glad to have the opportunity to buy inexpensive japanned tinware which would neither chip nor rust and was manufactured to fill a variety of needs. For such customers there was little reason to give articles a stylish appearance, still less a need for decorative *chinoiserie*. But by mid-century a greater variety of japanned ware was available, and both decoration and workmanship steadily improved. Soon Birmingham and other centers offered the novelty of papier-mâché as a substitute for tin. This indeed was a revolution, the effect of which was roughly comparable to that which followed the development of aluminium as a substitute for tin and ironware. Papier-mâché because fashionable not only because it was a novelty but also, in its early stage, because *chinoiserie* was the favored decoration. Toward the end of the eighteenth century the lacquermaster found his craft threatened by the growing industry. With japanned tin and later papier-mâché being gradually adopted by the fashionable world, and with light and elegantly fashioned papier-mâché chairs and tables substituted for those of wood, the battle for the market was joined.

There are good reasons why the japanning industry, like the japanners' craft, began in England at the time it did. Toward the end of the seventeenth century there was an urge among artisans to introduce new techniques or combine old ones to create new effects based on experiment rather than theory. In England this new movement was furthered by the formation of the Royal Society which developed out of the circle of Robert Boyle and his friends. It was typical of the English frame of mind that when Johann Joachim Becher, one of the most ingenious and creative men of the century, fled to England in 1681 because he had fallen into disgrace at court in Vienna, he was quickly invited to inform the king about his successful experiments in producing pitch and tar from coal. In England, Thomas Algood, in his time called a "projecting genius," had the same kind of creative and inquiring mind. Because he came from a Quaker family persecuted in Northamptonshire around 1680, Algood moved to Pontypool in Monmouthshire where Quakers were accepted. Undoubtedly he was also attracted by the availability of coal and iron in that section of Wales so that he might continue experimenting with those elements. The most important iron mill in the region was owned by the Hanbury family. Here Algood was employed as a kind of overseer. Originally the mill produced sheet iron, but after 1697 the mill fabricated both iron and tin sheets which were cheaper to produce, thinner, smoother, and more pliable than similar products from Saxony which hitherto had monopolized the market.

Such progress was probably due to knowledge gathered in 1666 by a small group of men led by Andrew Yarrenton who had been sent to Saxony by local mill owners who wanted them to ferret out the secrets of the Saxon iron mills and learn why they were so outstanding. John Hanbury, the owner of the mill at Pontypool, must have been a man of progressive character, evidenced by his success in making use of the information obtained by Yarrenton and his companions. Hanbury also must have encouraged Algood in his research, for he was undoubtedly eager to find a finish both protective and attractive for the iron sheets he produced.

Algood's work probably centered on ways in which coal could be made more useful as a combustion material and whether it might prove valuable for purposes other than fuel. It was years before he could report results, but eventually he achieved success. Whether Algood was able to extract oil suitable for lacquering from coal or coal shale remains an open question. Possibly he did find a substance, like a lacquer, which would serve to protect iron. All we know of this comes from a report obtained from the Algood family by W. Coxe, published in 1801, which asserts that Thomas Algood "made various experiments to extract coperas and oil from coal and finally invented the method of lacquering iron plates with a brilliant varnish.[8]

Originally the mill owner at Pontipool used linseed oil as the basis for lacquer. This was no novelty, for linseed oil had been used elsewhere and earlier and the process had been published. But the results of this and another method, using a combination of shellac or sandarac and spirits of wine, were not encouraging: the lacquer produced was neither durable nor effective when applied to metal, one reason being that only very weak stoving was utilized. What made Algood's method spectacular was that it produced a completely black varnish of extraordinary luster and great durability, resistant to rust, acid, and rough treatment. To achieve these qualities, a viscuous, quick-drying oil—that of Algood's invention?—was used in combination with heated raw linseed oil. This combination was oxydized by the addition of umber and litharge, and the black luster was achieved by introducing asphaltum. The black lacquer was coated several times and rubbed down after each stoving.

Another type of varnish produced was transparent and could be colored with pigment, usually vermilion or crimson, more rarely blue. A color effect typical of Pontypool but later much imitated was a tortoiseshell ground made by placing irregular pieces of silver foil under brown lacquer, thus giving it the appearance of gold. The brilliance of Algood's lacquer and its durability were achieved by the process of accurate firing, exposing the layers of lacquer to heat of varying degrees, and doing this two or three times for a certain period. This precisely timed procedure apparently was the secret of Pontypool.

Thomas Algood, who died in 1716, did not live long enough to see the practical results of his achievements, but in the years following his death the japanware factory established by his son, Edward, and his grandson, Thomas, became a most successful business. By 1732 their products must have been of rather good quality. Sir Charles Hanbury-Williams, a son of John Hanbury, was able to tell his wife, "Algood has found a new way of japanning which I think is so beautiful that I'll send you a couple of pieces of it."[9] Sir Charles, a diplomat, engaged in correspondence with Catherine the Great before she became empress of Russia. It is not inconceivable that the large group of Pontypool japannedware reported to be in the Hermitage Collection may have been a gift from Sir Charles to Catherine.

In 1763, perhaps because of family strife, the business was broken up and some of the family moved to Usk, a few miles from Pontypool, to start a new factory. At first there was strong rivalry between the two establishments, but in time it subsided. There is no way of distinguishing between the early production of the two plants. Only after the turn of the century do some individual marks from the Usk plant come to light. For instance, after 1810 the "stormont" pattern is frequently used at Usk to fill the center of trays—the name is said to have been derived from that of a statesman of the time known for his meandering speeches. The pattern corresponds to the "seaweed" decoration used in Worcester porcelain and Staffordshire earthenware. An Usk signature shows the name of Pyrke in raised fashion, and was used by John Pyrke when he owned the plant in the period 1814–26 (pl. 311). We find his signature on some sober crimson pieces now in the museum at Cardiff, but very likely only the lacquer was applied at Usk.

The Pontypool firm continued in operation until 1820 when the last owner, William Algood, removed to the United States. The plant at Usk passed out of the hands of the Algood family in 1791 and was carried on under different owners until 1870.

The fact that Pontypool has become the generic term for practically anything in tinware produced in Monmouthshire or in and around Birmingham makes it extremely difficult to distinguish between the various makes. If anything can characterize the wares from Pontypool and Usk it is simplicity, high quality of workmanship, and generally very high gloss. The early decoration is usually modest and never exaggerated, and the construction extremely solid. Large trays were made of sturdy black plate, while household items of smaller size were made of thin tin plate. Often the tortoiseshell pattern was applied to the underground, or it was colored in maroon or scarlet. An advertisement of the period describes some of the goods produced around 1765: "waiters" (bread baskets), tea kettles, coffee pots and urns, lamps, tea caddies, toast racks, chafing dishes, snuffboxes and other boxes, Dutch ovens, candlesticks, clock faces, and apparently even cut-outs to be placed in fireplace openings. The factories also decorated other objects suitable for japanning brought in by customers. That advertisements directed at "captains of ships" spoke of advantageous terms for purchases for export suggests that Pontypool merchandise was indeed exported in quantity. Philadelphia newspapers carried advertisements for the wares from Pontypool, and large shipments of snuffboxes were sent to Holland. Yet the often-told story that Dutch tinware was shipped to Pontypool to be japanned can hardly be correct; the reverse rather is true – japanned wares were exported to Holland and there sold as "Wallisch Lacwerk."

According to Richard Pockocke, writing in 1756, Pontypool decorated salvers with "China landscapes and figures in gold only, and not with colouring as at Birmingham." And yet in the same period we know that Benjamin Barker painted flower pieces for Pontypool trays in the manner of the Dutch painter Jan van Huysum. For a short time his son, Thomas Barker (1769–1847), also joined the firm, but about 1780 he moved to Bath and became known as "Barker of Bath." Still later he published designs in lithography to be used as patterns for decorations and presumably also for japanning.[10] Concerning the wares of Pontypool, a local poet was moved to celebrate in this fashion:[11]

> Figures gay the polish'd black adorn
> The swelling urn its lovely blue displays
> And beauteous tortoise shells are viewed on trays
> O'er brilliant line your pencils oft were wont
> To glide from narrow crimson to Stormont

Wherever possible, Pontypool wares of tin or papier-mâché were adapted from pieces produced from other materials – wooden tea caddies and knife boxes or tea kettles and urns modeled after silver patterns (pls. 307, 309, 312). The decoration of trays sometimes followed the patterns of Staffordshire earthenware or Derby porcelain. Among the most popular items were baskets (pl. 310), pin trays (pl. 317), and round trays, from 8 to 24 inches in diameter (pls. 315, 316). "Waiters" (pl. 314, 318) were either oblong, octagonal, or oval, and the rims of the trays, usually bent out at a 45° angle, were hand-punched with several rows of holes, lozenge-shaped or square, with the joints of the rims folded over and riveted (pl. 310). Later in the nineteenth century, a less-expensive method was devised, with rims stamped and soldered, not riveted (pl. 314). Chestnut "vases" or urns, extremely popular in France, were made with a somewhat elongated body, the finial ending in an acorn. Two such urns now in the museum in Cardiff are decorated with insects and flowers in natural colors (pl. 313). French imitations of somewhat the same shape are often misrepresented as products of Pontypool. Other items easily mistaken for Pontypool. wares are candlesticks shaped like Corinthian columns; or they may be claimed to be French *tôle* pieces.

In the Midlands, Bilston must be named as the first center for japanned ware, though on scant evidence. Between 1709 and 1719 three japanners were entered in the parish lists. Since we know that sheet iron was produced nearby, it is possible that these men produced some kind of tinware, probably of the crudest kind, with inadequate shellac or sandarac varnish applied before stoving. The only evidence for this supposition is the record of an accident in 1754, when a japanner was burned in his stove room.

In 1781 the Bilston directory listed a number of japanners in the town, and some of these men had another trade as well. In any case, japanning on tin cannot have been very remunerative at that time. Whatever trade there was only supplemented the production of the factories in Birmingham and Wolverhampton. On its own, Bilston probably would not have prospered. No pieces produced in Bilston have been identified, and we must presume that they were cheaply made. Perhaps because or in spite of this, Bilston's exports grew in time and customers were found as far afield as America, Spain, and Russia. It has been suggested that Bilston products, because of their poor quality, may now be regarded as popular "homemade" wares in some of the countries to which they were exported. Tea caddies, coal scuttles, trays, and boxes were among Bilston's stock in trade. In 1866, when ten factories employed some 400 workers, some two thousand tea caddies were produced in a single week, and the cheapest tray (12×30 inches) cost eight shillings and sixpence per dozen.[12]

Wolverhampton, like Bilston, was primarily involved in agricultural activities, although some farmers worked in the iron forges during the winter months. Japanning probably began some time after 1750 when the production of simple articles like buckles, hinges, and locks was transferred from Birmingham when the workers in that city became involved in the fabrication of more remunerative objects. In the early days japanning in Wolverhampton was only a sideline, and those working in this trade also followed other callings. Unlike Bilston, Wolverhampton soon must have begun to specialize in more important goods of better quality and higher value. Wolverhampton was known for the excellence of its japannedware both in the way of its material and its tasteful decoration. After 1810, the manufacturers of the town excelled in papier-mâché goods.

William Pitt remarked in 1817 that "there was a great and permanent demand both for home consumption and foreign supply of Wolverhampton japanned wares." Hundreds of women and children were busy making "the most elegant and expensive tea trays, both paper and iron, plate warmers, tea and coffee pots, caddies, inkstands, etc."[13] Among the earliest firms was that of Taylor and Jones, in 1770 occupying Old Hall, an ancient building in the town, and that of Barney and Ryton, a firm that succeeded to Taylor and Jones in 1787. Soon after 1810, papier-mâché was introduced. Some firms only manufactured blanks which were decorated in other shops or by independent artists who otherwise would not have had a chance to work in this field. One of the artists known to have worked at Old Hall was Edward Bird (1722–1819), who excelled in finely painted bouquets of flowers especially for trays. Following his father, Benjamin Walton, who had been in business with Ryton and later alone until the end of the 1840s, his son established the firm of F. Walton which remained in business from 1850 to 1880, when even the old Birmingham firms could no longer carry on. During the peak of activities, Walton employed some six hundred workers. As usual, trays as well as vases were the mainstay of production. A typical scheme of decoration in this period was an arrangement of flowers on a bronze stippled background. Another firm that managed to remain in business through the second half of the nineteenth century was that established by Edward and Richard Perry (1829–90) at Old Hall, the center of the lacquer business in Wolverhampton.

Some firms made tinware as well as papier-mâché goods. Until 1840 tin shapes were cut by hand; stamping became more common during the 1860s, although it cheapened the tinware. One result was that papier-mâché goods became more fashionable and were decorated in a more elegant manner. Among the goods made at Wolverhampton were waiters and small trays, vases, inkstands, sugar boxes, and the like (pl. 324).

Before going on to consider Birmingham, the center of the English lacquer industry, it may be of interest to mention the production of lacquer in three remote villages in Scotland, developed quite independently of English lacquer through the initiative and benevolence of a great philanthropist, Francis, Lord Gardenstone.[14] Members of the aristocracy often sought to encourage cottage industries to help poor country families make a better living. Lord Gardenstone, a so-called law lord, meaning judge, traveled abroad in 1787 and was impressed by the lacquer workshops at Chantilly established by the Duc de Bourbon Condé. When he reached Spa, he conceived the idea of hiring a lacquermaster to establish a shop at Lawrencekirk in Kincardineshire where Lord Gardenstone owned estates. The lacquermaster he approached was Vincent Brixhe (b. 1756), who for twenty years had worked with Antoine Lelou, one of the best known artisans in Spa whose speciality it was to decorate his work with landscapes. Brixhe was to receive thirty pounds for three years and was assured five guineas for every apprentice he hired. All of his work was to be at the disposal of Lord Gardenstone, who would furnish all materials. If Brixhe wished to stay on after three years he was welcome to do so and would receive a house free of rent for his lifetime. So successful was the arrangement that in 1791 Brixhe agreed to stay on. He was assisted by a compatriot from Spa, H. Henrard, who later returned home. As an aide to Brixhe, Lord Gardenstone hired a joiner, Charles Stiven, who had become known for the snuffboxes he whittled out of the solid. They were distinguished by "invisible" hinges cut out of lid and box, with rolls revolving around a wood or brass pin. Perhaps under the guidance of Brixhe, Stiven's son Jonathan was trained to decorate these boxes. Old Stiven, who was also a coachman, sold his boxes at coach stops.

By 1800 the fledgling industry was so successful that additional shops were opened at Cumnock and Mauchline in Ayrshire (pls. 308 a–d). In a description of the county published in 1811, the snuffboxes produced there were said to be fashioned of plane or American maple, curved to fit the pocket, approximately two inches square and half an inch deep, tinplated inside. They sold for two guineas and were decorated with "Egyptian, Roman or Chinese figures and other ingenious devices."[15] A later account, in 1837, suggests how the business had grown. Now there were sets of artists making the boxes while others decorated them, and women and children did the varnishing and polishing. If spirits of wine were used, each box was given thirty coats of varnish; if, as was more usual, copal was used, each box needed only fifteen coats of varnish and dried in a shorter time.

In 1825, the log of a plane tree, purchased for twenty-five shillings, was estimated to enable the production of articles worth three thousand pounds. In the period 1820–30, box makers easily earned a guinea a week, scene painters two guineas a week, varnishers twelve shillings a week, and children two shillings a week. There was hardly a family in the district that did not have at least one member working in the industry. Some of the family names are preserved: Chrichton, Crawford, Lammie, Drummond, and Buchanan. The majority of articles produced in the three villages were sold in London and Glasgow. The very finest boxes were sold for as much as seven pounds. Less-expensive boxes, selling for a guinea, were sold at the mailcoach stop at Cumnock. With the decline in the use of snuff, fewer boxes were produced in the 1830s.

Snuffboxes produced at Cumnock and Mauchline, like those at Lawrencekirk and Spa, were decorated with landscapes, genre scenes, and cats and rats (pl. 308 d). In addition there were local motifs – shooting and hunting scenes, horses, coaches, and copies of popular paintings first made by hand and later by transfer lithography. In Ayrshire, the land of Robert Burns, scenes illustrating his poems were popular. One such, based on the rousing ballad "Willie brewed a peck o' maut [malt]," depicted the consequences of overindulgence (pl. 308 b). Among those who painted in Cumnock were Daniel MacNeed, Horatio McCulloch, and William Leighton Leitch, all active in the 1820s. A sepia drawing by Leitch of Holford Bridge is typical of their work (fig. 16). Snuffboxes from Scotland were known on the continent; the firm of Alexander Fleck in Dresden exhibited some snuffboxes "in the Scottish manner" at an industrial exhibition in Mainz in 1842.

Vine leaves and grape leaves were popular patterns for the sides of boxes or as a background, as were undulating lines. Prior to 1837, a machine was designed to make checked patterns, and in turn this led to the use of tartans as background decoration. The use of tartans may have started in Mauchline where John Smith and his family were prominent manufacturers. Two members of the family, William and Andrew, published a guide to "authentic tartans" in 1850. John Smith himself was appointed furnisher to the king and was permitted to use the stamp "Smith, Mauchline. Manufacturer to His Majesty. Warranted out of the Solid" (pl. 308 c). A box of this make, showing an officer of the dragoons on horseback, signed I. Patterson, Cumnock, fecit, 1827, though made in Mauchline, is illustrated (pl. 308 a). When snuff-taking went out of fashion around 1840, the industry managed to survive by producing various trinkets including cosmetic jars, thread winders, brooches with tartan decoration, and tea caddies. The firm of Smith remained in business into the twentieth century and was dissolved only in 1937. Difficult as it is to distinguish the works produced in Mauchline, Cumnock, and Lawrencekirk unless they are marked in some way, they do differ from articles made in Wales, the Midlands, and Birmingham.

From its beginnings before the middle of the eighteenth century, japanning has been an important part of the metal industry in Birmingham. The transformation of small metal workshops into big establishments came quickly. For example, the estate of the owner of the earliest factory we know, John Taylor, who died in 1775, was valued at more than two hundred thousand pounds. To Taylor the city owed the introduction of gilt buttons, japanned and gilt snuffboxes, and enameling. Taylor charged as much as eighty guineas for a fine snuffbox and specialized in manufacturing gilt buttons at the rate of eight hundred per week. He was wise enough to avoid direct competition with one of the most successful manufacturers of the time, John Baskerville (1702–1775), who died in the same year as Taylor (pl. 319).

Baskerville is chiefly remembered today for his ability as a printer and for the type style he devised. A former stonecutter and writing master, Baskerville's interest in anything having to do with printing or lettering never waned. This great interest and the fascination he found in solving difficult technical problems led him to devote much of his energy to japanning and related problems in addition to the production of type fonts, paper, and ink. Baskerville began production of japanned tinware some time after 1740. In 1742 he was given a patent for mechanizing the production of sheet iron goods. Soon he was able to offer very thin sheet iron products lacquered and polished to a high gloss with a surface simulating mahogany veneer. According to its maker, sheet iron treated in this fashion would "not be impaired in several ages." It was used as a substitute for wooden picture frames, fronts of cabinets, and wainscoting. Sheets of this kind were probably used in decorating Baskerville's own carriage, considered "the pattern card of his trade." Each of its panels was decorated with a different picture, and the carriage was drawn by a stately pair of cream-colored horses.[16]

It is likely that Baskerville was the first in Birmingham to develop the mechanics of using papier-mâché as a substitute for tin. Since he made his own paper for printing and was constantly experimenting with paper, Baskerville had at hand the materials with which to produce papier-mâché. It seems only logical to suppose that he would envision papier-mâché built up of sheets pasted together into the required thickness rather than using pulp, a cheap and unreliable substitute. The Baskerville method was much like that of the Martins in Paris, whose methods could not have remained secret for long. Baskerville probably produced his first samples around 1750; unfortunately, none survive or have been recognized. According to a contemporary, Samuel Derrick, who visited Baskerville in 1760, he was then producing "candlestick stands, salvers, waiters, bread baskets, tea boards" – in short, articles of small or medium size. Considering the exquisite taste Baskerville showed in his printing work, we can assume that his japanned ware was impeccable in both quality and decoration. It is quite possible that this high standard obliged other Birmingham manufacturers to emulate him in order to compete.

Unaware of Baskerville's death in 1775, the German traveler Georg Christoph Lichtenberg, a professor of science at Göttingen, made a trip to Birmingham to become acquainted with its industrial development. In a letter to Dietrich, his publisher in Göttingen, Lichtenberg described in most enthusiastic terms the welcome he received from Baskerville's widow. Dressed in black silk, she received him most graciously: "... she lives in a splendid house next to the plant. She showed me the pleasure grounds, the herb garden, with beautiful walks between trees and hedges. The rooms are furnished in the fine taste of those people who instead of inheriting their wealth have earned it on their own."[17] The visitor goes on to describe the mechanics of papermaking; he was especially impressed by the way paper could be smoothed to order in various subtle degrees. Since Lichtenberg does not report on visits to lacquer shops, it seems likely that toward the end of his career Baskerville's chief interest lay in the printing business. Lichtenberg also visited establishments owned by Mathias Boulton and Henry Clay and greatly admired the spirit of these enterprising businessmen, typical of the period when British goods dominated the world market. What a difference there was between this flourishing industry and the struggles of japanners in London who sought to make a living!

A contemporary of Taylor and Baskerville, Stephen Bedford became one of the leading japanners in Birmingham. He is first mentioned by name in 1750 and his death is recorded in 1781. Like Baskerville, he attempted to improve mechanical methods, especially for the reproduction of ornamental designs, for which he received a patent in 1759. The idea of using some kind of mechanical transfer process was in the air at the time; Battersea had used it for enameling since 1753, just as Bow and Worcester, so close to Birmingham, had employed it for porcelain since 1756. In 1763 Bedford received an award given by the Society of Arts for the production of a "transparent and colorless varnish equal in all respects to that of 'Martins at Paris.'" This wording is revealing, for it indicates that hitherto there could not have been a varnish in England equal to that of the Martins. As for the durability of Bedford's varnish, Dossie mentions that Bedford produced some beautiful pieces of japanned ware but that his varnish was not as durable as the French.[18] On the other hand, it is known that French japannedware did sometimes flake, so Dossie's statement is to be questioned. Like Baskerville's production, Bedford's has remained unidentified.

Upon the death of Taylor and Baskerville, Henry Clay became the most prominent figure in the japanning trade in Birmingham. Apprenticed to Baskerville, he learned the making of papier-mâché. Later, Clay improved it, making it more easily workable as well as more durable. In 1772 he obtained a patent to manufacture a papier-mâché that could be sawed, mitered, and dovetailed just like wood. This, of course, opened the way to its use in making complete pieces of furniture. For decoration Clay introduced mother-of-pearl in 1778. The Birmingham directory of 1781 proudly states that several pieces of Clay's superb furniture adorned the royal residence.[19] And George III was "happy in every opportunity of expressing his utmost approbation and of giving his countenance to the undertaking." In 1793 Clay informed the king of "a new material for painting upon, infinitely superior to any substance hitherto used for its surface and durability." The reference probably is to papier-mâché furniture decorated with copies of famous oil paintings (such furniture was made after 1793). It is known that Clay ordered copies of paintings by Guido Reni and other artists (pls. 319, 320, 321), and lacquered copies were used to decorate a sedan chair presented to Queen Charlotte. Clay was the first to produce such large papier-mâché pieces as tables, cabinets, panels for doors and sedan chairs, toilette tables, and smaller pieces.

In 1775 Lichtenberg was among the prominent individuals who visited Clay. He wrote a friend in Germany, "I saw Clay's manufacture. Here most excellent lacquered tinware is made which is now imitated in Brunswick [by Stobwasser], also paper boxes, caddies, panels for coaches and sedan chairs, so you see that people in London now drive in paper coaches. Coffee trays and all sorts of vessels are made and decorated in black with orange color figures in the manner of Etrurian vases – they are beautiful beyond words. A tea caddie costs 3 guineas, – from here I went to Mr. Baskerville . . ."[20] Later, Lichten-

1

2

3

4

1. Ornamental engraving by Virgil Solis, Nürnberg, about 1550
2. Venetian lady at her toilet, woodcut, Venice, 1522
3., 4. Ornamental engravings by Jacques Androuet I. Ducerceau, Paris, about 1540

5 a

5 b

5 c

5 d

5 e

5 f

5 g

5 a. Orientals and Europeans, print, Dutch (?), end of seventeenth century
5 b. Lacquerworkers, print, after S. de Vries, 1682
5 c. *Chinoiserie*, print, Nürnberg, early eighteenth century
5 d., e. *Chinoiseries*, prints, Amsterdam, about 1707
5 f., g. *Chinoiseries*, prints, Nürnberg, eighteenth century

6 a

6 b

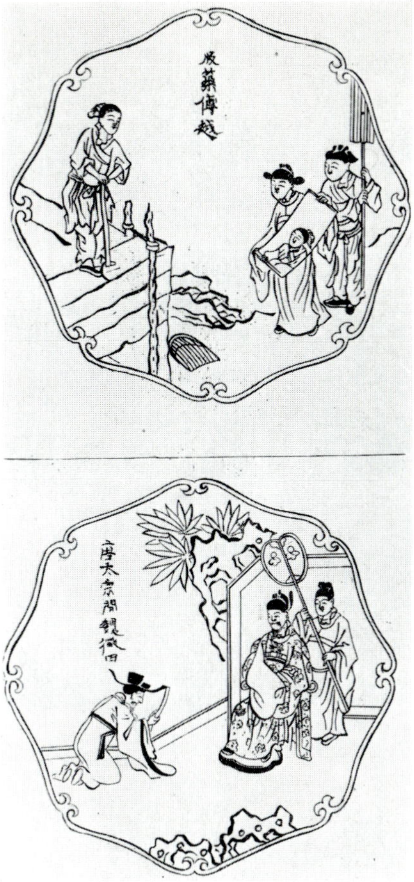

6 d

6 c

6 e

6 a. Design for *chinoiserie*, Dutch (?), late seventeenth century
6 b., c. *Chinoiseries*, prints, Amsterdam, about 1725–30
6 d. *Chinoiseries*, prints, Amsterdam, 1702
6 e. *Chinoiserie*, print, Amsterdam, 1702

7 a

7 d

7 b

7 c

8

7a., b., c. *Chinoiseries*, prints, London, 1688
7d. Ornamental engravings, Paris, 1762
8. *Chinoiserie*, print, Italian (?), eighteenth century

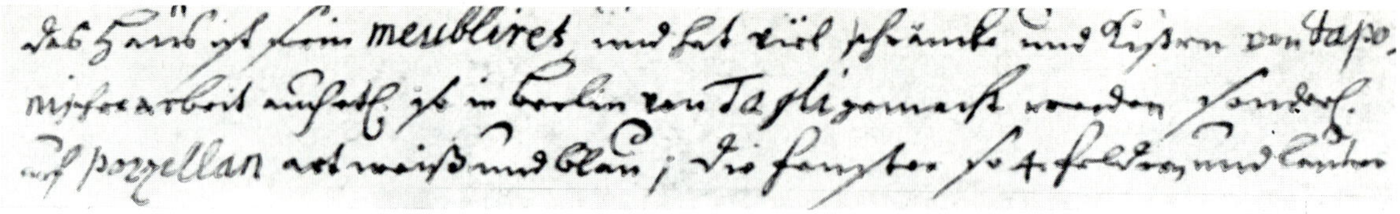

das Haus ist schön meubliret und hat viel schränke und tischen von tape-
zierarbeit [illegible] ist in berlin von [illegible] gemacht worden sonderl.
auf porzellan art weiss und blau; die fenster [illegible] 4 felder und lanter

9 a

9 b

10 a

10 b

9 a. Passage from diary kept by Christoph Pitzler concerning Dagly, 1694
9 b. Lady playing harpsichord, print, Paris, 1688
10 a., b. Engraved designs for lacquerwork, Berlin, about 1710

11

12

11. Design for harpsichord lid, Paris, about 1715
12. Design for harpsichord lid, Antoine Watteau, about 1708
13 a., b. Prints for use in lacca povera work, mid-eighteenth century, Italy

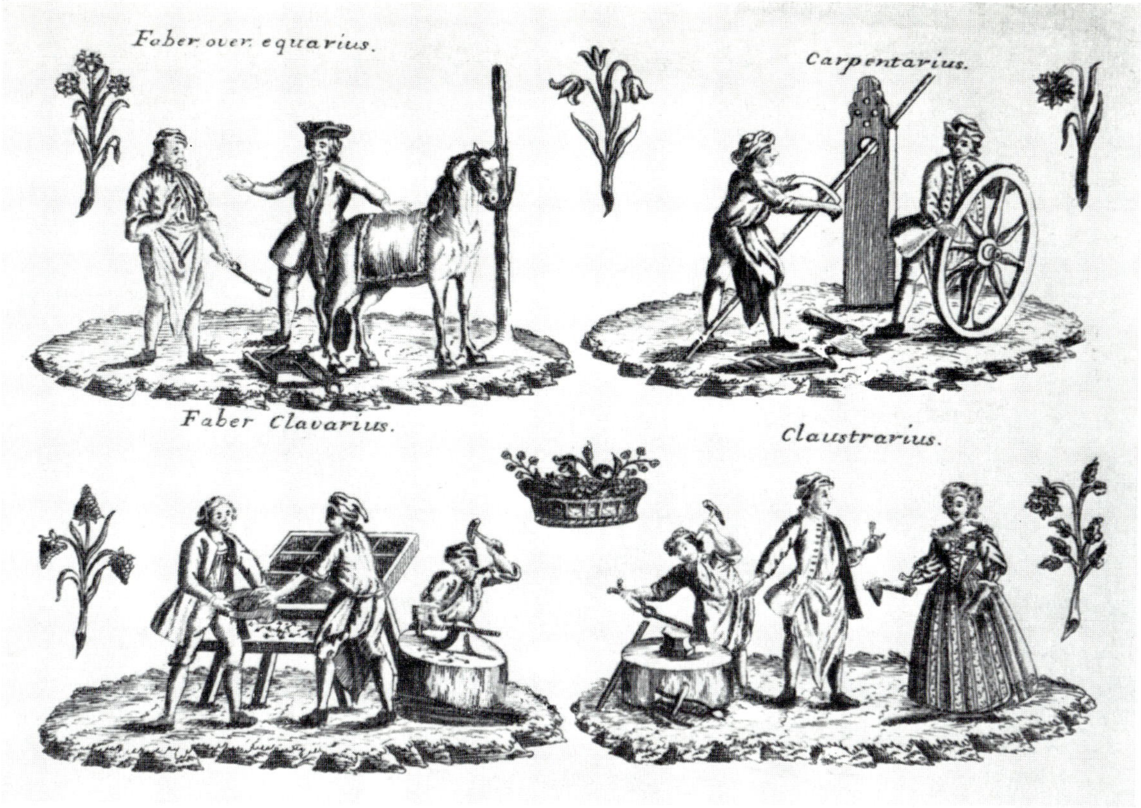

Faber over. equarius.
Carpentarius.
Faber Clavarius.
Claustrarius.

13 a

13 b

14

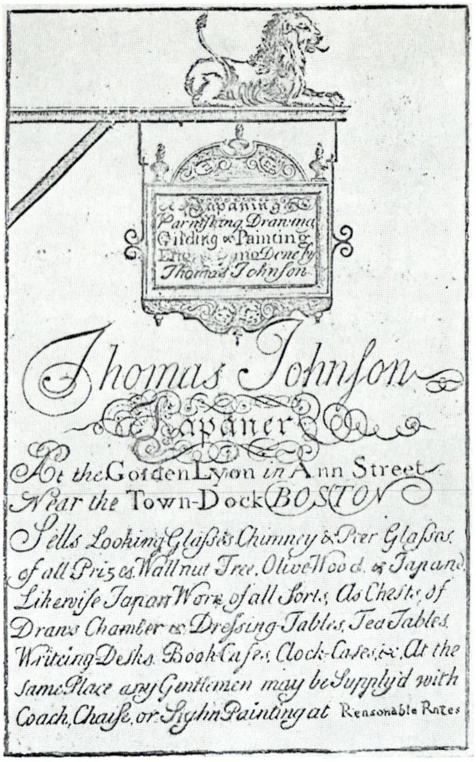

15

14. Trade card, Daniel Mills, japanner, London, mid-eighteenth century
15. Trade card, Thomas Johnson, japanner, Boston, 1932

16. "Holford Bridge," sepia sketch by W. L. Leitch, Cumnock (?), about 1820

Zu den vorzüglichsten, anderwärts kaum bekannten Leistungen in Papiermaché gehören diejenigen, welche wir auf dieser Seite abbilden. Sie sind Erzeugnisse des Etablissements von JOHN

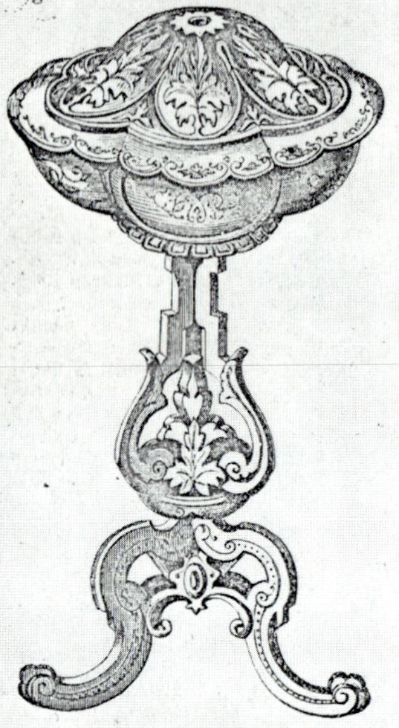

ARBEITSTISCHCHEN.

BETTRIDGE AND Co. (früher Jennings and Bettridge) in BIRMINGHAM, welches seit Beginn dieses Jahrhunderts den alten Ruf der Stadt aufrecht erhalten hat, die bekanntlich mit den Artikeln aus diesem

THEEBRET.

Material die halbe Welt versorgt. Aus der überaus zahlreichen Collection des genannten Hauses greifen wir zunächst heraus ein Damenarbeitstischchen von höchst zierlicher Form und praktischer Einrichtung, elegant modellirt und reich geschmückt. Interessanter ist noch das darunter abgebildete Theebret; dergleichen werden in allen Grössen und Formen angefertigt und gehen von Birmingham aus zu Hunderttausenden in die ganze theetrinkende Welt. Zwei Verzierungen, die sich

ORNAMENT.

auf Wandgetäfel, Füllungen u. s. w. anbringen lassen, nur erwähnend, kommen wir nunmehr zu dem Hauptstück der Ausstellung des Etablissements, das geeignet ist, allgemeine Aufmerksamkeit zu fesseln. Es ist dies eine Bettstelle in überaus prächtiger Ausführung, mit Ausnahme des nothwendigen Gerüstes ganz und gar in Papiermaché ausgeführt. Die geschmackvolle Anordnung ist ebenso bewundernswürdig wie die Trefflichkeit des Materials, die Schärfe der Ausprägung und Contouren aller Ornamente. Bekanntlich wird das gewöhnliche Papiermaché dargestellt durch

WANDVERZIERUNG.

Kochen von Papier in Wasser und Versetzung des entstandenen Breies mit Gummi- oder Leimlösung. Die dickliche Masse wird in hölzerne mit Oel ausgestrichene Formen gegossen. Nach dem Austrocknen nimmt man die Gegenstände aus den Formen, bemalt und lackirt sie. Gewöhnlich versetzt man die Masse noch mit weissem Sand, Kreide oder Thon u. dgl. Auf diesem Zusatz beruht meistens das Geheimniss der einzelnen Fabrikanten.

BETTSTATT.

17. Papier-mâché furniture, Bettridge and Company, London, 1862

berg mentions that upon return to London he spent over three hours alone with George III and his queen at Kew and reported on his travels. Undoubtedly he praised the two firms he had visited and may well have contributed to the king's interest in the vogue for japanned ware. In 1802 Clay moved his plant to London and continued there until his death in 1812. Clay's products carried the impressed marks "Clay Patent" under a crown (pl. 321) and after 1802 "Clay King St. Covt. Garden" (pls. 323 a, 323 b). Some relatives, working later, signed "Clay London," under a crown.

Clay's factory for the manufacture of papier-mâché was taken over in 1815 by Jennens and Bettridge who continued the progressive spirit of their predecessor and won immediate acclaim. The firm continued to serve as japanners to the court through the reigns of George IV, William IV, and Queen Victoria. When Bettridge died in 1864, Jennens carried on. Theirs was certainly the most enterprising firm in Birmingham. One of their most popular decorations was mother-of-pearl tinted in luster colors (pls. 326, 327a, b). This gave their bird, fruit, and flower arrangements a lively but not gaudy effect. A pattern much favored by the public and also offered by other firms was the so-called cockatoo and peacock design, a rich and colorful arrangement with gilt scrollwork. Although the basic elements for such oriental and rococo designs could be found in ornamental pattern books like Frederic Knight's *Fancy Ornaments*, published in London in 1834, the designers of the period developed a style of their own, doing honor to their inventive spirit.

In the catalogue of the Great Exhibition held in London in 1851, the firm of Jennens and Bettridge proudly announced that in addition to the usual tea trays and caddies the public could now avail itself of papier-mâché furniture of a rather substantial kind – beds, chairs, sofas for the drawing-room, and even entire casings for pianofortes (pls. 328–330, fig. 17). It should be added that chairs molded of papier-mâché were unusually comfortable, fitting the human figure as precisely as do modern chairs of plastic. This was the first time that a chair had been made comfortable without the use of upholstery; in addition they were lightweight, thus anticipating our own time. Jennens and Bettridge stamped their products on the underside or sometimes introduced their name on the front, hidden in the gilt ornament (pl. 327). A diamond mark occasionally to be found indicates that the object has been patented. For a brief period, in 1851, the firm opened a branch in New York. At the height of production, the firm had about sixty-four employees, including a number trained at the London School of Design.

In addition to the large firms mentioned, a number of smaller firms were in business in Birmingham (pl. 322). Alsager and Neville (both artists who specialized in very fine paintings) did not sign their decoration, but their work can be recognized by their unusually effective use of mother-of-pearl (pl. 325). The inlay was applied in such a fashion that some pieces were placed counter to the grain in various directions, thus producing an iridescence that contributed greatly to the color effects in floral and architectural pieces. There were also a number of other manufacturers who used the cheaper method of paper pulp and addded gaudy decoration.

At the time of the Great Exhibition in 1851, papier-mâché was at the apex of its popularity, with hardly a household item that could not be made of this wondrous material. Little was made of the fact that certain parts of the heavier pieces still had to be made of wood – bedposts and frames, for example, or the skeletons of pianofortes. In effect, papier-mâché was a form of make-believe.

By the time of the Great Exhibition of 1862 the papier-mâché industry had suffered considerably. In 1864 the firm of Jennens and Bettridge had to close its New York branch. This as much as anything confirms that lacquer as a fashion no longer existed, although the industry was not entirely given up. One or another of the flower painters continued in business to satisfy those of conservative taste, and toward the end of the nineteenth century Far Eastern imports once more attracted the curious and oriental patterns were used for some late pictorial papier-mâché work, although these products rarely drew more than passing attention.

In the United States as in England *chinoiserie* went out of style in the middle of the eighteenth century but revived to some extent during the classical period.[21] Certain types of Sheraton chairs, in vogue in the United States as "fancy chairs," provided space for decoration, either painting or japanning. These chairs enjoyed great popularity through the first three decades of the nineteenth century but later were cheapened for mass production. One of those who advertised his services as "a fancy chairmaker of all sorts of dyed and . . . japanned chairs" executed after "approved London patterns" was William Challen, who arrived from London in 1797.[22] In New York, two other specialists, John and Hugh Finlay, advertised their painted furniture in the period 1799–1838 and were supposed to have made chairs for the White House after drawings by Benjamin Latrobe.[23] But custom-made furniture of this kind was not to prove very profitable over the years. The most lucrative method of producing chairs was to make them in quantity, and this was done during the first decade of the nineteenth century by a number of firms in New York. The chairs were "painted, decorated and landscaped" to give them the appearance of being lacquered. As the population moved westward, there was a great market for inexpensive chairs shipped in quantity, and steamboats and packets were equipped with chairs called "steamboat fancies."

A decided change in the production as well as the marketing of chairs was introduced by Lambert Hitchcock, who was the first to make chair parts only and arrange to have them assembled at their place of destination.[24] When this method proved successful, Hitchcock built a large factory at Barkhamsted, Connecticut, in 1818 (pl. 331). Soon he was able to make as many as fifty chairs a day – the famous Hitchcock chair with turned front legs and rungs – for which he charged one dollar and fifty cents apiece. Later Hitchcock produced a variety of finished chairs, their mark of distinction being the way the slats were decorated by stenciling patterns in gold, bronze, or polychrome on dark backgrounds – an inexpensive way of giving the impression of japanning. For the most part these patterns of fruit, leaves, cornucopia, and similar elements were executed by women and children who acquired a moderate skill and even applied some personal touches.

Hitchcock's venture lasted into the 1860s and encouraged innumerable competitors. By mid-century the United States teemed with chair manufacturers producing lines similar to those of Hitchcock. Obviously this type of production had little in common with the activities of the japanner of old who tried to create a European version of Far Eastern lacquer, and yet there were some elements in the process that remained the same. In the first place, there was the wish to hide the underlying material under decoration. The dark background simulating a lacquered surface remained, and varnish covered the colorful decorations, lending a certain brilliance to the appearance of the chair. The Hitchcock chair went out of fashion in the late sixties when carved or veneered fine woods were introduced. Those few japanners who were left turned to decorating sewing machines and other household articles, generally using lithographed decals.

Shaping tin into household articles introduced another major industry to the American colonies about 1740, when two Irishmen, Edward and William Pattison, set up shop as tinsmiths in Berlin, Connecticut.[25] They depended entirely upon a supply of tin sheets, 10×4 inches, shipped from Wales. The Pattisons produced such household articles as pots, pitchers, caddies, and boxes for sugar, for pills, for deeds, and other trinkets. In shaping these objects, the tinsmiths were limited by the small size of the sheets, although a number could be joined by seams to make large trays. Such trays were hammered over molds, with the edge turned up to make the rim. Articles were coated with an asphaltum varnish, dried by stoving, decorated with oil colors, and varnished. After 1820 much of the painted decoration was replaced by stenciling.

Among the first in the tin trade we know by name were Zacharias Stevens, Thomas Briskos, Oliver Buckley, Eliza and Elijah North, Aaron Butler, and Oliver Filley. Stevens settled in Stevens Plains, near Portland, Maine, in 1789, and others soon followed until the hamlet became nearly as important a center for japanned tinware as Berlin, Connecticut (pl. 332). Oliver Filley (1721–1846), working in Bloomfield, Connecticut, started as a peddler and is known to have used a turning machine for his tin, enabling him to make large quantities and eventually to open other shops in Pennsylvania and New York.

The industry grew as turnpikes were opened in 1791. After the opening of the Erie Canal in 1825, tin plate could be shipped west as far as Ohio. In Ohio, lacquered tinware was produced in the Zoar community near Canton after 1817. There Pennsylvania Dutch patterns were followed as well as patterns developed at Stevens Plains. In those years it was a common sight to see on the road a peddler's cart piled high with sundry household articles, many of them made of tin, stowed away in various compartments.

Tin objects were decorated simply but in gay colors, vermilion, blue, yellow, and green, sometimes on a white ground with stripes and patterns of flowers and fruit and leaves. As a rule, tinsmiths copied the popular patterns of their competitors, although there were some attempts at originality. At the same time, of course, there was competition from Bilston. Although Bilston patterns are unknown today, it is probable that some American patterns are copies – or that even some Bilston ware is now considered to be of American origin. A report written in 1866 states that Bilston exported its cheapest products to the Americas and other countries because "a lack of wealth and education combine with specific instead of ad valorem duties to encourage an importation of the lightest and commonest goods of an ornamental character."[26]

In Pennsylvania, decorated tinware (pl. 333) was especially well received because its decoration was so much akin to the way Pennsylvania Dutch families customarily embellished their own household articles.[27] In their heyday, around 1832, the tinshops in Stevens Plains produced an amount of merchandise worth the not inconsiderable sum of $27,000. Tinware shipped to California was sold at three times the price asked in Boston.

Papier-mâché lacquerware had a late start in the United States and apparently never proved to be a great success, although Birmingham wares were exported to the United States and for a short while Jennens and Bettridge entertained an office in New York. In the early thirties lacquerworkers from the Midlands immigrated to the United States and settled in Connecticut. Unsuccessful on their own, they joined the Litchfield Manufacturing Company when it opened in 1850.[28] Litchfield began by manufacturing daguerreotype cases and a variety of small trinkets and later went into the production of clock cases of papier-mâché. The venture proved successful, and the company was soon able to offer finished products by obtaining clock works from Bristol, Connecticut. The cases were lacquered and richly decorated with flower arrangements, mother-of-pearl inlay, and gilt borders, looking quite as elegant as their English prototypes. The lacquer was not always quite smooth; the surface sometimes looked a bit "bubbly." Nevertheless, the clock were traded all along the Mississippi and even exported to South America. Because the clock works were accurate, these time pieces were used on railways and steamboats.

Occasionally Litchfield made small accessory furniture, including pole screens and sewing stands. In 1852, the company made fifty-five clocks a day, varying in price from one dollar to twenty-five dollars. In 1854 the company was sold to a firm in Bridgeport and the production of lacquer cases and other lacquerware was discontinued. Internal problems may have caused this abrupt end, but the change did happen to coincide with the end of the vogue for lacquer.

In France the activities of the Martin family had created a most favorable climate for the growing popularity of lacquerware. Their success in France may be measured by the number of imitators Watin describes as inundating Paris. The craftsmen worked in isolation and were highly competitive; neither in Paris nor elsewhere in France were there such centers as found at Birmingham and Pontypool. In the 1770s a vogue for English fashions swept Europe, and among these japannedware was much favored, thus encouraging the growth of English industry. A great quantity of English japannedware was imported to France and of course imitated as well – increasingly so in the period 1808–14 when Napoleon tried to throttle English trade by his "continental system."

When it became a fashion in the 1920s to collect *tôle*, the French equivalent of japannedware, there was much tinware on the art market which was claimed to be of French origin, although by reason of style it hardly could be distinguished from the English product.[29] It was different when the basic material used was copper, not tin. Copper had to be hammered into shape, and its surface was never quite smooth and would not provide a perfectly sound underground for japanning. Japanning on French *tôle* tended to be somewhat brittle. In addition, the French used bronze trimming for their tinware. To compound the confusion between English and French tinware, fakers were at work to "enrich" the market. Today there is not one piece of *tôle* ware that can be attributed to any known workshop in France.

Among favored items produced were chestnut urns, shaped like a shield, oval bowls with scalloped rims intended for the rinsing of glasses, candlesticks in the shape of Corinthian columns, lamps with reflecting shades (*abats-jour*), tea urns, coffeepots, and other objects which could have been made either in England or in France. Similar items were produced in Holland, Flanders, Bohemia, and Germany. One group of tinware in the Louis XVI style, rather crude in its execution, follows the shape of French silverware in designs for *cache-pots*, tureens, inkstands, and other pieces; its origin can only be guessed (pls. 334–339).

Around 1760 Philippe Jaubert established in Paris in the Faubourg St.-Honoré a shop called *Le petit Dunkerque* where he offered for sale all manner of lacquer merchandise including toilette utensils, trays, chimneypiece sets, and other items made of tin.[30] Jaubert also sold lacquered coffeepots, possibly made of copper, which, surprisingly, were copied from those introduced from Turkey. These pots probably had long, thin necks and small bodies covered with oriental decoration; so far none has been identified. Another enterprise that seems to have enjoyed the favor of the court was an establishment opened by François Samousat in 1767. It was called *Manufacture royale de vernis façon de Chine*. Here he exploited a lacquer his father-in-law, Gosse, had invented and submitted to the Académie des Science, pronounced to be "hard, brilliant, tough and of a brilliant black," applicable to wood, leather, papier-mâché, stone, and other materials. No product of this shop is known today even though each carried an identifying mark, *Veuve Gosse et Samousat*, or some abbreviation of this designation.[31]

Around 1762 we find a Sieur Destorges listed as a maker of lacquered copper panels to be used in the decoration of furniture. A shop called *La petite Pologne*, established in 1768 by Sieur Clément, is thought to be the first to produce articles in the English style. According to a note in *Mercure* (May, 1770), Sieur Clément also produced tin panels decorated with fruit and flowers to be used in the decoration of furniture. Although his varnish had been approved by the *Académie des Science* in 1769 and he attained considerable affluence, his work, as the Abbé Jombert recorded in 1773, was of inferior quality and eventually his business failed. Before his workmen disbanded, another *vernisseur*, Sieur Framéry, reorganized the shop with great success. Framéry did not copy the English style, that is, he did not attempt to imitate the typical Pontypool tortoiseshell ground; instead he used an aventurine ground, more popular in France, and decorated his wares with ornaments built up in relief. In 1792, another craftsman, name unknown, who had taken over a shop established in Clignancourt in 1778, boasted that he had learned his trade in England. He advertised "chimney and writing sets imitating the oriental style and decorated with ormulu."

In 1799 a number of *tôle* pieces made by Citizen Deharme were shown at the Exhibition of Industrial Arts; twenty years later, in 1819, Sieur Tavernier exhibited his tinware at the Louvre. A competitor of Tavernier, Sieur Pierre Leggard, is listed in 1823 as making lacquered lamps, some of which may have been of the kind called *bouillote*, in style at the time of the Restoration. The names of other lacquermasters are listed in the catalogues of exhibitions of industrial arts held in the early decades of the nineteenth century, but since they never signed their works it is impossible today to identify their products (pl. 339). Hubert Robert is known to have painted some *tôle* while in prison, but none is known today. One Paris firm, all but forgotten, was owned by Achille Robin, père et fils, who used lithographs either as patterns or by way of decalcomania. They also published a most attractive and now very rare book entitled *Traité de peinture sur bois blanc d'Ecosse et de Spa* (Paris, 1833). On the title page they advertised themselves as *Fabricans de tabletterie française et étrangère* and gave their address as Rue de Choiseul, no. 12. Eleven colored lithographs show patterns they recommended and probably used in their own shop, copying products from various places. Also included is a list of the various working materials they carried for sale. Toward mid-century lacquered tinware in France had become so cheap in style as well as in quality that it was not considered sufficiently elegant to be displayed during the second republic of Napoleon III.

Only in Brunswick and in Russia in the early nineteenth century were fully developed lacquer industries established whose products are known today. That Brunswick became a competitor of Birmingham did not happen by chance. Both Brunswick and Hanover had strong political and trade ties with England, and it was only natural that, sooner or later, a lacquer industry of importance in Brunswick was bound to become a rival of English firms. Brunswick was one of the few cities where lacquer had been produced since the early eighteenth century, but the trade had not flourished and its products had never been as distinguished as those made in Berlin or Dresden. When Johann Heinrich Stobwasser settled in Brunswick in 1763, the situation changed.[32]

Stobwasser, born in Saxony in 1740, was the son of a peddler. He accompanied his father on his journeys and while on the road young Stobwasser became acquainted with the lacquerware produced in Ansbach. It was purely commercial merchandise made for the military – swagger sticks for officers, belts, munitions cases, lacquered mugs, boxes, and trinkets of various kinds – and was sometimes decorated in a most primitive fashion. What distinguished this ware was its reliable quality and the sturdiness of its lacquer. A note found as late as 1787 in *Meusels Museum*, a well-known German magazine of the period, mentions the especially fine luster and the lasting quality of Ansbach lacquer. Living in the early years of mercantilism, and acquainted with imported English lacquer, Stobwasser must have realized that working with lacquer would open up rather promising industrial possibilities.

Eventually Stobwasser was able to wangle the secret of making Ansbach lacquer from a brother of the two most prosperous lacquermasters of the town, the family Eberlein. The brother, a pharmacist, was an easygoing fellow, so there was no great difficulty in prying the secret from him. At home in Lobenstein in Saxony, Stobwasser immediately began to improve on the work of the Ansbach craftsmen, decorating papier-mâché in a delicate style following the customary patterns of English japanned lacquerware. With this a success, he tried his hand at decorating tinware with figures and landscapes, using engravings as patterns. Probably the term *japanische lackiert Waren* found in Stobwasser's autobiography written in old age is a direct translation of the English "japanned ware" and does not indicate *chinoiserie*. Business grew quickly, and Stobwasser soon had his entire family at work. As was the custom in the home-production of paintings in reverse on glass, each member of the family had an especially assigned task. In 1763, the family heard that the duke of Brunswick was offering particularly favorable considerations to artisans who would settle in his domain. Soon the family—father Georg Siegmund, son Johann Heinrich, and three sisters—had been accepted and were settled in Brunswick. Within a few years the Stobwassers were turning out such merchandise as pipes, snuffboxes, mugs, cups, trays, tabletops, and pots of various kinds. Now and again they made furniture to order, including a desk, a commode, and a coffee table. In one of his routine reports to the duke, Stobwasser expressed the hope that in future he could provide lacquered military equipment; he also mentioned that he had attended the Leipzig fair and business was very successful. From the beginning the Stobwassers aimed at the industrialization of their shop and saw to it that individual commissions were kept to a minimum. This was in keeping with the trend of the time and with the direction the lacquer trade was taking elsewhere. Stobwasser was convinced that the more he enlarged the volume of his business and increased the variety of products offered, the better he would be able to compete with English products so much in favor on the continent.

In 1769 Stobwasser received the exclusive privilege to protect his merchandise against competitors who labeled their products Brunswick lacquerware. He reasoned successfully if not quite truthfully that the kind of work he was doing was quite unknown in England and France. To show that his shop was recognized as an industrial establishment, he was granted the right to display a sign naming the firm *Georg Siegmund Stobwasser und Sohn*. More important, he was granted permission to employ turners and cabinetmakers, masters and apprentices. Before this, soldiers had been employed in their off-hours. The new arrangement is a clear indication of the passing of the guild system and labor's eventual independence of the superannuated rules that once made industrial progress so difficult.

Among the soldiers to be employed by Stobwasser was Jean Guérin, of French descent and perhaps a Huguenot, a cabinetmaker by profession (pl. 346). An excellent craftsmen, Guérin was also inventive, and it was he who first began to make table tops of cardboard (pls. 341, 342). Although made for Stobwasser and decorated in his shop, for some time these were called Guérin tops. Guérin married Louise, the oldest and most business-minded of Johann Heinrich's three sisters, and in 1772 established a branch of the firm in Berlin in response to Frederick the Great's search for craftsmen to settle in Prussia. This new venture of the Stobwassers was an important step, for it provided additional protection of their merchandise within Prussian territory. By 1744 the firm kept stocks of merchandise in Hamburg, Berlin, Halberstadt, Leipzig, and Silesia with a total value of 1,354 thalers. The growth of the business can be assessed by the increase in the number of workers employed. The Brunswick branch employed 24 workers in 1774, 80 workers in 1796; the Berlin branch employed 15 workers in 1785 and sold merchandise worth 12,500 thalers, 3,000 of which came from the export of goods.

When production began in 1763, the firm used cardboard, papier-mâché, or wood as a base; in 1778 at the latest they began using tin, since in this year for the first time a tinsmith is mentioned among the personnel employed. Metals used were tin (*verzinntes Blech*) and rolled sheets (*gewalztes Eisenblech*) imported from England. Papier-mâché pipes were exported in great quantities to Hungary and Turkey as a kind of substitute for meerschaum, and much of the tinware produced went to Russia in spite of high duties and strong local competition. Stobwasser was probably able to acquire some business connections in Russia with the help of the Moravian brotherhood whose community he had joined and who had colonies there.

In 1810 Johann Heinrich Stobwasser retired and later married the widow of the famous cabinetmaker David Röntgen of Neuwied, who had also been a Moravian. Stobwasser's son, Christian Heinrich, his father's ablest assistant, sold the Brunswick business in 1832 but carried on in Berlin, although the production of lacquerware was discontinued. Instead, the firm made metal lamps. This branch continued under family management until well into the early decades of the twentieth century. The Brunswick firm went on producing lacquer goods under new management, Meyer und Ried. The report of an industrial exhibition held in Mainz in 1842 praises the firm which at that time employed twenty painters.

Even during the lifetime of Johann Heinrich Stobwasser, some of his employees left to establish their own business in Brunswick and elsewhere, and gradually the lacquer industry spread throughout Germany, Austria, and Bohemia. In the 1860s the industry reached a turning point and declined after transfer printing was substituted for the painting of lacquerware.

The importance of the products of Stobwasser's firm depends upon the quality and high artistic standards maintained. There was no great variety in forms and patterns, although certainly any novelty imported from England was immediately copied. Many favorite subjects used for decoration were taken from English prints. One of Guérin's table tops, mounted on a stand in the Louis XVI style, is decorated with a copy of such a print showing the sons of Edward IV in the Tower (pls. 341, 342). A secretary, one of the rare pieces of furniture made by Stobwasser, was decorated by the well-known Brunswick painter Friedrich Georg Weitsch, undoubtedly inspired by an engraving (pl. 340). Stobwasser production distinguished itself by good taste in design as well as a wide range of subjects, not excluding erotic themes painted inside snuffboxes and referred to in business accounts as *aequivoca*. The snuffboxes made by Stobwasser at the peak of production – though copied by others – can be easily recognized by their shape, with the rim between top and bottom curved inward (pl. 345). These boxes were first shaped in a mold, finished by a turner, and given five or more coats of lacquer. The piece was baked in an oven after each coating to give it a high gloss. The spaces to be painted were then covered with a ground of whiting, and the drawing to be used was transferred in outline. After the painter had completed his decoration in oil, it was covered with lacquer and dried in the air.

In order to secure the talent he needed, Stobwasser established an art school in Brunswick and undertook to collect painting by well-known artists. He also maintained a large collection of prints, supplemented by a library of illustrated books. All of this material was placed at the disposal of the artists, who made their outline drawings from these patterns or adapted them according to their own designs. Among the great variety of subjects used for decoration are found copies of works by Rembrandt, Rubens, Gerard Dou, Poussin, and Fragonard as well as contemporary battle scenes, landscapes, and topographical material. In addition there were portraits of contemporary celebrities and imaginative depictions of figures from fiction (pls. 343, 347).

For entertaining at tea or coffee in bourgeois society, service sets on trays were much in demand (pls. 351). The decoration of snuffboxes were done in an especially delicate style suitable to an age when miniature painting was so much appreciated. Snuffboxes were finished in modest fashion, never overwhelmed by an expensive and inappropriate setting, and yet the prices obtained for a good snuffbox might be as high as five or six louis d'or, out of which the painter received up to fifteen thalers. A fine example of a Stobwasser portrait is seen on a box in the Brunswick museum, the likeness of the dramatist Johann Anton Leisewitz, copied from a painting by J. H. Schröder (pl. 347). The increasing vogue for landscape painting during the romantic period brought favor to such subjects as "View of Brocken Mountain" (pl. 344). An elegant oval box bearing the name Guérin was probably made for his own use (pl. 346). A tobacco can, a tea kettle, and a casket show the style of Stobwasser tinware, scarcely to be distinguished from similar products from England and France (pls. 348–350).

Stobwasser's tin boxes are often gilt inside, his papier-maché boxes are brown, and later black, inside; the outside ground color is almost always red, with an overlay of black or green, producing a tortoiseshell effect. The mark which Stobwasser was privileged to use after 1775 is a horse over the letters *St*, but it was rarely applied. Many papier-mâché pieces were marked on the inside in a variety of ways –, for example, *Stobwasser's Fabrik* in red script, with the title of the painting indicated in the same way. Sometimes production numbers were added.

Ten years or so after the establishment of the firm, Stobwasser's products had won a reputation as wide as the continent. His fame lasted through two generations. By midcentury, when interest in lacquer was beginning to wane and its manufacture had been commercialized and cheapened, the Stobwassers left their business to others to continue in an industry that no longer seemed lucrative. Nevertheless, the lacquer trade lasted into the 1860s. Most lacquer firms on the continent produced articles resembling those made in Birmingham and the Midlands, seeking to capture the market by underbidding the original products and cheapening the output. Fuhse, the biographer of Stobwasser, collected much scattered material concerning this trade and was able to list over thirty lacquer firms working in the German-speaking areas of Europe.

Russia is the only western country where lacquer is produced as a work of art in an unbroken tradition extending from the eighteenth century to the present day. In recent years serious efforts have been made to adapt it to contemporary tastes. The use of lacquer in Russia developed along three distinctly different lines. The first, at the royal court, is similar to the custom-made products produced by skilled artisans throughout Europe. The decoration of *Mon Plaisir* at Peterhof is a splendid example of Russian lacquer influenced by European taste (pl. 296). The second, a lacquer industry, obviously followed English precedent, admired and copied all over the continent. The third, unique to Russia, is lacquer folk art, seemingly quite independent of European trends although perhaps influenced or inspired by traditional religious art.

The earliest printed information about an apparently successful industrial establishment comes from a report by the German scientist Peter Pallas who made a study of the remote provinces of Russia in 1769.[33] At Nizhni Tagil and Nevianskoi, both north of Sverdlovsk (the former Ekaterinburg), Pallas visited iron mills owned by the Demidov family. During the reign of Peter the Great, a metal craftsman from Tula, Nikita Demidovich Antufiev, exploited iron ore mines and worked the first blast furnace in the Ural. Later, his family, now called Demidov, established immense shops and forges, gained an enormous fortune, and received princely titles. In the mills Pallas was able to observe how sheets were forged, cannon founded, and other heavy metal work handled. The Demidov shops were also busy making copper and iron kettles, rolling tin to be used in lacquerwork, and also producing woodwork to be employed for the same purpose. Such items were decorated and lacquered in the Demidov's own shop, the outstanding lacquermaster being one Khudejarof of whom a signed tin box with the Demidov arms is known. Carriages, too, were produced, and one of them is included in the Hermitage Collection.

Trays decorated with landscapes (pl. 352) or historical scenes in western fashion are probably typical of the work done at Nizhni Tagil. The enterprise was well-organized, with a school to provide young craftsmen – probably former serfs – a chance to prepare for their jobs. The quality of the lacquer was high and is reputed to have been on a par with that of the Far East insofar as durability was concerned. Production lasted until well into the nineteenth century.[34]

Similar to the Demidov enterprises, although on a much smaller scale, was that of Prince Scheremetjev, who freed some of his serfs to do lacquerwork in Kuskovo near Moscow. Here we find the names of the Vishniakov family who worked until toward the end of the nineteenth century. That they were prosperous is attested by the fact that in 1876 they employed some 246 workmen (pls. 356e, 358). As the century advanced a number of daring entrepreneurs began business. One, A. I. Austin (the name suggests he may have been English), had an establishment near Moscow. In the workshop of A. Laboutin (pl. 354) trays were produced which follow the Pontypool style. Some of the production figures are known of another workshop maintained by a Captain Ternberg: in 1809 he produced 1,447 items and sold them for 11,723 rubles.

Since the nineteenth century the lacquer industry has continued to thrive in Russia and yields a considerable amount in taxes. The Russian government has done much to encourage it by placing protective customs duties on imports, making the export of lacquer tax-exempt, and, when needed, granting subsidies to help the industry prosper.

Another quite different kind of lacquer was on the market even early in the eighteenth century. These products – cups, bowls, and salvers turned of wood as well as tea caddies and other trinkets – were still well-known in western Europe before World War I. They were decorated in bold designs on a silver background, with evenly applied brushstrokes of black and red and stylized floral motifs. Their heavy varnish made the silver appear to be gold and lent the pieces a gay, even somewhat precious look. This treen ware was known as *Khokloma*, named for a village in the province of Gorki (formerly Nizhni Novgorod) where, as in nearby Semenova, the lacquerware was produced in the settlements of the so-called Old Believers, a group that seceded from the official church and fled to the eastern banks of the Volga toward the end of the seventeenth century. These cheap objects were sold at fairs along the Volga River and were found in the households of even the poorest farmers. To this day their production has never ceased, indeed is much encouraged as genuine folk art. It would be of great interest to discover if the prime impetus for this kind of woodware came from the Near East or from western Europe.

At Danilkovo (now called Fedoskino), twenty-two miles out of Moscow, lacquerware as it was introduced from the West became a veritable industry and continues today. Here, in 1798, Pavel Ivanovitch Korobov, who had visited the establishment of Stobwasser at Brunswick, opened a workshop of his own with the assistance of some workmen he had been able to lure away from Stobwasser (pl. 353). Korobov, who made visors for soldiers' caps, also produced decorated snuffboxes of various kinds. In 1824 this rather prosperous shop was taken over by Korobov's son-in-law, Piotr Vasielievich Lukutin (d. 1863), who developed it on a large scale. It was not long before the name Lukutin had the same connotation in Russia as did Martin in France, and Lukutin became the synonym for a lacquered snuffbox. Lukutin produced lacquerware by a meticulous process that guaranteed long life and assured that it would be chip-resistant. Since the present industry in Fedoskino is built on the Lukutin tradition, one may assume that the technique employed today closely corresponds to that used in the nineteenth century. The process begins by pressing sheets of cardboard around a block, the shape of the future box; bottom and lid are made separately. These parts are then dried naturally, soaked in heated vegetable oil, and baked in an oven at 200° Fahrenheit for several days. The material becomes as hard as wood and can be glued together; the lid is attached with hinges. The box is now ready to be grounded with black or possibly red to give it the look of tortoiseshell; then it is lacquered, red inside and black outside, and polished and baked in the oven after each application of lacquer. The piece then goes to the artisan who decorates the lid and covers the entire box with three or four coats of oil which give the colors and the background, possibly covered with gold or silver, a certain glow and an extraordinary transparency.

Lacquer products were decorated with landscapes or genre scenes, many copied from prints or other patterns and sometimes embellished with mother-of-pearl inlay, following the example of Stobwasser or English shops. Gradually a style developed distinctly Russian in appearance and subject matter. In time a number of smaller workshops in Danilkovo were taken over by Lukutin, and by the end of the nineteenth century his firm practically monopolized the production of lacquer in Russia (pls. 355, 357). The business remained in the hands of the family until the death in 1902 of the last owner, Nicolai Alexandrovitch Lukutin, a physician who could pay little attention to the family enterprise. His widow carried on for a time, but the factory was forced out of business in 1904.

Since 1828 the Lukutins had been permitted to mark their products with the imperial eagle painted in gold (pl. 356). In addition there was a mark with the letters FPL, standing for Factory Piotr Lukutin. After 1830 the letters were changed to the given names of the owners – F.P.&A.L. or F.A.L., standing for Piotr or his son Alexander who took over in 1859/60. After 1881 four eagles were shown, indicating the four czars under whom the Lukutins had served, to which was added *Factory Lukutin Moscow*. From 1902 to 1904 the letters L.R. stand as the initials of the widow of the last owner. After 1830 all

Russian lacquer had to be marked with the eagle and initials of the makers. How strictly this edict was adhered to remains a question.

The Lukutins sought to produce lacquer products to suit any number of strata of Russian society. Items for one and the same purpose were made in a variety of styles and qualities, and prices ranged from two rubles to three hundred rubles. In 1821 Lukutin employed four painters, three turners, and two lacquermen who turned out some 4,800 snuffboxes a year. By 1863 the firm produced some six hundred different items with a market value of about 23,000 rubles. Lukutin, who exported merchandise to the United States, achieved world-renown by displaying his products at international exhibitions.

That the Russian lacquer industry did not falter quite so soon as its western competitors at the end of the nineteenth century may be because objects were designed to appeal to Russian taste – decorated with such familiar scenes as a family at tea, a troika attacked by a wolf pack, a maiden strumming a musical instrument. Toward 1900, when the enterprising spirit of the Lukutins began to lag and conditions were no longer favorable to lacquer as a medium, even this industry had to narrow considerably. The knowledge of how to produce papier-maché boxes was carried on, in a small way, by a cooperative established by former Lukutin workers that managed to linger on until the Russian revolution.

With the revolution came attempts to preserve and celebrate the traditions of Russian folk art. Among those who sought to keep such crafts alive were Maxim Gorki, who had worked for an icon painter as a boy, and Anatoli Vasilievich Lunatscharski, the Bolshevik leader and commissar for education, who insisted that, whenever possible, "the golden chain of folk art" should not be broken. During the revolution the art of icon painting fell on evil days and was on the brink of perishing, but most propitiously a solution was found by adapting the skill of icon painters to the decoration of lacquerware. As a result, old Russian traditions were used in an entirely new way. At Palekh, Mstera, Koluy, and Zestovo, ancient centers of icon painting, artists now devoted to lacquerwork continued the old techniques, using egg tempera and subtle brushwork (pls. XVI b 359, 360). At Fedoskino, painting was practiced in a broader fashion and with oil paints. The subjects chosen for decoration were similar, usually taken from the rich sources of folklore and fairy tales or based on stories by Pushkin and others. At Fedoskino the artists emphasized a more realistic style, depicting home scenes as well, whereas the artists who worked in the older centers sought a more subtle artistry, preferring scenes in which fairies and demons disport with mortals amidst the glitter of a world of fantasy.

At present Fedoskino employs some three hundred workmen in the lacquer industry and produces some 4,000 boxes each month in many different styles and in a variety of patterns. Schools recruit craftsmen capable of continuing and developing the prosperous trade.

A number of reasons may be advanced for the slow death of the lacquer industry in Europe. For one, snuffboxes had gone out of fashion, and lacquer was not considered suitable for cigar cases. Materials had been cheapened in the face of enormous competition, and lacquer itself was discredited as apparently anything, regardless of quality, could be sold. Papier-mâché made of pulp pressed into molds was covered with inferior lacquer that chipped easily and was decorated with the newly invented aniline dyes in all-too-gaudy colors. Patterns were printed, no longer hand-painted, and anything at all in the way of design was offered as long as it pleased unassuming customers. In fashionable circles, lacquered tin and papier-mâché with its more or less borrowed splendor had long ceased to be of interest. Just as Sheffield plate was having difficulties because of the fierce competition offered by electroplated silver, so lacquer trays were replaced by electroplate which could be had at reasonable prices. As for lacquer beds and chairs, they were usurped by a change in fashion – the "new" material was brass or other metal tubing, polished and decorated with curlicue ornaments. Brass beds were considered more elegant and capable of more individual variegation than old lacquer models.

In these years, too, industrial art objects came under more severe scrutiny and were discussed by competent arbiters who ruled on taste. Discerning minds realized that the entire industry dealing with what were considered art objects was badly in need of improved designs. In 1851, the Great Exhibition in London offered a chance to compare the products of the "industry of all nations." To the group of men like Henry Cole, Augustus Pugin, Richard Redgrave, and others who had prepared the show with the encouragement and very active patronage of the prince consort, Albert, it was obvious that the exhibition demonstrated the need to improve the taste of manufacturers or the public or both. As a result, the English government set up a Department of Practical Art in 1852 to "increase the efficiency of the School of Design," which had been established in London in 1837. Located at Marlborough House under the direction of Henry Cole, this department entertained a little museum offering "specimens of ornamental art illustrating correct principles in decoration." At the same time a chamber of horrors was installed, exhibiting articles "considered to show wrong or false principles."[35] Among the eighty-four objects on exhibition was a lacquered papier-mâché tray about which the catalogue had this observation: "An example of popular but vulgar taste, of a low character, presenting numerous features which the student should carefully avoid: 1st the center is the piracy of a picture; 2d the picture, on which most labour has been bestowed, is thrown away." The student is further cautioned that the main painting is placed on the tray in such a way that it is obscured by the teapot. The tray is also criticized because the lines of the ornamentation do not follow the form of the tray and that the glitter of the mother-of-pearl inlay creates the impression that "the article is slopped with water perforated with holes." The catalogue, of which this is only a sample, scrutinized each object and spiced its observations with quotations from such critics as William Dyce, Richard Redgrave, and Augustus Pugin. Cole, responsible for the catalogue, made the tactical mistake of mentioning the names of the manufacturers of the goods he pilloried, thus bringing down upon him a storm of protest and causing the show to be closed. The show apparently did not attract the attention of aesthetes, who might have come to Cole's defense. However, in *Household Words*, (4 December 1852), a weekly journal meant to be read in the family, Charles Dickens discussed the "house full of horrors" over six pages. Although he poked some mild fun at the novel idea, he went into much detail and mentioned point by point the critical statements about the tray. In general, he said he liked the whole idea and agreed that "a little precise knowledge of some true principles of design is wanted just now quite as much by manufacturers as by the public . . . and it will be many years before mere abstract principles of choice in ornament can become familiar – I will not say to us, but to our children."

Taking advantage of the controversy, some manufacturers then offered prizes for designs, with the winners to be chosen by members of the Department of Practical Art. Jennens and Bettridge promised five pounds for a tray design and shrewdly advised the competitors to take as their model the ornamentation of the Indian examples in the collection of the department. It was well known, of course, that Richard Redgrave, quoted in the catalogue, expressed the opinion of the department when he pointed out that the beauty of the Indian patterns resulted from their adherence to the principles reiterated by the group around Cole. It might be added that the department and its successor, the South Kensington Museum (now the Victoria and Albert Museum), did not keep in the permanent collection the tray so severely castigated. The department did purchase six oriental lacquer trays, one of them Japanese, from an importer in London, and it was evidently these to which Jennens and Bettridge referred.

How successful the department and its successor were in improving public taste through the years is hard to judge. But we do know that the downfall of lacquer was not caused by the displeasure it aroused in this London circle. The correct interpretation was probably given by a Birmingham writer, W. C. Aitkin, who in 1866 sought to explain why such a misfortune had befallen the once-prosperous industry: "The tendency to over-elaboration of ornament fostered by the production of goods for foreign markets has . . . operated in checking the home demand, since purchasers are naturally shy of articles the majority of which, especially in the larger and more elaborate examples, are produced in a depraved taste."[36]

The aesthetic discussions which took place during the early Victorian era had been long forgotten when the art of the Far East, especially of Japan, once again gave inspiration and impetus to the arts of Europe toward the end of the nineteenth century. The influence was reflected in the work of the Impressionists and some of their followers and also in the *Art Nouveau* movement as expressed in the decorative arts. At that time a good many lacquer objects were imported from the Far East and did not fail to arouse interest. In the wake of such trends, an intermezzo deserving of attention took place – an encounter with the lacquer of the Far East experienced independently by two European artists. It was not the stylistic elements that interested them so much as Eastern lacquer techniques which they thought it possible to develop for the interpretation of European ideas. To appreciate this episode, which took place just after World War I, it is necessary to realize what it meant to be an artist in those years. When the holocaust ended in 1918, the entire world was once more accessible to European artists, and the creative imagination was again free to roam as it would. Inspiration might come from the Far East, the South Seas, or Africa, each offering ideas, forms, and rich materials foreign to Europe, which the artist might choose and shape to the satisfaction of his own imagination.

A sculptor in Brussels, Marcel Wolfers[37], had access to some Far Eastern resin and became involved in the task of putting it to his own use. Before the war he had become acquainted with the art of Japan and especially with the subtle ways of the lacquermasters, but at that time genuine *rhus vernicifera* was not available in Europe. Once the resin was available, Marcel Wolfers saw his opportunity. He did not choose the easy way, creating in the style of the Far East; rather, he kept in mind the lessons he had lately learned in studying Sung lacquer. He followed the basic principles that governed the Chinese use of the medium but strove through his sculpture and works of decorative art to express the spirit of his own time and to speak in the idiom of the European world. Although working with the strange material was to be a painful experience of trial and error, the artist succeeded in creating a number of most sensitively colored and occasionally ornamented vessels and jars (pl. 363). He then turned to sculpture, bringing lacquer within the orbit of European art – a head of Christ (pl. 361) lacquered on bronze, using the lost wax process, now owned by a museum in Barcelona, and a station of the Via Crucis molded in clay and then lacquered, now in the Church of Marcinelle, Charleroi (pl. 362). These triumphs bear witness to his talent and indicate that the possibilities inherent in Far Eastern lacquer are limited only by the potential of the artist who knows how to animate it. The qualities of lacquer are put to full use – the variety of shapes given to its surface, the colors selected to intensify the effect of this surface, and the subtle shapes allowing for the play of light and shadow. All this served to produce objects growing out of a specific medium well-suited to perform with color as well as to stress plastic values.

Another artist, the Franco-Swiss Jean Dunand, had a similar experience with the art of the Far East.[38] He first became acquainted with genuine lacquer about 1912. After the war he had an opportunity to meet some Annamese lacquer craftsmen who for a short while followed their trade in Europe. Although Dunand began his career as a sculptor, he was interested in discovering the possibilities in painting and decorating planes and surfaces which might be used for panels, screens, furniture, and entire rooms. Like Wolfers, Dunand declined to compromise by using timeworn *chinoiserie*. He adhered to Far Eastern principles only insofar as they allowed him to take advantage of color, luster, and translucency, without sacrificing his European point of view. Quite often Dunand's creations formed a nucleus for a setting to which other artists contributed a share to complete the ensemble. A decorative panel created in 1925 suggests Dunand's very advanced designs (pl. 364).

In each instance, a European artist used the Far Eastern medium in a novel way and quite contrary to the manner in which it had been used in Europe for so long. As it happens, these individual performances, promising though they were, were to remain unique.

The traditional production of lacquer, which had collapsed as an industry insofar as western Europe was concerned, did not remain in oblivion for long. When it was revived, the term lacquer was no more than a name for a substance which had changed completely in its basic ingredients and in the way it was to be used. It was divorced from any particular style or carrier with which it had been connected by tradition. Today, lacquer is a product of the chemical industry which has found radically new ways to produce a substance much richer in quality than anything concocted in the workshops of the lacquermasters. With its lucidity, sparkle, endurance, and great variety of colors, lacquer – or rather enamel as it is called today – is more in demand than ever. It is now within reach of everyone and has become independent of trends in fashion, to be put to use by industry as well as by individual artists and craftsmen.

1. [Achille] Robin, père et fils, *Traité de peinture sur bois blanc d'Ecosse et de Spa* (Paris, 1833), includes eleven color lithographs; Albin Body, *Essais Historiques sur les ouvrages peints, dits "Boîtes de Spa"* (Liège, 1898), pp. 9 ff.; *Catalogue de l'exposition de Liège* (1905); *Catalogue de l'exposition de l'art ancien au pays de Liège* (Paris, Musée des Arts Décoratifs, 1924), pp. 191–92; Georges Barzin, *Les bois de Spa* (Liège, 1946); *Trois siècles de bois de Spa* (Liège, Exposition Musée de la vie Wallone, 1967), includes an illustration of an old *bourdon* (no. 368, p. 88).
2. Edouard Nessel, *Traité des Eaux* (Liège, 1689).
3. K. L. Freiherr von Pöllnitz, *Les amusements de Spa* or *the gallantries of the Spaw in Germany* (2d ed., London, 1737), pp. 33, 37, 104, 149; G. A. Turner, *Amusements des eaux de Spa* (Paris, 1734); Prince Charles-Joseph de Ligne, "Contes immoraux," in *Mélanges militaires, etc.*, 34 vols. (Vienna, 1795–1811), 28:92–94.
4. J. Ph. de Limbourg, *New Amusements of the German* Spa (London, 1763), pp. 144–46.
5. *Catalogue of the exhibition "Kurfürst Clemens August" in Schloss Brühl* (Cologne, 1961), no. 404, p. 292.
6. Body, *Essais Historiques*, p. 158.
7. Most of the information on japanning in the nineteenth century was derived from F. Gibbs, "Historical Survey of the Japanning Trade," in *Annals of Science*, "III. Pontypool and Usk," 9 (1953): 197–213; "IV. The Midlands," 10 (1953): 214–32; W. P. John, *Pontypool and Usk Japanned Wares* (Newport, Monmouthshire, 1953); Jane Toller, *Papier-mâché in Great Britain and America* (London, 1962).
8. W. Coxe, *A Historical Tour through Monmouthshire* (1st ed., 1801; 2d ed., Brecon, Wales, 1904), p. 204.
9. Gibbs, "Japanning Trade," p. 201.
10. Gibbs, "Japanning Trade," pp. 202, 207.
11. John, *Pontypool*, pp. 57, 77, 79.
12. Gibbs, "Japanning Trade,", p. 217.
13. Gibbs, "Japanning Trade," p. 218.
14. Francis, Lord Gardenstone, *Traveling Memorandum*, 2 vols. (Edinburgh, 1791), 2:76, 77; Stuart Maxwell, "Craftsmen in Wood," in *Scotland's Magazine* (February, 1959), p. 26; *Trois siècles de bois de Spa*, pp. 12, 14.
15. William Aiton, *General view of the agriculture of Ayrshire*, 2 vols (1811), 2:605 ff.; *New Statistical Account for Old Cumnock*, 6 vols. (Edinburgh, 1837), 5:485-86; John Warnick, *The History of Old Cumnock* (Paisley, 1899); James Edward Shaw, *Ayrshire* (Edinburgh, 1953), p. 52; N. Talbot Rice, "19th Century Tartan Keepsakes," in *Connaissance*, 159 (1958), 242–45; J. Strawhorn, *The New History of Cumnock* (Glasgow, 1966); Martin Kemp, "William Leighton Leith and the Mauchline Snuff Box Trade in Burns's Souvenirs," in *Connaissance*, 170 (1969), 148–52.
16. Gibbs, "Japanning Trade," p. 222.
17. Georg Christoph Lichtenberg, *Briefe*, edited by Albert Leitzmann and Carl Schüddekopf, 2 vols. (Göttingen, 1901), 1:230.
18. Robert Dossie, *Memoirs of Agriculture*, 3 vols. (London, 1768), 1:192–94.
19. Gibbs, "Japanning Trade," p. 228.
20. Lichtenberg, *Briefe*, p. 233.
21. Rufus Porter, *Curious Arts* (Concord, New Hampshire, 1826); Esther Stevens Brazer, *Early American Decoration* (Springfield, Massachusetts, 1946; augmented reprint, 1960); Erwin Christensen, *Early American Design* (New York, 1950); Beatrice Powers and Olive Floyd, *Early American Tinware* (New York, 1957); Shirley S. DeVoe, "Japanned Tinplate," in *The Concise Encyclopedia of American Antiques* (New York, 1958); Z. R. Lee, *The Ornamented Chair* (Rutland, Vermont, 1960).
22. Lee, *The Ornamented Chair*, p. 36.
23. *Antiques*, 91 (1967), 483 and illustration.
24. Scott Graham Williamson, *The American Craftsman* (New York, 1940), pp. 44–46; Lee, *The Ornamented Chair*, pp. 81–87.
25. Esther Stevens Brazer, "The Tinsmiths of Stevens Plains," in *Antiques*, 35 (1939), 294–96.
26. Gibbs, "Japanning Trade," p. 216.
27. Francis Lichten, *Folk Art of Rural Pennsylvania* (New York, 1946), pp. 149–50; Elizabeth S. Hoke, *Pennsylvania German Painted Tin* (New York, n. d.).
28. Jane Toller, *Papier-mâché in Great Britain and America* (London, 1962), pp. 97–103, contains many illustrations of Litchfield ware.
29. Henri d'Allemagne, *Les accessoires du costume*, 2 vols. (Paris, 1928), 1:196–200, 2:489; Lady Walston, "Tôle," in *Connoisseur*, 73 (1925), 144–52, and *Connoisseur*, 87 (1931), 240–43; James Rambo, "Some French and English Tôle in the Cooper Union Museum, New York," in *Cooper Union Mus. Chronicle*, II (1951), no. 2.
30. Jean Robiquet, *L'Art et le goût de la restauration* (Paris, 1928), p. 144.
31. A. Jacquemart, "Une Manufacture de laque à Paris en 1767," in *Gazette des Beaux Arts*, 9 (1861), 311–13.
32. C. H. Stobwasser, *Die merkwürdigsten Begebenheiten aus der Lebensgeschichte von Johann Heinrich Stobwasser* (Brunswick, 1830); F. Fuhse, *Vom Braunschweiger Tischlerhandwerk und Stobwasserarbeiten* (Brunswick, 1925). Both volumes also contain information about lacquer in Germany and Austria.
33. Peter S. Pallas, *Voyages en différentes provinces de l'Empire de Russie*, 3 vols. (Paris, 1789), 2:243–60; I. N. Ouchanova, *Laques russes au l'Ermitage* (Leningrad, 1964), contains bibliography.

34. A. B. Bakushinskij, *Russian Lacquer* (Moscow, 1926); A. B. Bakushinskij, *The Art of Palekh* (Moscow, 1934); D. M. Semenov, *Mstera* (Moscow, 1939); G. Yalovenko, *Fedoskino* (Moscow, 1959); the four volumes listed above are in Russian; Richard Mare, *The Art and Artists of Russia* (London, 1965), contains many illustrations in color; Y. Protopopov, "The Palekh Revival," in *Soviet Life* (January, 1965), pp. 31–40, with illustrations in color; Boris Korolyov, "Fedoskino," in *Soviet Life* (January, 1967), pp. 30–35, with illustrations in color.
35. Winslow Ames, *Prince Albert and Victorian Taste* (New York, 1968), pp. 94–95; *Department of Practical Art. A catalogue of the articles of ornamental art in the museum of the department ... with an Appendix* (2d ed.; London, 1852), pp. 79, 83, 84; *First Report of the Department of Practical Art* (London, 1853), p. 326.
36. Toller, *Papier-mâché*, p. 23.
37. For Marcel Wolfers (born 1886) see Hans Vollmer, *Allgemeines Lexikon der bildenden Künstler des 20. Jahrhunderts*, 6 vols. (Leipzig, 1961); 5:162; M. H. Lelong, *Chemin de la Croix* (Brussels, 1932). Exposition Marcel Wolfers, (exhibition catalogue, *à l'Ecuyer, Bruxelles, Mai–Juin 1970*).
38. For Jean Dunand (1877–1942) see Vollmer, *Lexikon*, 1:608.

SELECTED BIBLIOGRAPHY

Volumes are listed in chronological order. Unless otherwise noted, the date given is the date of first publication.

1550 *De Secreti del Reverando Don Alessio Piemontese.* Venice.

1564 Fioravanti, Leonardo. *Compendio di secreti rationali.* Venice.

1567 Fioravanti, Leonardo. *Dello specchio di scientia naturale.* Venice, 1567, 1572.

1615 Lendsiedel, B. Schnur von. *Kunst und Wunderbüchlein.* Frankfurt.

1619 Caneparius, Pedro Maria. *De atramentis cuiuscunque generis. Opus sane novum hactenus a nemini promulgatum.* Venice, 1619; English ed., London, 1660.

1622 *Museum Calceoloarium.* Verona.

1650 *Museum Wormianum.* Batavia, 1655.

1655 Martinius, P. Martin. *Novus Atlas Sinensis.* Amsterdam.

1658 Sanderson, William. *Graphice: The Use of Pen and Pencil.* London.

1664 Evelyn, John. *Sylva.* London.

1665 Nieuhoff, John. *Het Gezantschaft der Neerlandtsche Oost Indische Compagnie.* Leyden.

1667 Kircher, Athanasius. *China monumentalis qua sacris qua profanis illustrata.* Amsterdam.

1669 Montanus, Arnold. *Denkwürdige Gesandschaften.* Amsterdam, 1669; German ed., n.p., 1670.

1670 Dapper, Olfert. *Gedenkwaerdig Bedryf der Nederlandsche Oost-Indische Maetschappye. Beschryving van geheel Sina.* Amsterdam.

1670 Franciscus, Erasmus. *Neupolierter . . . Spiegel ausländischer Völker.* Nürnberg.

1672 Salmon, William. *Polygraphice, or the arts of drawing, engraving, varnishing, Japanning and gilding.* London, 1672, 1685, 1701, 1735, 1778, 1781.

1674 d'Emery, Antoine. *Recueil des Curiosités rares et nouvelles.* Paris, 1674; English ed., n.p., 1685.

1680 Tylkowski, Adalbert. *Physique curieuse.* Paris.

1681 *Kunstbüchl . . . auf mancherley Weiss Farben zu bereiten.* Augsburg.

1685 Zahn, P. Johannis. *Fundamentum tertium, practico-mechanico Syntagma.* Vol. 3. *Oculus officialis.* Herbipolensis.

1688 Parker, George, and Stalker, John. *A Treatise on Japanning and Varnishing.* London, 1688. Reprinted, London, 1960.

1688 [C. B.] *Traité de mignature, le secrèt de faire le verniz de la Chine.* The Hague, 1688. Italian ed., n.p., 1694.

1689 Kunckel, Johannes. *Ars vitraria experimentalis.* Frankfurt.

1693 Love-Morley, Christopher. *Collectanea Chymica Leydensia.* Lyons.

1693 Coronelli, Vincenzo. *Epitome cosmographica.* Colonia Julia Fanestris. Also inserted in *Bibliotheca Universale Sacra et Profana,* Tom. 1. Venice, 1701.

1696 *Der Curieuse Kunst- und Werckspiegel.* Nürnberg.

1696 *Curieuse Kunst- und Werckschul, erster und anderer Theil.* Nürnberg, 1696, 1705, 1732.

1697 Pollexfen, John. *A discurse of Trade, Coyn and Paper Credit.* London.

1697 [C. K.] *Art's Masterpiece; or a companion for the Ingenious of either Sex; the newest experiments in Japanning.* London, 1697; five later editions, the last 1710.

1702 T. S[now] [Richard Neve]. *Art's improvement.* London, 1702, 1703, 1723.

1702 *Natürliches Zauberbuch oder neuer Spielplatz der Künste. Aus dem Niederländischen.* Nürnberg.

1703 *Die den Frauenzimmerschmuck liebende Kammerjungfer.* Nürnberg.

1703 *Anweisung in der schönen Lacier- und Schildkröten Arbeit.* Nürnberg.

1703 *Der zu vielen Wissenschaften dienstlich anweisende cüriöse Künstler, vorgestellt in einem neu verfertigten und in zwey Theile eingerichtetem Kunst- Haus- und Wunderbuch.* Nürnberg.

1704 Harris, John. *Lexicon technicum.* London, 1704, 1735.

1704 Valentini, M. B. *Museum Museorum.* Frankfurt, 1704–14.

1709 Kochertaler, Caroline. *Neu entdeckte Lacquier-Kunst.* Leipzig, 1709; abridged ed., Dresden, 1754.

1711 Lockyer, Charles. *An account of the trade in India.* London.

1712 Gundling, Jacob Paul von. *Nachricht von den Commercien und Manufacturen.* 1712, 1795.

1712 Kaempfer, Engelhard. *Amoenitatum Exoticarum Fasciculi.* Lemgo.

1713 *Miscellanea Berolinensia.* Vol. 1, see "Vernis." Berlin, 1723–46.

1713 Pictorius, Joh. Baptist [pseud.?]. *Die mit vielen raren und curiösen Geheimnüssen angefüllte Illuminierkunst.* Nürnberg, 1713, 1730.

1715 *Neue und wohl-approbierte Haus und Kunstübung.* Nürnberg.

1717 *Gründlicher Untericht von der Graphice oder Zeichen und Malkunst.* Halle.

1718 Sincerus, Alexander. *Kunst und Nutz.* Nürnberg.

1720 Bonnani, Filippo. *Trattato sopra la vernice.* Rome, 1720, 1731, 1786; French ed., n.p., 1723, 1733; pirated ed., n.p., 1772, 1780; German ed., n.p., 1746.

1728 Chambers, Ephraim. *Cyclopedia.* 3 vols. London, 1728, 1740.

1728 *Der nützliche und curiöse Künstler.* Nürnberg.

1730 *Grundmässige und sehr deutliche Art zu der schönen Laccier- und Schildkrötenarbeit.* Nürnberg, ca. 1730, 1738.

1730 *Introduction in the Art of Japanning with the true India varnish.* London.

1731 *Neuentdeckte Lacquier-Kunst.* Dresden.

1732 *Der curieuse Kunst- und Handwerksnotarius.* Nürnberg.

1732 [Robert Boyle.] *The method of learning to draw in Perspective, chiefly from the Manuscripts of the great Mr. Boyle.* London. 1732; 3rd ed., 1735.

1734 Weber, Georg Christian. *Neueröffnete Guldene Kunstpforte.* Nürnberg, 1734, 1772.

1735 *Dictionarium Polygraphicum,* or *whole body of Arts.* London.

1735 Zedler, J. H. *Grosses vollständiges Universallexikon.* Halle–Leipzig. Vol. 9, p. 2143, see "Fürnis"; vol. 11, p. 1381, see "Gummi lacca"; vol. 16, p. 41, see "Lacciren," and p. 123, see "Lack."

1736 *Der wohlausführende Mahler, welcher curieuse Liebhaber lehret.* Jena.

1738 Smith, Gerry. *The Laboratory,* or *School of Arts.* London, 1738, 1740, 1750.

1748 Guidotti, Alexandro. *Methodo facile per formare qualunque sorta di Vernici.* Rimini, 1748, 1764, 1791; German ed., n.p., 1793.

1752 *Sehr geheim gehaltene . . . Kunststücke die schönsten und rarsten Farben zu verfertigen.* Zittau, 1752, 1777.

1753 Lindenbergh, J. F. *Nieuwe verligtes lerende bereiding voor vernisseurs lakers.* Amsterdam, 1753; German ed., n.p., 1754.

1754 Roslin, *L'esprit du commerce.* Paris.

1754 Müller, Joh. Friedrich. *Kurze und auf Erfahrung gegründete Anweisung zum Lackieren.* Frankfurt, 1754, 1756, 1770, 1771.

1754 Edwards, E., and Darly, Mathew. *Design for use upon lacquered furniture.* London.

1755 *Gründliche Anweisung zur Lackierkunst.* Nordhausen.

1756 Teuber, J. *Vollständiger Unterricht von der Drehkunst und Lackierkunst.* Regensburg.

1756 *Neueröffnete Vorratskammer . . . Kunststücke . . . lackieren.* Frankfurt, 1756, 1758.

1758 Dossie, Robert. *The Handmaiden to the Arts.* London, 1758, 1764.

1758 *Ökonomische Nachrichten.* 15 vols. Leipzig, 1749–63, 1758.

1760 *The Ladies Amusement,* or *the whole Art of Japanning Made easy,* edited by Robert Sayer. London, 1760, 1762.

1760 d'Incarville, P. "Mémoir sur le vernis de la Chine," in *Memoirs de l'Académie Royale des Sciences.* Vol. 15. Paris, 1760; German ed., 1767.

1761 Justi, Joh. Heinr. Gottlob von. *Vollständige Abhandlungen von den Manufakturen und Fabriken.* Copenhagen, 1758–61.

1762 Lalande, J. J. de. "Précis de l'art du cartonnier," in *Déscription des arts et métiers.* Paris, 1762; German ed., 1763.

1762 Brulons, Jacques Savary des. *Dictionaire Universel de commerce.* Nouvelle edit. Vol. 4, p. 118. Copenhagen, 1762; English ed., 1774.

1762 Bondaroy, A. D. Fougeroux de. "Art de travailler les cuirs dorés ou argentés," *Déscription des arts et métiers.* Paris, 1762; German ed., 1763.

1764 Anderson, Adam. *An historical and chronological deduction of commerce.* 2 vols.; Vol. 2, p. 48, see "Lacquer." London.

1765 Halle, Joh. Samuel. *Werkstätten der heutigen Künste.* 4 vols. See vol. 4, p. 154. Brandenburg, 1761–79.

1765 Lewis, William. *Commercium Philosophico Technicum.* London, 1763–65.

1766 *Trattato di Minature.* Venice.

1767 *Der gründlich belehrende Lakiermeister.* Leipzig, 1767, 1769.

1771 Cocq, H. *De Konst van Bereiding van Lakken en Vernissen.* Amsterdam.

1771 *Encyclopaedia Britannica.* 3 vols. Edinburgh, 1768–71.

1772 *Le vernisseur parfait ou manuel du vernisseur.* Pirated from Bonanni, 1772; German ed., n.p., 1773.

1772 *Dictionnaire économique.* Paris.

1772 Watin, Jean Felix. *L'art de faire et d'employer le vernis.* Paris, 1772; enlarged ed., 1773; 14th ed., 1916; German ed., 1774, 1788, 1834.

1773 [P. J. Macquer.] *Dictionnaire des arts et métiers.* Nouvelle ed. by Ch. A. Jombert. See p. 273, "Tôle." Paris.

1773 Sprengel, P. N. *Handwerke und Künste.* Berlin, 1778–95.

1774 *Modern dictionary of arts and sciences.* London.

1780 *Traité de la composition des vernis en général.* Nyon.

1782 Jacobson, J. K. G. *Technologisches Wörterbuch.* Berlin, 1781–84.

1784 Bücking, J. J. *Gründliche Abhandlung von Lackfirnissen.* 3 vols. Stendal.

1788 Krünitz, Joh. Georg. *Ökonomische Encyclopädie,* Brno, 1788–1817. See "Firnis," vol. 13, pp. 434–67; see "Lack," vol. 58, pp. 337–411; see "Lackieren," vol. 58, pp. 522–614.

1788 Agricola, F. *Trattenimenti sulle vernici ed altri materie utili.* Ravenna.

1790 *Mahler-Farb-Illuminier- und Firnisbuch.* Cologne.

1792 *Kunstmappe eines Karthäusers.* Altona, 1792, 1807.

1792 de Salivet, L. *Manuel du tourneur.* Paris.

1793 Coler, I. A. *Gründliche Anweisung zur Lacquirkunst.* Nordhausen.

1794 Kok, J. *Onerrichting... verschiedene soorten van lakken en vernissen te maken.* Amsterdam.

1796 Schubert, S. G. *Der ökonomische Künstler.* Frankfurt.

1796 Le Comte, P. Louise. *Nouveaux mémoires sur l'état présent de la Chine.* Paris.

1798 Schreck, J. L. *Von der sogenannten Laccirkunst.* Nürnberg.

1800 Thomsen, W. *Die Kunst Firnisse und Lackfirnisse zu bereiten.* Quedlinburg, 1800, 1832.

1800 Stegmüller, A. *Der Lackfirnissfabrikant.* Berlin.

1801 Müller, J. C. *Praktische Anweisung zum Lakkiren.* Leipzig, 1801; Graz, 1803.

1804 Tingry, P. F. *The Painter and Varnisher's Guide.* London, 1804, 1816. First published in French and German, 1804.

1804 Stöckel, H. F. *Handbuch für Künstler, Lakkierliebhaber.* Nürnberg, 1804, 1818, 1820, 1822, 1829.

1807 Poppe, Joh. Heinrich. *Geschichte der Technologie,* 3 vols. Göttingen, 1807–10.

1809 [A. R.] *Kunst und Wunderbuch oder verborgene Geheimnisse.* Nürnberg.

1811 Blasche, B. H. *Der Papparbeiter.* Schnepfental, 1811; 5th ed., 1847.

1811 *Praktische Anweisung zum Lackieren.* Leipzig.

1817 Poppe, Joh. Heinrich. *Handbuch der Erfindungen in den mechanischen und technischen Künsten.* Hannover.

1825 Thon, Chr. F. G. *Vollständige Anleitung zu der Lackierkunst.* Ilmenau.

1827 Hyot, L. *Der Damenfreund.* Quedlinburg.

1833 Robin, [Achille], père et fils. *Traité de peinture sur bois blanc d'Ecosse et de Spa.* Paris.

1834 Bickes, F. A. *Das Ganze der Kunst des Lackierens.* Heilbronn.

1836 Stolz, F. *89 Rezepte zu Lacken, etc.* Quedlinburg.

1841 Keller, W. *Neueste und vollständige Farben und Lackkunde.* Berlin.

1845 Sinfer, C. F. W. *Der industriöse Geschäftsmann.* Quedlinburg.

1851 Rikey, J. V. *Der praktische Glasmaler, Wagenlackierer, etc.*

1855 Byron, M. *The artist's and trades man's companion.* London.

1863 Schedel, J. C. *Allgemeines Warenlexikon.* Leipzig.

1865 Creuzberg, Heinrich. *Neues Lehrbuch der Lackierkunst.* Weimar, 1865 (7th ed. of Thon, 1825), 1876, 1884.

1898 Body, Albin. *Essai historique sur les Ouvrages Peints dits Bois de Spa.* Liège.

1901 Brown, W. N. *Handbook on Japanning.* London, 1901, 1913.

1923 Symonds, R. W. *Old English walnut and lacquer furniture.* New York.

1925 Koizumi, G. *Lacquerwork, practical exposition of the art of lacquering.* London.

1927 Stephan, Karl. *Die Lackierkunst der Völker.* Munich.

1929 *Il settecento Italiano, Catalogo della Mostra delle Lacche Veneziane del Settecento.* Venice.

1938 Lorenzetti, Giulio. *Le Lacche Veneziane del Settecento.* Venice.

1954 Morazzoni, Giuseppe. *Mobili Veneziani Laccati.* Milan.

1955 Huth, Hans. *Europäische Lackarbeiten, 1600–1850.* Darmstadt.

1958 Holzhausen, Walter. *Lackkunst in Europa.* Brunswick.

1962 Toller, Jane. *Papier-mâché in Great Britain and America.* London.

1962 Baccesci, Eduard. *Mobili Laccati Veneziani del Settecento.* Venice, 1962, 1966.

1963 Mariacher, G. "Lacquer," in *Encyclopedia of World Art.* Vol. 8, pp. 1003 ff. New York.

1964 Ouchanova, I. N. *Laques russes au l'Ermitage.* Leningrad.

1966 de Sandão, Artur. *O movel pintado em Portugal.* Oporto.

1967 Levy, S. *Lacche Veneziane Settecentesche.* Milan.

1967 *Trois siècles de bois de Spa.* Catalogue, Exhibition Musée de la Vie Wallone. Liège.

ILLUSTRATIONS

Color Plates

Figures (following p. 118)

Figures (continued)

Plates (following p. 158)

20b. Casket, gilt, wood setting for cut glass, Venice, end of sixteenth century (Salford Museum and Art Gallery, Lancashire)
21. "La cassette," detail from engraving by François Guibert, early eighteenth century, after painting by follower of Titian, second half of sixteenth century (From: J. Couché, *Les tableaux du Palais Royal*, Paris, 1786–1808, *Planche* XII)
22. Casket, framework wood, silver-gilt setting, stonework including sardonyx and lapis lazuli, Italian, end of sixteenth century (Geistliche Schatzkammer, Vienna)
23. Casket, framework gilt wood, metal setting, rock crystal, bronze fittings, Venice, about 1600 (S. A. Le Duc de Mouchy, Paris)
24. Casket, framework gilt wood, metal setting, rock crystal, Venice, about 1600 (Museu de Arte Antiga, Lisbon)
25. Casket, interior, similar to plate 23, Venice, about 1600 (Sale Robiony, Nice, 15 February 1965)
26. Casket, interior, similar to plate 23; *see also* color plate I (City Art Museum of St. Louis)
27. Casket, polychromed and gilded, wood, silver-gilt metalwork, Venice, about 1580 (Metropolitan Museum of Art, New York), detail, plate 2
28. Casket, polychromed and gilded, wood, bronze fittings, Venice, about 1550 (Staatliche Stiftung Preussischer Kulturbesitz, Kunstgewerbe-Museum, Berlin-West)
29. Folding table, polychromed, Italian, before 1591 (Museum für Angewandte Kunst, Vienna)
30. Tabletop, gilt (?), Italian, end of sixteenth century (From: *Burlington Magazine*, 29 [1934], 153)
31. Virginal, detail, polychromed and gilded, Italian, about 1570 (Victoria and Albert Museum, London)
32. Virginal, detail, gilt, Benedetto Floriani, Venice, 1571 (Universitäts-Museum, Leipzig)
33. Virginal, detail, gilt on bone and wood, Giovanni Celestini, Venice, 1593 (Royal College of Music, London)
34. Virginal, detail, gilt, Giovanni Antonio Baffo, Venice, 1574 (Victoria and Albert Museum, London)
35. Harp, polychromed and gilded, wood, possibly decorated by Giulio Marescotti in 1587, made for Duke Alphonso II d'Este at Ferrara (Pinacotheca Estense, Modena)
36. Detail of harp, plate 35
37. Cabinet, polychromed wood, Florence (?), about 1600 (Staatliches Kunstgewerbe-Museum, Berlin-Köpenick)
38. Saddlers' Guild ballot box, gilt, wood, London, dated 1619 (The Saddlers' Guild, London)
39. Cabinet, gilt, wood, London, about 1620 (Victoria and Albert Museum, London)
40. Door of cabinet, plate 39
41. Portable cabinet, gilt, wood, London, about 1620 (Victoria and Albert Museum, London)
42. Cabinet, interior, plate 41
43. Trencher, gilt, wood, London, about 1620 (Victoria and Albert Museum, London)
44. Trencher, gilt, wood, London, about 1620 (Victoria and Albert Museum, London)
45. Box, gilt, wood, Holland (?), seventeenth century (Rijksmuseum, Amsterdam)
46. Box, gilt, wood, Holland (?), seventeenth century (Palazzo Doria-Pamphilij, Rome)
47. Plate, gilt, wood, Holland (?), seventeenth century (Musée d'Art et Histoire, Geneva)
48. Plate, gilt, wood, Goa, early seventeenth century (Universitets Konsthistoriska Institution, Upsala)
49. Box, gilt, wood, Augsburg, about 1630 (Universitets Konsthistoriska Institution, Upsala)
50. Box, gilt, wood, Augsburg, about 1630 (Universitets Konsthistoriska Institution, Upsala)
51. Panel, gilt, decorated with battle scene, Augsburg, dated 1628 (Städtisches Kunstgewerbemuseum, Frankfurt am Main)
52. Carbine, detail of shaft, gilt, wood, French, about 1630 (Metropolitan Museum of Art, New York)
53. Cabinet, red, green, and gold raised work, silvered stand, English, about 1675–80 (Victoria and Albert Museum, London)
54. Cabinet, composed of pieces of Coromandel screens, England, about 1680 (Ham House, Richmond)
55. Cabinet, gilt, English, end of seventeenth century (courtesy of the Trustees of the Lady Lever Art Gallery, Port Sunlight)
56. Cabinet, gilt, English, about 1700 (Messrs. French and Company, New York)
57. Bureau-cabinet, polychromed on yellow, England, about 1710 (Palazzo Pallavicini, Rome)
58. Bureau-cabinet, gilt, England, about 1715 (Palazzo Pallavicini, Rome)
59. Bureau-cabinet, red and gilt, England, about 1715 (Palazzo Pallavicini, Rome)
60. Bureau-cabinet, interior, plate 59
61. Dressing table, blue, white, and gilt, raised work, England, about 1690 (Schloss Schlobitten, East Prussia, now destroyed)
62. Chest on stand, gilt, England, about 1710 (Art Institute of Chicago)
63. Mirror, made up of Coromandel pieces, polychromed, fashioned in England about 1690 (Ham House, Richmond)
64. Side table, in the manner of Coromandel work, polychromed, English, about 1690 (Ham House, Richmond)
65. Tea table, from painting "The Strong Family," by Philips, English, about 1730 (Metropolitan Museum of Art, New York)
66. Card table, gold on red, raised work, Giles

Grendey, London, about 1730 (Metropolitan Museum of Art, New York)

67. Top of card table, plate 66
68. Leather screen, polychromed, England, middle of the eighteenth century (Messrs. M. Harris and Son, London)
69. Leather screen, detail, polychromed, signed: Coventry, London, English, mid-eighteenth century (formerly Schloss Wilhelmshöhe, Kassel)
70. Screen, detail of signature, "Coventry, London," plate 69
71. Bed, canopy gilt, posts scarlet, Thomas Chippendale, London, about 1755 (Victoria and Albert Museum, London)
72. Wardrobe, green on yellow, Thomas Chippendale, London, 1770 (Victoria and Albert Museum, London)
73. Bookcase, gilt, raised work, England, about 1755 (Private collection, Chicago)
74. Long-case clock, polychromed, England, about 1735 (Messrs. Mallett and Son, London)
75. Bracket clock, gilt, England, about 1730 (Victoria and Albert Museum, London)
76. Toilet mirror, gilt, England, about 1710 (Colonial Williamsburg, Virginia)
77. Toilet mirror, gilt, England, about 1720 (courtesy Cooper Union Museum, New York)
78. Casket, polychromed on metal, decorated and signed by Marmaduke Craddock, London, 1660–1716 (Victoria and Albert Museum, London)
79. Casket, gold on white, initialed JW or ML, silver containers marked Thomas Heming, London, 1753 (Philadelphia Museum of Art)
80. Chair, polychromed, coronet and cipher of Elizabeth, Duchess of Lowderdale, English, about 1683 (Ham House, Richmond)
81. Chair, green and gold, England, late seventeenth century (Victoria and Albert Museum, London)
82. Chair, gilt, England, about 1695 (courtesy Museum of Fine Arts, Boston)
83. Chair, gilt, England, about 1710 (Victoria and Albert Museum, London)
84. Armchair, gold on red, England, about 1710 (Palazzo Pallavicini, Rome)
85. Chair, gilt, England, about 1710 (Victoria and Albert Museum, London)
86. Daybed, gold on red, Giles Grendey, London, about 1730 (Victoria and Albert Museum, London)
87. Chair, polychromed on yellow, England, about 1735 (Messrs. Mallet and Son, London)
88. Chair, gold on green, Giles Grendey, London, about 1730 (Colonial Williamsburg, Virginia)
89. Chair, detail, plate 88
90. Highboy, polychromed, North American, about 1700 (Metropolitan Museum of Art, New York)
91. Highboy, polychromed, North American, about 1730 (Henry Francis Du Pont Winterthur Museum, Delaware)
92. Highboy, polychromed, Boston, about 1725–1730 (courtesy Museum of Fine Arts, Boston)
93. Highboy, polychromed, Boston, 1725–30 (courtesy Museum of Fine Arts, Boston)
94. Highboy, gilt, raised work, carries name of cabinetmaker "Pimm," attributed to japanner Thomas Johnson, Boston, 1735 (Henry Francis Du Pont Winterthur Museum, Delaware)
95. Highboy, gilt, raised work, attributed to japanner Thomas Johnson, Boston, 1735 (Metropolitan Museum of Art, New York)
96. Lowboy, gilt, attributed to japanner Thomas Johnson, Boston, about 1735 (Metropolitan Museum of Art, New York)
97. Chair, gilt, Boston, 1700 (Los Angeles County Museum)
98. Chair, detail, plate 97
99. Long-case clock, work by Gavin Brown, Boston, 1766 (Henry Ford Museum, Dearborn, Michigan)
100. Mirror, gilt, New York, about 1730–40 (Henry Francis Du Pont Winterthur Museum, Delaware)
101. Panel, polychromed, North American, about 1750 (Metropolitan Museum of Art, New York)
102. Cabinet, Augsburg (?), seventeenth century, and table, Venice (?), end of seventeenth century, both decorated with *chinoiseries*, polychromed, table with mother-of-pearl inlay (Cà Rezzonico, Venice)
103. Frame, Guido Reni, S. Francis, dark-green lacquer, gilt, mother-of-pearl inlay, after 1650 (Národni Galerie, Prague)
104. Frame, detail, plate 103
105. Crucifix stem, detail, polychromed, mother-of-pearl inlay, Venice, about 1650 (San Zaccaria, Venice)
106. Bureau-cabinet, polychromed, Venice, about 1700 (Messrs. Loewi-Robertson, Inc., Los Angeles)
107. Bureau-cabinet, polychromed and gilded, Venice, early eighteenth century (Museo Castello Sforcesco, Milan)
108. Bureau-cabinet, polychromed on yellow, Venice, middle of the eighteenth century (Madame Georges A. Salman, Paris)
109. Bureau-cabinet, *lacca povera* work, polychromed, Venice, about 1740 (Metropolitan Museum of Art, New York)
110. Console table, gold on green, Venice, about 1750 (Cà Rezzonico, Venice)
111. Commode, gold on green, Venice, about 1750 (Cà Rezzonico, Venice)
112. Commode, polychromed on blue, Venice, about 1750 (Stanford University, Palo Alto)
113. Stand, polychromed and silver, Venice, about

1750 (Messrs. Loewi-Robertson, Inc., Los Angeles)

114. Blackamoor, polychromed and gilt, linden wood, Giovanni Giuliani, St. Florian, 1729 (Stift St. Florian, Austria)
115. Frame, polychromed on green, with Rezzonico coat of arms, Venice, about 1750 (Private collection)
116. Ridotto Venier, Venice, after 1750 (Ponte dei Baratteri, no. 4939, Venice)
117. Armchair, polychromed on blue, Venice, about 1750 (Messrs. Loewi-Robertson, Inc., Los Angeles)
118. Chairs, polychromed on white, Venice, late eighteenth century (Collection Tullio Silva, Milan)
119. Toilette set, polychromed on yellow and black, Venice, about 1750 (Metropolitan Museum of Art, New York)
120. Game of Lotto, polychromed, *lacca povera* work, Venice, after 1750 (Messrs. Loewi-Robertson, Inc., Los Angeles)
121. Game tabletop, polychromed, *lacca povera* work, Venice, about 1740–50 (private collection, Milan)
122. Stringed instrument, gilt, Venice (?), about 1700, case later (Messrs. Loewi-Robertson, Inc., Los Angeles)
123. Stringed instrument, gilt, Venice (?), 1730–40 (Palazzo Doria-Pamphilij, Rome)
124. Sales desk, polychromed on gold and black, Venice, about 1750 (Messrs. Loewi-Robertson, Inc., Los Angeles)
125. Commode, polychromed on blue, from Falier family, Venice, late eighteenth century (Cà Rezzonico, Venice)
126. Lacquer room, polychromed, Pietro Massa, Turin, about 1735–38 (Palazzo Reale, Turin)
127. Lacquer room, detail, plate 126
128. Paneling, polychromed, Turin, about 1720–30 (Palazzo Reale, Turin)
129. Lacquer room, detail, plate 126
130. Door and paneling, polychromed on white, Turin, about 1770 (Casa di Caccia, Stupinigi)
131. Corner cupboard, polychromed on white, Turin, about 1750 (Casa di Caccia, Stupinigi)
132. Lacquer room from Villa Vacchetti at Gerbido, near Turin, polychromed on white, North Italy, about 1740 (Nelson Art Gallery, Kansas City, Missouri)
133. Secretary, gold and polychrome on blue, Turin, about 1730 (private collection)
134. Commode, green and gold, Turin, about 1750 (Sale, Christie's, London, 19 March 1959)
135. Corner cupboard, red and gold, Turin, about 1750 (Private collection, on exhibition at *Mostra del Barocco Piemontese*, Turin, 1963, no. 240)
136. Bed table, *lacca povera* work, polychromed on cream, Turin, about 1750 (Private collection, on exhibition at *Mostra del Barocco Piemontese*, Turin, 1963, no. 83)
137. Tabletop, polychromed and gold on cream, Turin, about 1750 (Private collection, on exhibition at *Mostra del Barocco Piemontese*, Turin, 1963, no. 85)
138. Stool, gilt, Turin, about 1750 (Palazzo Reale, Turin)
139. Table, red and green, Turin, about 1750 (Private collection, on exhibition at *Mostra del Barocco Piemontese*, Turin, 1963, no. 86)
140. Microscope, gilt, instrument made by P. Paulus Maria Petrini, Rome, about 1750 (S. A. Principe Urbano Barberini, Rome)
141. Commode, gold on purple, Rome, about 1750 (S. A. Principe Urbano Barberini, Rome)
142. Commode, detail, plate 141
143. Commode, polychromed on white, Rome, about 1750 (Los Angeles County Museum)
144. Commode, gold on white, Rome, about 1750 (Palazzo Pallavicini, Rome)
145. Lacquer room, gold on black, Sicily, mid-eighteenth century (Villa Vizcaja, Miami, Florida)
146. Panel from ballroom, polychromed on light color, Sicily, about 1750 (Musée des Arts Décoratifs, Paris)
147. Commode, polychromed on light colors, Sicily, after 1750 (Messrs. Loewi-Robertson, Inc., Los Angeles)
148. Clavichord, by H. A. Hass, Hamburg, 1723, polychromed, gold on tortoiseshell ground (Musik Historisk Museet, Copenhagen)
149. Clavichord, by Christian Zell, Hamburg, 1728, polychromed (Museum für Kunst und Gewerbe, Hamburg)
150. Clavichord, by H. A. Hass, Hamburg, 1732, gold on red (Kunstindustri Museet, Oslo)
151. Clavichord, by H. A. Hass, Hamburg, 1732, interior, polychromed (Kunstindustri Museet, Oslo)
152. Cabinet, polychromed on green, Hamburg, about 1730 (Kunstindustri Museet, Oslo)
153. Cabinet, detail, plate 152
154. Clavichord, by J. A. Hass, Hamburg, 1755, green and red on white (Musik Historisk Museet, Copenhagen)
155. Detail of window frame, Catarinenstrasse 9, Hamburg, destroyed during the war, polychromed on wood, early eighteenth century (Photo Denkmalsamt, Hamburg)
156. Chest on stand, polychromed, J. C. Lesieur, Brunswick, about 1730 (S. K. H. Herzog von Hannover)
157. Cupboard, polychromed on red, Danzig (?), early eighteenth century (Sale Stucker, 1964, Bern, Switzerland)
158. Cabinet, polychromed, North German (?), early eighteenth century (Dansk Folke Museum, Copenhagen)

159. Cabinet on stand, raised work, gold and black on white, attributed to Gérard Dagly, Berlin, about 1700 (Schloss Charlottenburg, Berlin)
160. Cabinet on stand, blue on white, Gérard Dagly, Berlin, about 1690 (Schloss Charlottenburg, Berlin)
161. Cabinet, interior, polychromed on white, plate 160
162. Cabinet, Japan, raised work, gilt, seventeenth century; stand and decoration of sides, Dagly workshop, Berlin, about 1700 (Schloss Charlottenburg, Berlin)
163. Cabinet, detail, plate 162, Dagly workshop, Berlin, about 1700 (Schloss Charlottenburg, Berlin)
164. Cabinet on stand, gilt, attributed to Gérard Dagly, Berlin, about 1700 (K. Husgerads Kammeren, Stockholm)
165. Cabinet, detail, plate 160, blue on white
166. Cabinet on stand, raised work, once in curio room shown in plate 167, Gérard Dagly, before 1696 (Staatliches Kunstgewerbe Museum, Berlin-Köpenick)
167. Curio room, once in Berlin palace (now destroyed), with four cabinets by Gérard Dagly (engraving from: Lorenz Beger, *Thesaurus Brandenburgicus*, Cologne, 1696, plate 1)
168. Cabinet, detail, plate 166
169. Table, polychromed, Dagly workshop, about 1700 (Schloss Charlottenburg, Berlin)
170. Table, detail, plate 169
171. Table, gilt, Berlin, about 1700 (formerly Schloss Schlobitten, East Prussia)
172. Armchair, red and gold, chair Far East (?), japanning Berlin (?), about 1700 (Schloss Charlottenburg, Berlin)
173. Armchair, detail, plate 172
174. Cupboard, gold on red, Berlin, about 1725 (Schloss Charlottenburg, Berlin)
175. Cupboard, detail, plate 174, interior gold on green
176. Firescreen, gold on red, Berlin, about 1725 (Schloss Charlottenburg, Berlin)
177. Panel, polychromed, David Pennewitz, from the manor of Plaue, about 1715 (Märkisches Museum, Berlin-East)
178. Table, polychromed on red, Sebastian Chevalier, Berlin, about 1775 (Neues Palais, Potsdam)
179. Table, detail, plate 178
180. Drawing of furniture in the bedroom of Frederick the Great, including oval table by Chevalier beside the chair in which the king died (present whereabouts of drawing and table unknown)
181. Oval room, polychromed on yellow, Sebastian Chevalier, about 1767 (Neues Palais, Potsdam)
182. Pilgrim bottle, red stoneware, polychromed, japanning attributed to Martin Schnell, Meissen, about 1715 (Metropolitan Museum of Art, New York)
183. Coffeepot, red stoneware, polychromed, japanning attributed to Martin Schnell, about 1715 (Sale, Sotheby's, London, 1952)
184. Vase, faïence, decorated with blue underglaze, partly covered with brown lacquer, Frankfurt, 1680–90 (Bayrisches National Museum, Munich)
185. Vase, porcelain, polychromed on red, Far East (?), decorated in Berlin (?), about 1800 (formerly Private collection, Berlin)
186. Vase, porcelain, polychromed on red, Far East (?), decorated in Berlin (?), about 1800 (formerly Private collection, Berlin)
187. Vase, faïence, decorated with blue underglaze, partly covered with brown lacquer, Ansbach, about 1720 (Bayrisches National Museum, Munich)
188. Cabinet on stand, gold and silver on red, Schnell workshop (?), Dresden, about 1710–20 (formerly Bergpalais, Pillnitz)
189. Cabinet, interior, plate 188
190. Tabletop, gold on red, Schnell workshop (?), Dresden, about 1720–30 (Bergpalais, Pillnitz)
191. Tabletop, gold on red, Schnell workshop (?), Dresden, 1720–30 (Bergpalais, Pillnitz)
192. Cabinet, gilt, Schnell workshop (?), Dresden, about 1715 (Rijksmuseum, The Hague)
193. Cabinet, interior, plate 192
194. Bureau-cabinet, gold on red, Schnell workshop (?), Dresden, about 1720–30 (Bergpalais, Pillnitz)
195. Bureau-cabinet, gold on red, Schnell workshop (?), Dresden, about 1720–30 (Bergpalais, Pillnitz)
196. Bureau-cabinet, gold on red, Dresden, about 1740 (Schloss Moritzburg, Dresden)
197. Bureau-cabinet, gold on red, interior gold on blue, Dresden, about 1740 (Museum für Kunsthandwerk, Frankfurt)
198. Screen, oil painting on canvas, J. G. Näcke, Dresden, about 1726 (Museum für Kunsthandwerk, Dresden)
199. Mirror back, royal coat of arms of Saxony on front, polychromed and gilded, Dresden, about 1720 (Rijksmuseum, Amsterdam)
200. Chair, polychromed on white, leather cover with embossed coat of arms of Saxony, on rear embossed initials MSG and date 1719, Schnell workshop (?), Dresden, 1719 (Lack Museum Herbig-Haarhaus, Cologne)
201. Chair, detail, plate 200
202. Oval room, panels bottom row, door, polychromed, Munich, 1717, restored 1769 (Pagodenburg, Nymphenburg)
203. Corner of room, oblong panels polychromed, J. G. Höringer, Munich, 1763 (Schloss Nymphenburg)
204. Clock on stand, polychromed, movement B. Firstenfelder, 1725, Friedberg, near Augsburg (Bayrisches National Museum, Munich)

205. Bracket clock, polychromed on yellow, movement Paulus Graf, Munich, about 1760 (Mr. Karl Leuthenmayr, Munich)
206. *Chinoiserie* panel, detail (B. Verwaltung der staatl. Schlösser, Gärten u. Seen Museumsabteilung, Schloss Nymphenburg, Munich)
207. *Chinoiserie* print copied for panel, plate 206, engraving before 1756 by M. Engelbrecht, Augsburg (Graphische Sammlung, Munich)
208. Sedan chair, silver on blue, Munich, about 1750 (Schloss Nymphenburg, Munich)
209a. Margrave Ludwig Wilhelm of Baden (nicknamed "Türkenlouis") in Turkish costume, red and gilt frame, German, about 1700 (Schloss Favorite, near Baden-Baden)
209b. Prince Carl Joseph of Baden (?) in Turkish costume, red and gilt frame, German, about 1710 (Schloss Favorite, near Baden-Baden)
210a. Carved table, gilded, Dutch (?), about 1700 (Schloss Favorite, near Baden-Baden)
210b. Table, detail, plate 210a, polychromed and gilded
211. Chinese room, gilt, J. J. Sänger, 1717 (Schloss Ludwigslust, near Stuttgart)
212. Chinese room, large panels Coromandel work, oblong and lower panels incised and polychromed on stucco by Margravine Wilhelmine about 1740 (Eremitage, Bayreuth)
213. Lacquer room, walls polychromed, oval panels blue on white, Johann Adalbert Kratochwil, Prague, 1709 (Palais Sternberg, Kinsky pavilion, now Národni Galerie, Prague)
214. Detail from plate 213
215. Cabinet, gilt, Johann Konrad Hoffmann, about 1711 (Schloss Weikersheim)
216. Door of cabinet, plate 215
217. Desk secretaire, gilt, Bamberg, about 1730 (Bayrisches National Museum, Munich)
218. Panel from Dutch room, center gold on blue, borders blue and white, German or Dutch, about 1705 (Neue Residenz, Bamberg)
219. Fragment of door of lacquer room formerly at the palace of Brühl near Cologne, polychromed, German (?), about 1705 (Denkmalsamt, Cologne)
220. Bureau, gilt, bearing coat of arms of Rabutin-Sévigné, Far East (?), about 1680 (Musée Carnavalet, Paris)
221. Commode, polychromed and gilded, France, about 1725 (formerly Messrs. A. and R. Ball, New York)
222. Commode, gilt, Japanese cabinet mounted in France, about 1715 (Pagodenburg, Nymphenburg)
223. Panel, lacquered and decorated, X-ray photograph of underground of Watteau's *Leçon d'amour*, painted about 1716–17 (National Museum, Stockholm)
224. Box, gold on red, French, about 1720 (Victoria and Albert Museum, London)
225. Desk, gilt, French, attributed to Bernard van Risenburgh, about 1735 (Residenz Museum, Munich)
226. Commode, polychromed and gilded, Mathieu Criaerd (signed), Paris, about 1740 (Palazzo Pallavicini, Rome)
227. Drop-front secretary, gilt, Japanese lacquer except for drawer front, Jean-François Dubut (signed), Paris, about 1740–50 (Mr. and Mrs. Charles B. Wrightsman, New York)
228. Desk, gilt, Jacques Dubois (signed), Paris, about 1745 (formerly Duc de Talleyrand, Sagan, Silesia)
229. Desk, gilt, Paris, about 1745 (Sale, Sotheby's, 7 July 1961, London)
230. Desk, gold on blue, Paris, about 1745 (Musée des Arts Décoratifs, Paris)
231. Table, Sèvres top, originally lacquered white with green lozenges and gold, Bernard van Risenburgh (signed), Paris, about 1761, lacquer probably Martin workshop (J. Paul Getty Museum, Malibu)
232. Table, Sèvres top, originally lacquered white, green lozenge pattern, R. Lacroix (signed), Paris, about 1765, lacquer probably Martin workshop Musée du Louvre, Camondo Collection, Paris)
233. Table, Sèvres top and shelf, blue, Bernard van Risenburgh (signed), Paris, about 1760, lacquer probably Martin workshop (Metropolitan Museum of Art, New York)
234. Corner cupboard, polychromed and gilded, Jacques Dubois (signed), Paris, about 1745 (J. Paul Getty Museum, Malibu)
235. Corner cupboard, gilt, scarlet frame, Bernard van Risenburgh (signed), Paris, about 1745–49 (by gracious permission of H. M. Queen Elizabeth II, copyright reserved)
236. Corner cupboard, gilt, from the Château de Bellevue, Martin Carlin (signed), Paris, about 1785 (Musée du Louvre, Paris)
237. Commode, gilt, Jean Desforges (signed D. F.), Paris, about 1740 (Widener Collection, National Gallery of Art, Washington, D.C.)
238. Commode, polychromed and gilded, raised work, Bernard van Risenburgh, Paris, about 1740 (J. Paul Getty Museum, Malibu)
239. Commode, black and gold, Paris, about 1770 (formerly Messrs. Duveen, New York)
240. Commode, raised lacquer, gilt, E. Levasseur (signed), Paris, about 1780 (Sale, Sotheby's, 17 April 1964, London)
241. Corner cupboard, blue on white, from Château de Choisy, Paris, about 1773 (Musée du Louvre, Paris)
242. Writing table, polychromed and gold on yellow, Paris, about 1760 (formerly Messrs. A. and R. Ball, New York)
243. Commode, blue on white, Pierre Roussel (signed), Paris, about 1750 (formerly Messrs. A. and R. Ball, New York)

244. Commode, polychromed on yellow, François Rubestuck (signed), Paris, about 1775 (formerly Messrs. A. and R. Ball, New York)
245. Box, polychromed on gold, papier-mâché, *vernis Martin*, Paris, about 1745 (Victoria and Albert Museum, London)
246. Box, polychromed on gold ground, papier-mâché, *vernis Martin*, Paris, about 1745 (Metropolitan Museum of Art, New York)
247. Pinbox, gold on purple, papier-mâché, *vernis Martin*, Paris, about 1745 (Lack Museum Herbig-Haarhaus, Cologne)
248. Pinboxes, polychromed on lavender, papier-mâché, *vernis Martin*, Paris, about 1745 (Lack Museum Herbig-Haarhaus, Cologne)
249. Toilette table, with set of utensils, polychromed on black, Paris, about 1770 (Antique Company of New York, Inc.)
250. Bed table, rosewood veneer, top of table polychromed on green, France, 1740–50 (formerly collection Wilhelm von Bode, Berlin)
251. Bed table, detail of polychrome decoration, plate 250
252. Spinettino, gilt, France, about 1740 (Musikinstrumentensammlung, Berlin-West)
253. Spinettino, detail, plate 252
254. Sedan chair, polychromed on gold, Paris, about 1750 (formerly Mr. A. Seligmann-Rey, New York)
255. Carriage seat, gold on red lacquer, now transformed into chair, Paris, early eighteenth century (Palazzo Pallavicini, Rome)
256. Sledge seat, detail polychromed, inscribed DAGLY (?), Paris, before 1750 (Carriage Museum, Château de Compiègne, France)
257. Harpsichord, polychromed on green, Johannes Goermans, Paris, 1754 (Metropolitan Museum of Art, New York)
258. Harpsichord, detail, plate 257
259. Gentleman playing harp, oil painting, Danish (?), about 1760 (Kunstindustri Museet, Oslo)
260. Harp, detail, polychromed decoration, French, about 1760 (Kunstindustri Museet, Oslo)
261. Octavina spinet, polychromed on cream, Pascal Taskin, Paris, about 1778 (Belle Skinner Collection of musical instruments, Yale University, New Haven)
262. Chinese room, gilt, Netherlands, about 1680 (Rosenborg, Copenhagen)
263. Chinese room, detail of paneling, plate 262
264. Secretary, polychromed on white, raised work, Antwerp (?), about 1680 (Schloss Charlottenburg, Berlin)
265. Secretary, detail, plate 264
266. Cabinet, polychromed, Netherlands, about 1690 (formerly Schloss Königsberg)
267. Cabinet, gilt outside, interior polychromed on white, Netherlands, about 1680 (Schloss Mosigkau near Dessau, East Germany)
268. Cabinet, gilt, Netherlands, about 1700 (formerly Schloss Berlin)
269. Cabinet, gilt, Netherlands, about 1700 (Kölnisches Stadt Museum, Cologne)
270. Cabinet, gold on red, Netherlands, about 1700 (Jonkheer J. Beelarts van Blokland, Osterbeek, Holland)
271. Cabinet, gilt, Netherlands, about 1700 (Messrs. Loewi-Robertson, Inc., Los Angeles)
272. Chinese room, polychromed and gilded, Netherlands, about 1750 (from Buitenrust, now Gemeente Museum den Haag)
273. Cabinet, gilt, Netherlands, about 1700 (Kölnisches Stadt Museum, Cologne)
274. Cabinet on stand, Netherlands, about 1700, stand about 1740 (Kölnisches Stadt Museum, Cologne)
275. Writing desk, gold on green, Netherlands (?), about 1725 (Private collection, Munich)
276. Writing desk, detail of top, plate 275
277. Cabinet, gilt, Netherlands, about 1740 (Schloss Mosigkau, near Dessau, East Germany)
278. Chinese room, gold on red and black, Netherlands, about 1780 (Huis ten Bosch, den Haag)
279. Cabinet, gilt, from dollhouse by Christof van Brant, Amsterdam, about 1740 (Rijksmuseum, Amsterdam)
280. Folding table from dollhouse by Christof van Brant, polychromed, Amsterdam, about 1740 (Rijksmuseum, Amsterdam)
281. Stand, gilt, Netherlands, early eighteenth century (Dr. A. Staring, Vorden, Holland)
282. Pastel, detail, by Cornelis van Troost, Netherlands, about 1711 (Rijksmuseum, Cat. 2968, Amsterdam)
283. Cabinet, silver on black, Sweden, 1730–40 (Nordiska Museet, Stockholm)
284. Corner cupboard, polychromed, Sweden, early eighteenth century (Nordiska Museet, Stockholm)
285. Cabinet, *lacca povera*, Sweden, early eighteenth century (Nordiska Museet, Stockholm)
286. Long-case clock, gilt, English movement by John Davies, japanning by Niels Lochstoer (signed), about 1750 (privately owned, Svanoy, Norway)
287. Long-case clock, gold on blue, Sweden, Dalarna, about 1740 (Nordiska Museet, Stockholm)
288. Long-case clock, gilt, Denmark, about 1750, work signed by Mathiesen, Copenhagen (Dansk Folke Museum, Copenhagen)
289. Long-case clock, detail, plate 286
290. Long-case clock, detail, signature of Lochstoer, plate 286
291. Bracket clock, gold and silver on green, Niels Lochstoer (signed), about 1750 (Norsk Folke Museum, Oslo)
292. Bracket clock, gold and silver on green, Sweden, Smaland, about 1740 (Nordiska Museet, Stockholm)

293. Bracket clock, detail, plate 292
294. Desk, green on yellow, Sweden (?), about 1740–50 (Sale, Sotheby's, April, 1966, London)
295. Desk, gilt, Japanese lacquer, Niels Dahlin, Stockholm, about 1765 (Nordiska Museet, Stockholm)
296. Lacquer room, gilt, Ivan Tikhanov and Perfil Fjodorov, Russia, 1720–22 (Mon Plaisir, Peterhof)
297. Desk, gilt, Russia, early eighteenth century (Hermitage Museum, Leningrad)
298. Desk, detail, plate 297
299. Box, polychromed, inlay of pewter and mother-of-pearl, wood, Spa, after 1650 (Musée Communal de Spa)
300. Box, black, inlay of mother-of-pearl, papier-mâché, Spa, about 1700 (Musée de la Vie Wallone, Liège)
301. Box, with chips, gilt, inlay of mother-of-pearl, coat of arms of Clemens August, Elector and Archbishop of Cologne, Spa, about 1740–50 (Rheinisches Landesmuseum, Bonn)
302. Box, polychromed on white, Vincent Rousseau (signed), Spa, about 1750 (Victoria and Albert Museum, London)
303. Desk, polychromed, Spa (?), about 1750 (Messrs. Loewi-Robertson, Inc., Los Angeles)
304. Tea caddy, polychromed, Spa (?), about 1750 (Victoria and Albert Museum, London)
305. Set of boxes, polychromed on white, Spa, before 1750 (Lack Museum Herbig-Haarhaus, Cologne)
306. Toilet set, with views of Spa, polychromed on white, Spa, about 1750 (formerly Frau Elfriede Langeloh, Cologne)
307. Box from toilet set, tin, gilt on tortoiseshell, with Battersea enamel plaque, Pontypool, about 1750 (Colonial Williamsburg)
308 a. Snuffbox, with portrait of Colonel John Ferrier Hamilton, polychromed on wood, signed: I. Patterson, Comnock, 1827, made and marked by John Smith, Mauchline (Mrs. J. B. Findlay, Carnell, Hurlford, Scotland)
308 b. Snuffbox, scene from a poem by Robert Burns, polychromed wood, Scotland, about 1830 (National Museum of Antiquities of Scotland)
308 c. Snuffbox, gilt on wood, made and marked by John Smith, Mauchline, before 1837 (Mrs. J. B. Findlay, Carnell, Hurlford, Scotland)
308 d. Snuffbox, cat and rat story, polychromed wood, Scotland, about 1840 (Colonel B. Knox, Kerseland, Monckton, Scotland)
309. Knife boxes, tin, polychromed and gilded on tortoiseshell, Pontypool, about 1755–60 (formerly collection of Mr. Arthur J. Sussell, Philadelphia)
310. Tin basket, remainders of tortoiseshell, Pontypool, about 1775 (National Museum of Wales, Cardiff)
311. Tin maker's mark, tin soldered on base of sugar basket: "Japan'd by Pyrke of Usk, Monmouthshire," Usk, 1814–26 (National Museum of Wales, Cardiff)
312. Tea urn, tin, polychromed on crimson, Pontypool, about 1770 (National Museum of Wales, Cardiff)
313. Chestnut vase, tin, gold, silver, and red, Pontypool (?), about 1795 (National Museum of Wales, Cardiff)
314. Tilt-top table, tray, tin, polychromed and gilded on tortoiseshell, Pontypool, about 1765 (Colonial Williamsburg)
315. Tray, tin, gilt on crimson, Pontypool, about 1760 (National Museum of Wales, Cardiff)
316. Tray, tin, gilt on tortoiseshell, Pontypool or Usk, about 1810 (National Museum of Wales, Cardiff)
317. Pin tray (5 in.), tin, gilt on crimson, Pontypool, about 1790 (National Museum of Wales, Cardiff)
318. Tray, "Capture of Fort Detroit," 1812, polychromed, tin, Pontypool, after 1812 (National Museum of Wales, Cardiff)
319. Snuffbox, with portrait of John Baskerville, signed by S. Raven (1775–1847), papier-mâché, Birmingham, end of the eighteenth century (City Museum and Art Gallery, Birmingham)
320. Snuffbox, with coat of arms of the Society of Planemakers, probably painted by S. Raven, papier-mâché, polychromed, Birmingham, end of eighteenth century (City Museum and Art Gallery, Birmingham)
321. Tray, papier-mâché, with Italian Renaissance motifs, polychromed and gilded, impressed mark "Clay Patent" under crown, Henry Clay, Birmingham, about 1800 (City Museum and Art Gallery, Birmingham)
322. Tray, "Gathering of the Unions," polychromed, tin, Birmingham, after 1832 (City Museum and Art Gallery, Birmingham)
323 a. Tray, papier-mâché, polychromed and gilded on black, Henry Clay, London, after 1800 (City Museum and Art Gallery, Birmingham)
323 b. Tray, impressed mark: Clay Kingst Covt. Garden, plate 323 a
324. Sugar box, tin, polychromed, Wolverhampton, 1810–20 (Henry Francis Du Pont Winterthur Museum, Delaware)
325. Stereoscope, papier-mâché, gilded on black with mother-of-pearl inlay, Birmingham, about 1850 (City Museum and Art Gallery, Birmingham)
326. Blotter, papier-mâché, polychromed on black tinted mother-of-pearl inlay, Birmingham, about 1855 (Victoria and Albert Museum, London)
327 a. Writing box, tin, polychromed and gilded on black, Jennens and Bettridge, Birmingham, about 1850 (Victoria and Albert Museum, London)

327 b. Writing box, impressed mark: Jennens and Bettridge, Makers to the Queen, plate 327 a
328. Chair, papier-mâché, polychromed and gilded on black, inlay of mother-of-pearl, Birmingham, about 1860 (Art Institute of Chicago)
329. Toilette table, with mirror, papier-mâché with wooden structure, polychromed and gilded on black, mother-of-pearl inlay, Birmingham, 1850–60 (formerly Miss Elizabeth Day McCormick Collection, Chicago)
330. Bed, papier-mâché and wood, polychromed and gilded on black, mother-of-pearl inlay, Birmingham, 1850–60 (formerly Miss Elizabeth Day McCormick Collection, Chicago)
331. Chair, black and gold, American, bearing stencil on back "L. Hitchcock, Hitchcockville, Conn.," 1825–28 (Henry Ford Museum, Dearborn, Michigan)
332. Bread basket, tin, polychromed on yellow, Stevens Plains, early nineteenth century (Henry Francis Du Pont Winterthur Museum, Delaware)
333. Cookie box, tin, polychromed, Pennsylvania, 1800–50 (Philadelphia Museum of Art)
334. Tureen, copper gold on black, French, about 1750 (Lack Museum Herbig-Haarhaus, Cologne)
335. Câche pot, copper gold on black, French, about 1750 (courtesy of the Cooper Union Museum, New York)
336. Tea kettle and stand, tin gold on black, French, about 1750 (Colonial Williamsburg)
337. Jardiniere, tin, polychromed on black, French, about 1770 (Musée des Arts Décoratifs, Paris)
338. Inkstand, tin, polychromed on green, French, about 1780 (Musée des Arts Décoratifs, Paris)
339. Urn, tin, polychromed on white, French, end of eighteenth century (Musée des Arts Décoratifs, Paris)
340. Secretary, decorated with allegorical paintings by F. A. Weitsch, signed and dated 1794, tin, plates polychromed, Stobwasser workshop, Brunswick (Städtisches Museum, Brunswick)
341. Table, with tray, polychromed on tortoiseshell, Stobwasser workshop, Brunswick, before 1800 (Städtisches Museum, Brunswick)
342. Tray, detail of plate 341, showing sons of Edward IV in the Tower of London, taken from print
343. Snuffbox, "Amor and Psyche," after painting by Johann Enter, papier-mâché, grisaille, Stobwasser workshop, Brunswick, about 1800 (Städtisches Museum, Brunswick)
344. Snuffbox, "View of Brocken Mountain," papier-mâché, polychromed, Stobwasser workshop, Brunswick, about 1800 (Städtisches Museum, Brunswick)
345. Snuffbox in silhouette, Stobwasser workshop, Brunswick (Städtisches Museum, Brunswick)
346. Snuffbox, inscribed "Jean Guérin, Vernisseur, Brunswick," papier-mâché, gilt, Stobwasser workshop, Brunswick, about 1800 (Städtisches Museum, Brunswick)
347. Snuffbox, with portrait of the dramatist Johann Anton Leisewitz after painting by J. H. Schröder, papier-mâché, polychromed, decorated by H. Krevel about 1811, Stobwasser workshop, Brunswick (Städtisches Museum, Brunswick)
348. Tobacco jar, tin, silver and gold on black, Stobwasser workshop, Brunswick, about 1800 (Städtisches Museum, Brunswick)
349. Tea kettle, tin, gilt on red, Stobwasser workshop, Brunswick, about 1800 (Städtisches Museum, Brunswick)
350. Casket with tea caddies, polychromed views on wood, Stobwasser workshop, Brunswick, end of eighteenth century (Städtisches Museum, Brunswick)
351. Tray, papier-mâché, polychromed on tortoiseshell, Stobwasser workshop, Brunswick, about 1800 (Städtisches Museum, Brunswick)
352. Tray, "Italian fountains at Peterhof," polychromed on tin, Demidov workshop, Russia, early nineteenth century (Hermitage Museum, Leningrad)
353. Tray, "Triple Alliance of 1815," polychromed on papier-mâché, P. I. Korobov workshop (?), Russia, about 1815 (Hermitage Museum, Leningrad)
354. Tray, polychromed on tin, A. Laboutin, Russia, about 1840 (Hermitage Museum, Leningrad)
355. Tray, "Czar Nicholas I and Czarina and monument to Peter I," polychromed on papier-mâché, P. and A. Lukutin, Danilkovo (Fedoskino), about 1850 (Valentin, Count Zoubov, Paris)
356. Russian lacquer marks:
    a. Eagle and initials P. P. L. for Factory Piotr Vasielievich Lukutin, 1828–30 (Hermitage Museum, Leningrad)
    b. Eagle and initials F. A. L. for Factory Alexander Pietrovitch Lukutin, used after 1830 (Lack Museum Herbig-Haarhaus, Cologne)
    c. Eagle and P. A. Lukutin (in script), used after 1830 (Lack Museum Herbig-Haarhaus, Cologne)
    d. Four eagles and Russian for Factory Lukutin, Moscow, used between 1881 and 1902 (Hermitage Museum, Leningrad)
    e. Mark showing name Vishniakov and Son, Kuskovo, used around 1870 and later. Mark also exists with five medals and without crown (Lack Museum Herbig-Haarhaus, Cologne)
357. Snuffbox, "View of Moscow," polychromed on papier-mâché, P. A. Lukutin, Danilkovo (Fedoskino), about 1850 (Hermitage Museum, Leningrad)

358. Snuffbox, "Family at tea," polychromed on papier-mâché, Vishniakov, Kuskovo, about 1875 (Hermitage Museum, Leningrad)
359. Box, "Fairy tale scene," polychromed on papier-mâché, V. V. Kotukhin, Palekh, 1945 (courtesy *A la vieille Russie*, New York)
360. Box, "Holiday scene," polychromed on papier-mâché, N. Vikhrev, Palekh, 1960 (courtesy *Soviet Life Magazine*, Washington, D.C.)
361. Head of Christ, Chinese lacquer on bronze, Marcel Wolfers, Brussels, about 1930 (Museo de Bellas Artes, Barcelona)
362. Relief, "Fourteenth Station of the Cross," Chinese lacquer on clay, Marcel Wolfers, Brussels, about 1925 (Church of Marcinelle, Charleroi)
363. Vases, clay, Chinese lacquer, Marcel Wolfers, Brussels, about 1920 (Marcel Wolfers, Brussels)
364. Decorative panel, polychromed on wood, Jean Dunand, Paris, about 1925 (California Palace of the Legion of Honor, San Francisco)

INDEX

PLATES

1. Bookbinding, Venice, 1570–77

2. Casket lid, Venice, about 1580

3. Shield, Venice, end of sixteenth century

4. Salver, damascened and signed by Mahmud al Kurdi, early sixteenth century

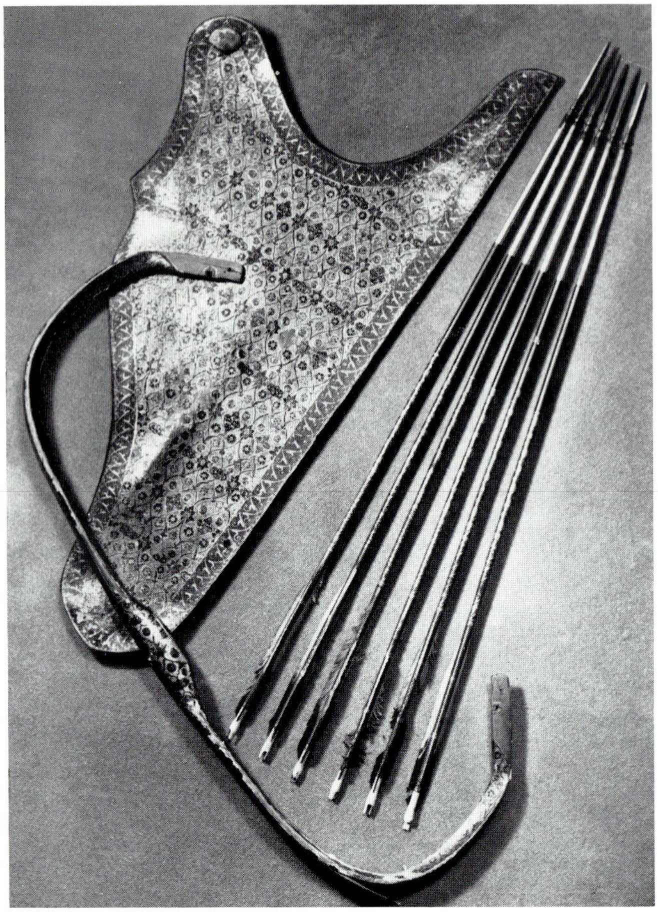

5

6

5. Quiver, Turkish, about 1550
6. Quivers, Venetian, end of sixteenth century
7. Box with toilette utensils, Venice, about 1550
8. Box, Venice, about 1550

7

8

9

10

9. Casket, Venice, about 1550
10. Casket, damascened and signed by Paolo Rizzio, Venice, about 1570
11. Venetian lady, portrait attributed to Bernardino Licinio, Venice, about 1550
12. Box, Venice, after 1550

11

12

13

14

13. Mirror, Venice, about 1575
14. Frame with inlay, portrait, school of Corneille de Lyon, Venice (?), about 1580

15. Frame, portrait by Francesco da Segala, Venice, end of sixteenth century

16. Frame, "Madonna and Saints," reverse on glass, Venice, end of sixteenth century

17

18

17. Cabinet, with inlay of stone, Venice, about 1580
18. Interior view of cabinet, plate 17

19. Cabinet, with inlay of stone, Venice, about 1580

20 a

20 b

21

22

20 a. Cabinet, with inlay of enamel, signed Jean Le Court, 1562
20 b. Casket, with cut glass, Venice, end of sixteenth century
21. "La cassette," engraving after painting by follower of Titian, 1500–1600
22. Casket, stone work in metal setting, Italian, end of sixteenth century

23

24

25

26

23. Casket, wood and metal setting for rock crystal, Venice, about 1600
24. Casket, wood and metal setting for rock crystal, Venice, about 1600
25. Casket, interior, similar to plate 23, Venice, about 1600
26. Casket, interior, similar to plate 23; *see also* color plate I

27

28

27. Casket, Venice, about 1580
28. Casket, Venice, about 1550
29. Folding table, Italian, before 1591
30. Tabletop, Italian, end of sixteenth century

29

30

31

32

33

34

31. Virginal, Italian, about 1570
32. Virginal, Benedetto Floriani, Venice, 1571
33. Virginal, Giovanni Celestini, Venice, 1593
34. Virginal, Antonio Baffo, Venice, 1574

35

36

35. Harp, possibly decorated by Giulio Marescotti, Ferrara, 1587
36. Detail of harp, plate 35
37. Cabinet, Florence (?), about 1600

37

38. Saddlers' Guild ballot box, London, 1619

39. Cabinet, London, 1619

40

40. Door of cabinet, plate 39
41. Cabinet, London, about 1620
42. Cabinet, interior, plate 41

41

42

The lawe my callinge is, my roobe, my tounge, my penn, wealth and opynion
knowen dishonest cause I neuer did defend, nor spun out suits in length,
did bewraie, nor of both parties take, nor neuer tooke I fee,

43

44

45

46

43. Trencher, London, about 1620
44. Trencher, London, about 1620
45. Box, Holland (?), seventeenth century
46. Box, Holland, seventeenth century

47

48

47. Plate, Holland (?), seventeenth century
48. Plate, Goa, early seventeenth century
49. Box, Augsburg, about 1630
50. Box, Augsburg, about 1630
51. Panel decorated with battle scene, Augsburg, 1628
52. Carbine, France, about 1630

49

50

51

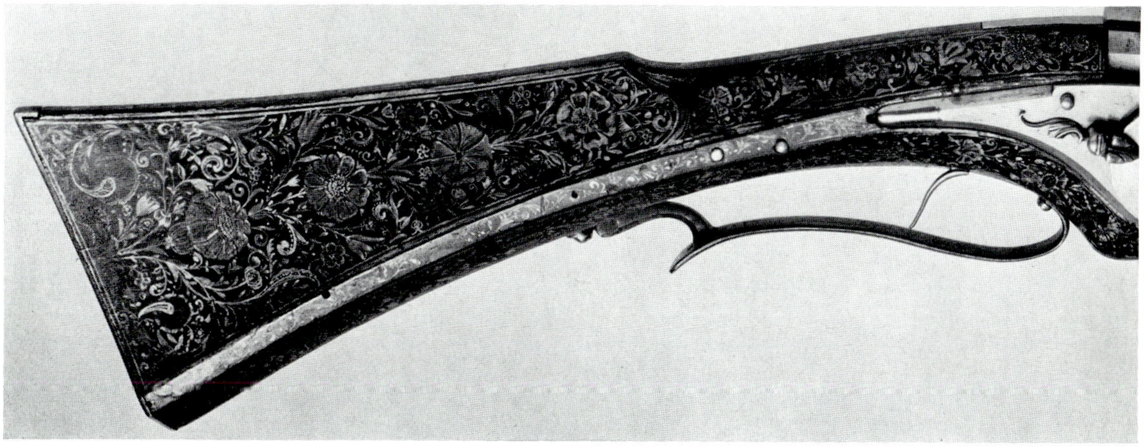

52

53

53. Cabinet, England, about 1675–80
54. Cabinet, Coromandel, England, about 1680

55

55. Cabinet, England, end of seventeenth century
56. Cabinet, England, about 1700

57

58

57. Bureau-cabinet, England, about 1710
58. Bureau-cabinet, England, about 1715

59

60

59. Bureau-cabinet, England, about 1715
60. Cabinet, interior, plate 59

61

62

61. Dressing table, England, about 1690
62. Chest on stand, England, about 1710
63. Mirror, Coromandel, England, 1690
64. Side table, Coromandel, England, about 1690

63

64

65

65. Tea table, from painting by Philips, England, about 1730
66. Card table, Giles Grendey, London, about 1730
67. Top of card table, plate 66

66

67

68

69

70

71

68. Leather screen, England, about 1750
69. Leather screen, detail, London, about 1750
70. Signed screen, "Coventry, London," plate 69
71. Bed, Thomas Chippendale, about 1755

72. Wardrobe, Thomas Chippendale, 1770

73. Bookcase, England, about 1755

75

74. Long-case clock, England, about 1735
75. Bracket clock, England, about 1730
76. Toilet mirror, England, about 1710
77. Toilet mirror, England, about 1720
78. Casket, decorated and signed by Marmaduke Craddock, about 1700

74

76

77

78

79

79. Casket, set, several marks, London, 1753
80. Chair, England, about 1683
81. Chair, England, late seventeenth century
82. Chair, England, about 1695
83. Chair, England, about 1710

80

81

82

83

84

85

86

87

84. Armchair, England, about 1710
85. Chair, England, about 1710
86. Daybed, made by Giles Grendey, London, about 1730
87. Chair, England, about 1735

88

89

88. Chair, made by Giles Grendey, London, about 1730
89. Detail of chair, plate 88
90. Highboy, North American, about 1700

91. Highboy, North American, about 1730

92. Highboy, Boston, about 1725–30

93. Highboy, Boston, 1725–30

94. Highboy, carries name of cabinetmaker "Pimm," decorations attributed to Thomas Johnson, Boston, 1735

95

95. Highboy, decorations attributed to Thomas Johnson, Boston, about 1735
96. Lowboy, decorations attributed to Thomas Johnson, Boston, about 1735
97. Chair, Boston, 1700
98. Chair, detail, plate 97

96

97

98

99

100

99. Long-case clock, work by Gavin Brown, Boston, 1766
100. Mirror, New York, about 1730–40
101. Panel, North American, about 1750

101

102

102. Cabinet, Augsburg (?), seventeenth century, and table, Venice, end of seventeenth century
103. Frame, mother-of-pearl inlay, after 1650
104. Frame, detail, plate 103
105. Crucifix stem, detail, mother-of-pearl inlay, Venice, about 1650

103

104

105

106. Bureau-cabinet, Venice, about 1700

107

108

107. Bureau-cabinet, Venice, early eighteenth century
108. Bureau-cabinet, Venice, about 1750

109

109. Bureau-cabinet, *lacca povera* work, Venice, about 1740
110. Console table, Venice, about 1750
111. Commode, Venice, about 1750

110

111

112

112. Commode, Venice, about 1750
113. Stand, Venice, about 1750
114. Blackamoor, by Giovanni Giuliani, St. Florian, 1729
115. Frame, with Rezzonico coat of arms, Venice, about 1750

113

114

115

116. Ridotto Venier, Venice, after 1750

117. Armchair, Venice, about 1750

118a

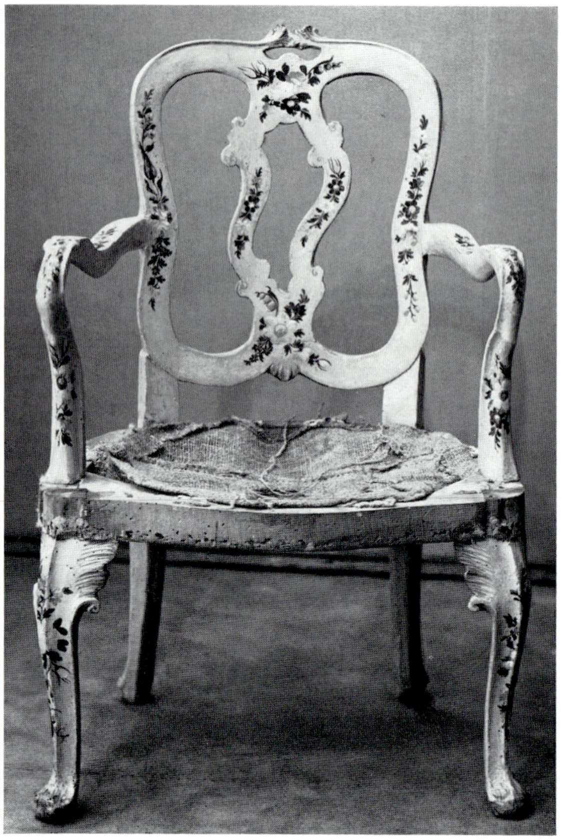

118b

118. Chairs, Venice, late eighteenth century

119. Toilette set, Venice, about 1750

LOTTO REALE
UOMO
DONNA
PARI
DISPARI
FIORE
FRVT.
DISPARI DENTRO
DISPARI FUORI
FARFALLA
NANO
FUORI
DENTRO
QUADRV PEDE
PARI & FUORI
ALBERO
PARI DENTRO
VOLA

120

121

122

123

120. Game of Lotto, Venice, after 1750
121. Game tabletop, Venice, about 1740–50
122. Stringed instrument, Venice (?), about 1700
123. Stringed instrument, Venice (?), about 1730–40

124. Sales desk, Venice, about 1750

125. Commode, Venice, late eighteenth century

126. Lacquer room, Pietro Massa, Turin, about 1735–38

127

128

127. Lacquer room, detail, plate 126
128. Paneling, Turin, about 1720–30

129. Lacquer room, detail, plate 126

130. Door and paneling, Turin, about 1770

131. Corner cupboard, Francesco Servorcelli, Turin, about 1770

132. Lacquer room, Villa Vacchetti, near Turin, about 1740

133

134

133. Secretary, Turin, about 1750
134. Commode, Turin, about 1750

135

136

135. Corner cupboard, Turin, about 1750
136. Bed table, *lacca povera*, Turin, about 1750

138

139

140

137

137. Tabletop, Turin, about 1750
138. Stool, Turin, about 1750
139. Table, Turin, about 1750
140. Microscope, instrument made by P. Paulus Maria Petrini, Rome, about 1750

141

142

141. Commode, Rome, about 1750
142. Commode, detail, plate 141
143. Commode, Rome, about 1750
144. Commode, Rome, about 1750

143

144

145

146

145. Lacquer room, Sicily, about 1750
146. Panel from ballroom, Sicily, about 1750

147. Commode, Sicily, after 1750

148

149

148. Clavichord, by H. A. Hass, Hamburg, 1723
149. Clavichord, by Christian Zell, Hamburg, 1728

150

151

150. Clavichord, by H. A. Hass, Hamburg, 1732
151. Clavichord, inside lid, plate 150

152

153

152. Cabinet, Hamburg, about 1730
153. Cabinet, detail, plate 152
154. Clavichord, by J. A. Hass, Hamburg, 1755
155. Detail of window frame, Hamburg, early eighteenth century

154

155

156. Chest on stand, Johann Christoph Lesieur, Brunswick, about 1730

157. Cupboard, Danzig (?), early eighteenth century

159

158. Cabinet, North German (?), early eighteenth century
159. Cabinet on stand, attributed to Gérard Dagly, Berlin, about 1700

160. Cabinet on stand, Gérard Dagly, Berlin, about 1690

161. Cabinet, interior, plate 160

162

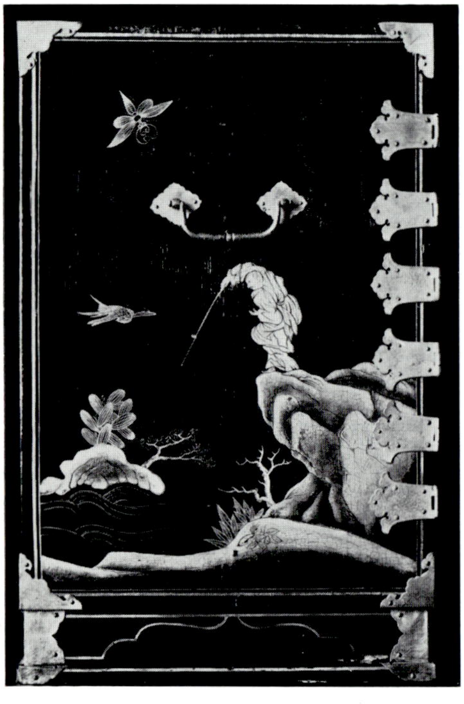

163

162. Cabinet, Japan, seventeenth century; stand and decoration of sides, Dagly workshop, Berlin, about 1700
163. Cabinet, detail, plate 162
164. Cabinet on stand, attributed to Gérard Dagly, Berlin, about 1700
165. Cabinet, detail, plate 160

164

165

166

167

166. Cabinet on stand, once in curio room shown in plate 167, Gérard Dagly, before 1696
167. Curio room, once in Berlin palace, with four cabinets by Dagly (engraving, 1696)
168. Cabinet, detail, plate 166

170

169

171

169. Table, Dagly shop, Berlin, about 1700
170. Table, detail, plate 169
171. Table, Berlin, about 1700
172. Armchair, Far East (?), japanned in Berlin (?), about 1700
173. Armchair, detail, plate 172

172

173

174

175

174. Cupboard, Berlin 1725
175. Cupboard, detail, plate 174
176. Firescreen, Berlin, about 1725
177. Panel, David Pennewitz, from the manor of Plaue, about 1715

176

177

178

180

179

181

178. Table, Sebastian Chevalier, Berlin, about 1775
179. Table, detail, plate 178
180. Table, with chair in which Frederick the Great died, anonymous drawing, 1786
181. Oval room, in the New Palace, Potsdam, Sebastian Chevalier, about 1767

182

183

184

182. Pilgrim bottle, red stoneware, japanning attributed to Martin Schnell, about 1715
183. Coffeepot, red stoneware, japanning to Martin Schnell, about 1715
184. Vase, faïence, Frankfurt, 1680–90
185. Vase, porcelain, Far East (?), decorated in Berlin (?), 1800
186. Vase, porcelain, Far East (?), decorated in Berlin (?), 1800
187. Vase, faïence, Ansbach, about 1720

185

186

187

188

189

190

191

188. Cabinet on stand, Schnell workshop (?), Dresden, 1720–30
189. Cabinet, interior, plate 188
190. Tabletop, Schnell workshop (?), Dresden, 1720–30
191. Tabletop, Schnell workshop (?), Dresden, 1720–30

193

192. Cabinet, Schnell workshop (?), Dresden, 1720–30
193. Cabinet, interior, plate 192

195

194. Bureau-cabinet, Schnell workshop (?), Dresden, 1720–30
195. Bureau-cabinet, Schnell workshop (?), Dresden, 1720–30

196. Bureau-cabinet, Dresden, about 1740

197. Bureau-cabinet, Dresden, about 1740

198

199

198. Screen, oil painting on canvas, J. G. Näcke, Dresden, about 1726
199. Mirror back, Dresden, about 1720
200. Chair, dated 1719, Schnell workshop (?), Dresden
201. Chair, detail, plate 200

200

201

202. Oval room, panels, bottom row, door, Munich, 1717; restored 1769

203. Corner of room, J. G. Höringer, Munich, 1765

204

206

204. Clock on stand, movement B. Firstenfelder, 1725, environs of Augsburg
205. Bracket clock, movement Paulus Graf, Munich, 1760
206. Chinoiserie panel, detail
207. Chinoiserie print copied in panel, plate 206

205

207

208. Sedan chair, Munich, about 1750
209 a. Margrave Ludwig Wilhelm of Baden in Turkish costume, German, about 1700
209 b. Prince Carl Joseph of Baden (?) in Turkish costume, German, about 1700
210 a. Carved table, Dutch (?), about 1700
210 b. Table, detail, plate 210 a

208

209 a

209 b

210a

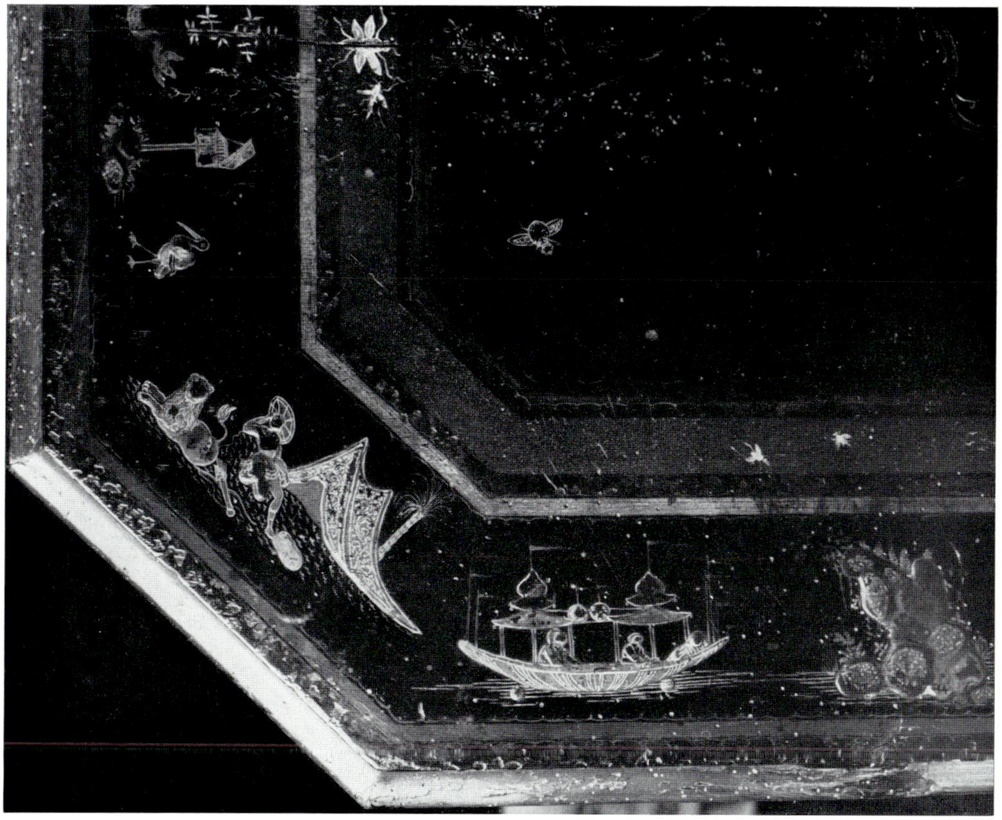

210b

211. Chinese room, J. J. Sänger, Ludwiglust, 1717

212. Chinese room, large panels Coromandel work, oblong and lower panels incised and polychromed on stucco by Margravine Wilhelmine about 1740

213. Lacquer room, Johann Adalbert Kratochwil, Prague, 1709

214. Detail from plate 213

215

216

217

215. Cabinet, Johann Konrad Hoffman, about 1711
216. Door of cabinet, plate 215
217. Desk secretaire, Bamberg, about 1730

218

219

218. Panel from Dutch room, German or Dutch, about 1705
219. Fragment of door, formerly at palace of Brühl near Cologne, German (?), about 1705

220. Bureau, bearing coat of arms Rabutin-Sévigné, Far East, about 1680

221

222

223

224

221. Commode, France, about 1725
222. Commode, Japanese cabinet mounted in France, about 1715
223. Panel, X-ray photograph of underground of Watteau's *Leçon d'amour*, painted about 1716–17
224. Box, French, about 1720

225

226

227

225. Desk, attributed to Bernard van Risenburgh, Paris, about 1735
226. Commode, Mathieu Criaerd, Paris, 1740
227. Drop-front secretary, Japanese lacquer except for drawer front, Jean-François Dubut, Paris, about 1740–50

228

229

230

228. Desk, Jacques Dubois, Paris, about 1745
229. Desk, Paris, about 1745
230. Desk, Paris, about 1745
231. Table, Sèvres top, Bernard van Risenburgh, Paris, about 1761
232. Table, Sèvres top, R. Lacroix, Paris, about 1765
233. Table, Sèvres top and shelf, Bernard van Risenburgh, Paris, about 1760

231

232

233

234

235

236

234. Corner cupboard, Jacques Dubois, Paris, about 1745
235. Corner cupboard, Bernard van Risenburgh, Paris, about 1745–49
236. Corner cupboard, from the Château de Bellevue, Partin Carlin, Paris, about 1785
237. Commode, Jean Desforges, Paris, about 1740
238. Commode, Paris, about 1770

237

238

239

240

239. Commode, Paris, about 1770
240. Commode, E. Levasseur, Paris, about 1780
241. Corner cupboard, from the Château de Choisy, Paris, 1775
242. Writing table, Paris, about 1760

241

242

243

244

245

246

247

248

243. Commode, Pierre Roussel, Paris, about 1750
244. Commode, François Rubestuck, Paris, about 1745
245. Box, *vernis Martin*, Paris, about 1745
246. Box, *vernis Martin*, Paris, about 1745
247. Pinbox, *vernis Martin*, Paris, about 1745
248. Pinboxes, *vernis Martin*, Paris, about 1745

249

251

250

252

253

249. Toilette table, with set of utensils, Paris, about 1770
250. Bed table, France, 1740–50
251. Bed table, detail of polychrome decoration, plate 250
252. Spinettino, France, about 1740
253. Spinettino, detail, plate 252

255

256

254. Sedan chair, Paris, about 1750
255. Carriage seat, transformed into chair, Paris, early eighteenth century
256. Sledge seat, inscribed DAGLY (?), Paris, before 1750

257

258

259

260

261

257. Harpsichord, Johannes Goermans, Paris, 1754
258. Harpsichord, detail, plate 257
259. Gentleman playing harp, oil painting, Danish (?), about 1760
260. Harp, detail, French, about 1760
261. Octavina spinet, Pascal Taskin, Paris, about 1778

262

263

262. Chinese room, Netherlands, about 1680
263. Chinese room, detail of paneling, plate 262
264. Secretary, Antwerp (?), about 1680
265. Secretary, detail, plate 264

264

265

266

267

268

266. Cabinet, Netherlands, about 1690
267. Cabinet, Netherlands, about 1680
268. Cabinet, Netherlands, about 1700
269. Cabinet, Netherlands, about 1700

269

270

271

270. Cabinet, Netherlands, about 1700
271. Cabinet, Netherlands, about 1700
272. Chinese room, Netherlands, about 1750

19

273

275

274

276

273. Cabinet, Netherlands, about 1700
274. Cabinet on stand, Netherlands, about 1700
275. Writing desk, Netherlands (?), about 1725
276. Writing desk, detail of top, plate 275

277

278

277. Cabinet, Netherlands, about 1740
278. Chinese room, Huis ten Bosch, Netherlands, about 1780
279. Cabinet from dollhouse by Christof van Brant, Amsterdam, about 1740
280. Folding table from dollhouse by Christof van Brant, Amsterdam, about 1740
281. Stand, Netherlands, early eighteenth century
282. Pastel, detail, by Cornelis van Troost, Netherlands, about 1711

279

280

281

282

283

284

285

286

287

288

283. Cabinet, Sweden, 1730–40
284. Corner cupboard, Sweden, early eighteenth century
285. Cabinet, *lacca povera*, Sweden, early eighteenth century
286. Long-case clock, English movement, japanning by Niels Lochstoer, Norway, about 1750
287. Long-case clock, Sweden, about 1740
288. Long-case clock, Denmark, about 1750

289

290

289. Long-case clock, detail, plate 286
290. Long-case clock, detail, signature of Lochstoer, plate 286
291. Bracket clock, Niels Lochstoer, Norway, about 1750
292. Bracket clock, Sweden, about 1740
293. Bracket clock, detail, plate 292

291

292

293

294

295

296

294. Desk, Sweden (?), about 1740–50
295. Desk, Japanese lacquer, Niels Dahlin, Stockholm, about 1765
296. Lacquer room, Iwan Tikhanov and Perfil Fjodorov, Russia, 1720–22

297

298

297. Desk, Russia, early eighteenth century
298. Desk, detail, plate 297
299. Box, with inlay, Spa, after 1650
300. Box, with inlay, Spa (?), about 1700

299

300

301

302

301. Box, with coat of arms of Clemens August, Elector of Cologne, Spa, about 1740–50
302. Box, signed Vincent Rousseau, Spa, about 1750

303

304

303. Desk, Spa (?), about 1750
304. Tea caddy, Spa (?), about 1750

305

306

305. Set of boxes, Spa, before 1750
306. Toilet set, with views of Spa, about 1750
307. Box from toilet set, with Battersea enamel plaque, Pontypool, about 1750
308 a. Snuffbox, with portrait of Colonel Hamilton, signed I. Patterson, Cumnock, 1827, marked John Smith, Mauchline
308 b. Snuffbox, scene from a poem by Robert Burns, Scotland, about 1830
308 c. Snuffbox, marked John Smith, Mauchline, before 1837
308 d. Snuffbox, cat and rat story, Scotland, about 1840

307

308 a

308 b

308 c

308 d

309

310

309. Knife boxes, Pontypool, about 1755–60
310. Tin basket, Pontypool, about 1775
311. Tin maker's mark, Pyrke of Usk, 1814–26
312. Tea urn, Pontypool, about 1770
313. Chestnut vase, Pontypool (?), about 1795
314. Tilt-top table, Pontypool, about 1765

312

313

314

311

315

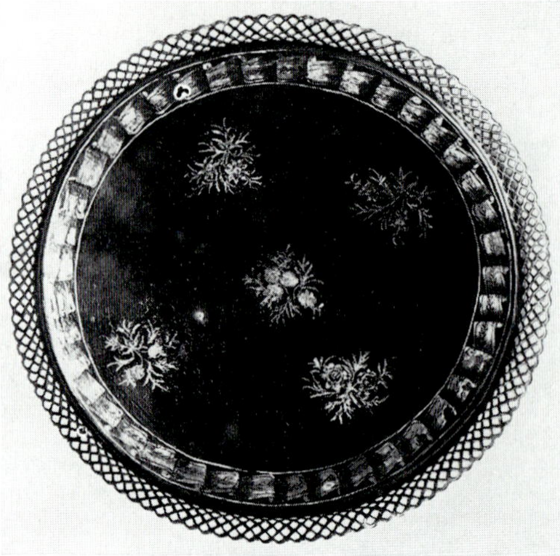
316

317

318

330

328. Chair, mother-of-pearl inlay, Birmingham, about 1860
329. Toilette table, with mirror, mother-of-pearl inlay, Birmingham, 1850–60
330. Bed, mother-of-pearl inlay, Birmingham, 1850–60

331

332

333

331. Chair, bearing stencil on back "L. Hitchcock, Hitchcockville, Conn.," 1825–28
332. Bread basket, Stevens Plains, early nineteenth century
333. Cookie box, Pennsylvania, 1800–50
334. Tureen, French, about 1750
335. Câche pot, French, about 1750

334

335

337

338

336

339

336. Tea kettle and stand, French, about 1750
337. Jardiniere, French, about 1770
338. Inkstand, French, about 1780
339. Urn, French, end of eighteenth century
340. Secretary, paintings by F. A. Weitsch, signed and dated 1794, Stobwasser workshop, Brunswick
341. Table, with tray, Stobwasser workshop, Brunswick, before 1800
342. Tray painting, "Sons of Edward IV in the Tower of London," taken from print, plate 341

340

341

342

343

344

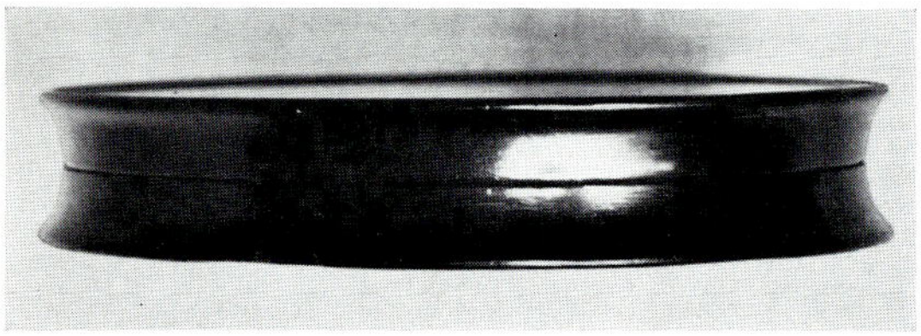

345

346

347

343. Snuffbox, "Amor and Psyche," after painting by Johann Enter, Stobwasser workshop, Brunswick, about 1800
344. Snuffbox, "View of Brocken Mountain," Stobwasser workshop, Brunswick, about 1800
345. Silhouette of snuffbox, Stobwasser workshop, Brunswick
346. Snuffbox, inscribed "Jean Guérin, Vernisseur, Brunswick," Stobwasser workshop, about 1800
347. Snuffbox, portrait of the dramatist Johann Anton Leisewitz after painting by J. H. Schröder, Stobwasser workshop, Brunswick, about 1811
348. Tobacco jar, Stobwasser workshop, Brunswick, about 1800
349. Tea kettle, Stobwasser workshop, Brunswick, about 1800
350. Casket with tea caddies, Stobwasser workshop, Brunswick, end of eighteenth century
351. Tray, Stobwasser workshop, Brunswick, about 1800

349

348

350

351

352

353

352. Tray, "Italian fountains at Peterhof," Demidov workshop, Russia, early nineteenth century
353. Tray, "Triple Alliance of 1815," P. I. Korobov workshop (?), Russia, about 1815

354

355

354. Tray, A. Laboutin, Russia, about 1840

355. Tray, "Czar Nicholas I and Czarina and monument to Peter I," P. and A. Lukutin, Danilkovo (Fedoskino), about 1850

356 a

356 b

356 c

356 d

356 e

357

358

356. Russian lacquer marks:
 a. Eagle and initials P. P. L. for Factory Piotr Vasielievich Lukutin (1828–30)
 b. Eagle and initials F. A. L. for Factory Alexander Pietrovitch Lukutin, used after 1830
 c. Eagle and P. A. Lukutin (in script), used after 1830
 d. Four eagles and Russian for Factory Lukutin, Moscow, used between 1881–1902
 e. Mark showing name Vishniakov and Son, Kuskovo, used around 1870 and later. Mark also exists with five medals and without crown

357. Snuffbox, "View of Moscow," P. A. Lukutin, Danilkovo (Fedoskino), about 1850

358. Snuffbox, "Family at tea," Vishniakov, Kuskovo, about 1875

359. Box, "Fairy tale scene," V.V. Kotukhin, Palekh, 1945

360. Box, "Holiday scene," N. Vikhrev, Palekh, 1960

359

360

361. Head of Christ, Marcel Wolfers, Brussels, about 1930

362. Relief, "Fourteenth Station of the Cross," Marcel Wolfers, Brussels, about 1930

363

364

363. Vases, Marcel Wolfers, Brussels, about 1920
364. Decorative panel, Jean Dunand, Paris, about 1925